The Garbage Generation

The Garbage Generation:

The Consequences
of the Destruction of the Two-Parent Family
And The Need to Stabilize It
By Strengthening Its Weakest Link,
The Father's Role

Daniel Amneus

Primrose Press : Alhambra, CA

By Daniel Amneus

Back to Patriarchy
The Mystery of *Macbeth*
The Three *Othellos*
The Garbage Generation

Copyright © 1990 by Daniel Amneus

Primrose Press
2131 S. Primrose Ave.
Alhambra, CA 91803

First printing 1990

ISBN   0-9610864-4-0 (Hard cover)
       0-9610864-5-9 (Paperback)

For Clayton

Contents

Glossary

Agnation: kinship through males. It is the argument of the present book that the social system based on male kinship is undergoing a breakdown and being replaced by the older (Stone Age) system of social system based on female kinship.

Field direction: Doing what everyone else does.

First Law of Matriarchy: "Women control our own reproduction." This is identical to the Promiscuity Principle and the antithesis of the Legitimacy Principle.

Garbage Generation: The underachieving, undisciplined sexually anarchic generation produced by family breakdown and the feminist/sexual revolution since the 1960's.

Legitimacy Principle: Every child must have a sociological father (who may not be identical with his biological father).

Matriarchy: As Steven Goldberg has shown in his *The Inevitability of Patriarchy* there is no such thing as matriarchy in the sense of "government by women." In the present book the word is sometimes used to refer to family arrangements from which fathers are excluded.

Promiscuity Principle: "A woman's right to control her own sexuality." Identical with the First Law of Matriarchy; antithetical to the Legitimacy Principle, which requires a woman to share her reproductive life with a man.

Sexual Constitution: Sexual law-and-order based on monogamy, stable, patriarchal families, the Legitimacy Principle and the Double Standard.

The Garbage Generation

I

Introduction:

The Pathology Of The Female-Headed Family

"Women," wrote Ramsey Clark in 1970, in his celebrated book *Crime in America,* "are not a threat to the public."[1] But he also wrote, in discussing the male juvenile criminals who *are* a threat to the public, that "three-fourths came from broken homes."[2] That means mostly female-headed homes. That means that while the single mothers of these criminals do not themselves commit crimes and go to prison, the socialization they give their children has an extraordinarily high correlation with the male crime of the next generation. This socialization, in fact, is the "root cause of crime" which Clark wrote his book to explore. He had found the explanation he sought and he didn't know it. It was concealed by the generation-long time-lag between cause and effect and by the sex-switch between generations: like hemophilia, crime is manifested in males but carried and transmitted by females—or rather by single females. Instead of seeing the true connection, Clark gave his readers this:

> *If we are to deal meaningfully with crime, what must be seen is the dehumanizing effect on the individual of slums, racism, ignorance and violence, of corruption and impotence to fulfill rights, of poverty and unemployment and idleness, of generations of malnutrition, of congenital brain damage and prenatal neglect, of sickness and disease, of pollution, of decrepit, dirty, ugly, unsafe, overcrowded housing, of alcoholism and narcotics addiction, of avarice, anxiety, fear, hatred, hopelessness and injustice. These are the fountainheads of crime.*[3]

---

1. Ramsey Clark, *Crime in America: Observations on Its Nature, Causes, Prevention and Control* (New York: Pocket Books, 1970) p. 216
2. Clark, p. 39
3. p. 5; emphasis in original.

3

Not so. If we are to deal meaningfully with crime, what must be seen is its relationship with the female-headed family. Most criminals come from female-headed families. Most gang members come from female-headed families. Most addicts come from female-headed families. Most rapists come from female-headed families. Most educational failures come from female-headed families. Every presidential assassin before Hinckley came from a female-headed family or one in which he had an impossibly bad relationship with his father. Most illegitimate births occur to females who themselves grew up in female-headed families.

If we are to deal meaningfully with crime, what we must do is reduce the number of female-headed families; what we must do is prevent the divorce courts from expelling half of society's fathers from their homes; what we must do is terminate a welfare system which displaces millions of men from the principal male role, that of family-provider. What we must do is make the father the head of the family.

The female role, says Margaret Mead, is a biological fact; the male role is a social creation.[4] This is the primary reality concerning human society. Motherhood has been the dominant feature of mammalian life since its beginning some two hundred million years ago, most conspicuously since the great reptiles became extinct and the Age of Mammals began sixty-five million years ago. Fatherhood in the sense of major male participation in reproduction is only a few million years old. Fatherhood in the sense of male headship of families is only a few thousand years old.

What is happening to our society is that it is discarding patriarchal sexual regulation and reverting to the primeval mammalian pattern of a reproductive unit consisting of the mother and her offspring, the male putting in an appearance to perform his minuscule sexual function and then disappearing or being hauled away to the sausage factory or being reduced to the role of stud who can be discarded when his female tires of him. "Men and women," rejoices feminist-anthropologist Helen Fisher, "are moving toward the kind of roles they had on the grasslands of

---

4. "Human Fatherhood Is a Social Invention" is the title of Chapter IX of Mead's *Male and Female: A Study of the Sexes in a Changing World* (New York: William Morrow and Company, 1949).

4

Africa millions of years ago....Human society is now discovering its ancient roots....The recent trend toward divorce and remarriage is another example of a throwback to earlier times....[T]he so-called new extended family [read: broken family] may actually have evolved millennia ago....At long last, society is moving in a direction that should be highly compatible with our ancient human spirit....The 'traditional' role of women is a recent invention."[5]

Biologically speaking, it is indeed a recent invention, scarcely older than the civilization which it made possible and which emerged coevally with it and created the wealth which reconciled women to accepting it. But women's new economic independence is leading them to yearn for a return to the prehistoric mammalian arrangement. "[W]herever women are economically powerful," says Fisher, "divorce rates are high. You see it in the Kung and you see it in the United States."[6]

Let's say, wherever women are economically powerful and there are no social guarantees to ensure male headship of families, divorce rates are high—such being the case among the Kung and the Americans. The Kung have no social guarantees to ensure male headship of families because the Kung never emerged from the Stone Age. The Americans have no social guarantees to ensure male headship of families because there exists an elementary confusion in the heads of policy makers, lawmakers and judges, who imagine that the obvious strength of the biological tie between the mother and the infant (the "biological fact" Margaret Mead refers to) means that it requires their assistance. A biological fact does not require the services of the legal system. What does require these services is the weakest biological link in the family, the role of the father. It was the creation of this role—only a few thousand years ago—which made patriarchal civilization possible. Prior to that, mankind had to muddle through the million years of the Stone Age with the female-headed reproductive arrangements of the ghetto, the barnyard and the rain forest.[7]

---

5. Conversation with Kathleen McAuliffe in *U.S. News and World Report.* 8 August, 1988.
6. *Ibid.*
7. Documentation for the assertations made in this chapter is given in *Annex to Chapter I.*

Annex to Chapter I

The Annex is an essential part of the argument of this book and logically belongs at this point in the text. To place it here, however, would be placing a stumbling block in front of the reader, asking him to plow through seventy pages of tedious documentation, filled with repetitious overkill, proving the assertions made in Chapter I. Like the textual notes in an edition of Shakespeare, which nobody reads and which only one reader in hundreds consults, it has to be in the book but it does not have to be read. It is enough that the reader should know that there exists (and can be consulted on pages 215-285) proof that the high-crime, low-achieving areas of society are those with the greatest numbers of families headed by women and that the low-crime, high-achieving groups in society are those with stable, patriarchal families—that the feminist/sexual revolution and its attempt to impose a social organization based on female kinship is a failure and that it is necessary to return to a social organization based on male kinship.

.

.

II

The Once and Future Matriarchy:

The Stone Age, The Ghetto and The Promiscuity Principle

In the Matriarchal System the reproductive unit consists of the mother and her offspring, the father playing a marginal role, wandering into and out of the "family," subject to dismissal at the mother's bidding. The central fact about this kind of family is its *naturalness.* Roman jurists spoke of maternity as a natural fact, "natura verum," and of paternity as merely a matter of civil law. "In all but a few species," writes Sarah Hrdy, "females are permanent residents in social groups, males mere transients."[1] This is the reproductive arrangement of all lower mammals. It has been the reproductive arrangement of the human race itself until recently. Its biological backup is awesome—what Margaret Mead meant by saying the female role is a "biological fact."

It is the reproductive pattern which re-emerges in times of social catastrophe. When men are killed on battlefields or cast into prisons, female-headed families carry on. When there is divorce, the mother takes custody of the children. When ghetto males sit on curbsides and get stoned, ghetto females and children stay home and watch T.V.

The matriarchal family may result from catastrophe, but it may also result from doing *nothing*, from biological and social drifting. It is always on standby, always waiting to resurface and re-establish itself. It is what society lapses into when the upkeep and maintenance of the patriarchal system is neglected. It is the pattern which is re-emerging at the present time under the aegis of the feminist/sexual revolution.

It is the pattern found in surviving Stone Age societies. A 19th century German ship's doctor described the situation in the German African colony of Cameroon thus:

---

1. Cited in Marilyn French, *Beyond Power: On Women, Men and Morals* (New York: Summit Books, 1985), p. 28.

9

With a large number of tribes, inheritance is based on maternity. Paternity is immaterial. Brothers and sisters are only the children of one mother. A man does not bequeath his property to his children, but to the children of his sister, that is to say, to his nephews and nieces, as his nearest demonstrable blood relatives. A chief of the Way people explained to me in horrible English: "My sister and I are certainly blood relatives, consequently her son is my heir; when I die, he will be the king of my town." "And your father?" I inquired. "I don't know what that means, 'my father,' answered he. Upon my putting to him the question whether he had no children, rolling on the ground with laughter, he answered that, with them, men have no children, only women.[2]

"Originally," writes W. Robertson Smith, "there was no kinship except in the female line and the introduction of male kinship was a kind of social revolution which modified society to its very roots."[3] "Kinship through females," says John McLennan, must be a more archaic system of relationship than kinship through males—the product of an earlier and ruder stage in human development than the latter—somewhat more than a step farther back in the direction of savagery. To prove its existence on such a scale as to entitle it to rank among the normal phenomena of human development, is, we may now say, to prove it the most ancient system of kinship." "Wherever non-advancing communities are to be found," he informs us, "—isolated in islands or maintaining their savage liberties in mountain fastnesses—there to this day exists the system of kinship through females only."[4] "The maternal totemic clan," writes Robert Briffault in reference to this female-headed reproductive unit and to the larger matrilineal ties it creates,

---

2. Cited in August Bebel, *Women and Socialism* (New York: Socialist Literature, 1910), p. 213.
3. *Kinship and Marriage in Early Arabia* (London: A. and C. Black, 1903), p. 213.
4. *Primitive Marriage* (Chicago: University of Chicago Press, 1970; originally published, 1865), pp. 66, 92.

was by far the most successful form that human association has assumed—it may indeed be said that it has been
the only successful one....All human associations that
have subsequently arisen have been bound by loose and
feeble ties compared with the primitive maternal clan.
Political organizations, religious theocracies, States,
nations, have endeavored in vain to achieve real and
complete social solidarity. They are artificial structures;
social humanity has never succeeded in adequately
replacing the primitive bond to which it owes its existence. Even those loyalties which took its place have
now to a large extent lost their reality, and individualis-
tic interests rule supreme. Human society finds itself in
the precarious position of being no longer held together
by those bonds of sentiment which constitute the distinction between a social group and an aggregate of individuals.[5]

The term "family" properly refers to the male-headed patriarchal unit. "The relations arising out of the reproductive
functions, which constitute the only analogue of social relations
to be found in the animal world," says Briffault,

differ conspicuously from those generally connoted by
the term "family." That term stands, in the tradition of
civilised societies, for a group centering round the interests, activities, and authority of a dominant male. The
husband is the head of the family; the other members of
the group, wife and children, are his dependents and
subordinates. The corresponding group arising out of
the reproductive functions among animals presents no
trace of that constitution. It consists of the mother and
her offspring. The male, instead of being the head and
supporter of the group, is not an essential member of it,
and more often than not is altogether absent from it. He
may join the maternal family, but commonly does not.
When he attaches himself to the female's family his
association with it is loose and precarious. He has no

---

5. Robert Briffault, *The Mothers* (New York: Macmillan, 1927) II, 491f.

functional place in it. The parental relation is confined to that between mother and brood. Paternity does not exist. The family among animals is not, as the human family is supposed to be, the result of the association of male and female, but is the product of the maternal functions. The mother is the sole centre and bond of it. There is no division of labour between the sexes in procuring the means of subsistence. The protective functions are exercised by the female, not by the male. The abode, movements, and conduct of the group are determined by the female alone. The animal family is a group produced not by the sexual, but by the maternal impulses, not by the father, but by the mother.[6]

"In the great majority of uncultured societies," writes Arthur Evans, "women enjoy a position of independence and of equality with the men and exercise an influence which would appear startling ,in the most feministic modern civilized society."[7] "Women," he adds,

had a very high status in the Stone Age, as we have seen. Archeology, myth and comparison to still existing na- ture societies all point to their dominant position.

He quotes Jacquetta Hawkes:

There is every reason to suppose that under the life conditions of the primary Neolithic way of life, mother- right and the clan system were still dominant [as they had been in the paleolithic period], and land would generally have descended through the female line. In- deed, it is tempting to be convinced that the earliest Neolithic societies throughout their range in time and space gave woman the highest status she has ever known.[8]

---

6. Robert Briffault, *The Mothers*, abridged ed. (New York: Macmillan, 1931), pp. 22f.

7. Arthur Evans, *Witchcraft and the Gay Counterculture* (San Francisco: Fag Rag Press, 1978) p. 16. He cites Briffault, *The Mothers*, I, 311.

8. Evans, p. 30, citing Hawkes, "Prehistory," *History of Mankind*, I, 264.

The matriarchal family pattern is being restored by the welfare system, by the feminist/sexual revolution, by women's growing economic independence and by the legal preference for mother-custody following divorce. Writing of the educated and economically independent women created by women's liberation, Elizabeth Nickles and Laura Ashcraft say, "The Matriarchal woman who finds that her relation with a man is undermining her sense of self-esteem will not consider it necessary to cling to the relation for the traditional reasons, and she will have the self-sufficiency to stand on her own."[9] Because "the Matriarchal woman" can afford it, she reverts to the mammalian/matriarchal family pattern. The choice is hers; the father has nothing to say about it. She knows she has the chivalrous support of lawmakers and judges who suppose that a biological fact needs the help of lawyers, whereas merely social arrangements such as the marriage contract do not—these can be set aside if Mom decides they should be set aside. The result: educated, economically independent women have a divorce rate five times greater than the fifty percent divorce rate of other women.[10] The man who marries such a woman will find himself without bargaining power and, if his wife chooses, without children, without home, without a large part of his future income.

9. *The Coming Matriarchy: How Women Will Gain the Balance of Power* (New York: Seaview Books, 1981), p. 217.

10. *The Coming Matriarchy*, pp. 42ff. Cf. George Gilder, *Sexual Suicide* (New York: Quadrangle/ The New York Times Book Company, 1973), p. 67: "Women with high incomes and/or graduate degrees have the highest divorce rate—a rate far higher than successful men" [Citing Carter and Glick, *Marriage and Divorce* (Cambridge, Mass.: Harvard University Press, 1970), pp. 313-20]; Gilder, *Men and Marriage* (Gretna, LA: Pelican Publishing Company, 1986), pp. 205f. quotes Isabel V. Sawhill, "Economic Perspectives on the Family," *Daedalus*, Spring 1977, p. 119: "One of the most dramatic and consistent findings has been the greater prevalence of marriage and the lower probability of divorce where women's wages or labor-market participation are relatively low." Vassar economist Shirley Johnson computes that each additional $1,000 of a woman's earnings increases her likelihood of divorce by two percent. (Quoted by Caroline Bird, *The Two-Paycheck Marriage* (New York: Rawson, Wade, 1979), p. 13.) Summing up the evidence, Bird concludes: "The more money a woman earns, the less likely she is to be married. The relationship cannot be denied..."

For further documentation of the fact that most divorce actions are initiated by wives see Chapter VII, note 62.

"In the coming matriarchy," continue Nickles and Ashcraft,

> families will be thought of as sets of divers individuals
> rather than homogeneous social clusters, and the defini-
> tion of "family" will broaden to include many kinds of
> living arrangements, as is happening now without wide-
> spread social recognition. We may see the advent of the
> rotational family, in which there is no single, stable cast
> of characters for a lifetime, but rather a series of indi-
> viduals—male and female—who will be added to or
> phased out of a continually reconstituted family unit as
> the needs, interests, and emotional commitments of the
> couple, individual, or group dictate. The first five years
> of a woman's adult life may be spent living with male and
> female roommates; the next five years with a male mate;
> the next five with a husband and a child; the next three
> with two female friends, and so on. This pattern is
> already emerging, but when it occurs on a large scale, we
> will see the rotational family replacing the nuclear
> family as the status quo.[11]

The family pattern is called "rotational," but it does its
rotating around the fixed figure of Mom, who remains at its
center while males make their entrances, do their orbiting, and
make their exits.

It is the pattern of the Hopi Indians, of whom Fred Eggan
gives the following description:

> The central core or axis of the household is composed of
> a line of women—a segment of a lineage. All the
> members of the segment, male and female, are born in
> the household and consider it their home, but only the
> women normally reside there after marriage. The men
> of the lineage leave at marriage to reside in the house-
> holds of their wives, returning to their natal home on
> various ritual and ceremonial occasions, or in case of
> separation or divorce, which is frequent. Into the house-

---

11. *The Coming Matriarchy*, p. 220.

hold in turn come other men through marriage....The household revolves about a central and continuing core of women; the men are peripheral with divided residences and loyalties.[12]

A. I. Richards calls this pattern the "institution of the visiting husband or the visiting brother," and remarks that the pattern is characterized by unstable marriages: "A man who cannot stand the situation in his wife's village leaves and goes elsewhere. This might be described as the solution of the detachable husband."[13]

It is the pattern of the ghettos, where illegitimacy now exceeds 50 percent and where men and boys grow increasingly roleless and violent—and where women live in poverty and complain of their insufficient subsidization.

It is the pattern of increasing numbers of households in the larger society. According to the Washington-based National Center for Policy Alternatives, 40 percent of girls in school today will be heads of households.[14] "Ten percent of the nation's families are headed only by a woman," writes Joreen, "but 40 percent of the families classified as poor have female heads."[15] Implying, naturally, that society should do more to help these poor Moms and their kids.

The matriarchal days of the Stone Age are thus nostalgically described by feminist Marilyn French:

From 3.5 million years ago to about 10,000 years ago, was a peaceful period, when "marriage" was informal, casual.... Yes, there was a garden and in it we gathered fruits and vegetables and sang to the moon and played and worked together and watched the children grow. For the most part life was good, and we made art and rituals celebrating our participation in the glorious spectacle and process of life within nature.[16]

12. "The Hopi and the Lineage Principle," in *Social Structure*, pp. 131-21; cited in Evelyn Reed, *Women's Evolution* (New York: Pathfinder Press, 1975), pp. 320f.

13. "Some types of Family Structure Amongst the Central Bantu," in *African Systems of Kinship and Marriage*, pp. 246-48; cited in Reed, *loc. cit.*

14. Janice Mall in the *Los Angeles Times*, 12 April, 1987.

15. "The 51 percent Minority Group," in Robin Morgan (ed.) *Sisterhood Is Powerful* (New York: Vintage Books, 1970), p. 39.

16. Marilyn French, *Beyond Power* (New York: Summit Books, 1985) pp. 38, 39, 63.

Referring to those same happy days, feminist Evelyn Reed writes,

> A woman did not need a husband as a means of support; she was herself economically independent as a producing member of the community. This gave women, like men, the freedom to follow their personal inclinations in sex relations. A woman had the option of remaining for life with one husband, but she was not under any legal, moral or economic compulsion to do so.
>
> This freedom was destroyed with the advent of class society, private property and monogamous marriage.[17]

It was destroyed by the advent of class society, private property, monogamous marriage *and the creation of wealth and civilization which stable marriage made possible.* The promiscuity which characterizes the matriarchal system denies men a secure role within families and the motivation provided by that secure role. The absence of that motivation is why the ghettos are the mess they are—why the women of the ghettos enjoy the "freedom to follow their personal inclinations in sex relations," but find that the families in which they enjoy their freedom are impoverished and underachieving.

Ms. Reed lauds the freedom of such women. But there is a complementary freedom which is denied them. If they exercise their freedom to be promiscuous, they cannot enter into a stable and binding contract to share their reproductive lives with men who need to rely on their loyalty and chastity as a precondition for having legitimate children and stable families. Once women get the freedom to make the marriage contract non-binding, then they may suppose they have the "option" of either remaining for life with one husband or of not so remaining, but since the husband has no comparable option—the woman's freedom includes the freedom to throw the man out and take his children from him (and in the American matriarchy to take part of his paycheck as well)— the man is forced to share the woman's view of the marriage as non-binding. He becomes roleless and de-mo-

---

17. *Problems of Women's Liberation* (New York: Pathfinder Press, 1971) p. 56.

tivated, likely to become a drifter or a disrupter of society, likely to be regarded by women as poor marriage material, to be pointed to by feminists as proving the anti-sociality of males and the need for more feminism.

"If motherhood and sexuality were not wedged resolutely apart by male culture," says Adrienne Rich (she means wedged resolutely *together*), "if women could *choose* both the forms of our sexuality and the terms of our motherhood or non-motherhood freely, women might achieve genuine sexual autonomy." Quite so. Women *are* choosing it and thereby wrecking the patriarchal system. It is the declared purpose of feminists (including Ms. Rich) to do so.

"Our liberation as women and as lesbians," write Barbara Love and Elizabeth Shanklin,

> will never be accomplished until we are liberated to be mothers. Until we have the power to define the conditions under which we exercise our biological potential, until we define for ourselves the role of motherhood to include the power to determine the conditions of motherhood and to determine the environment in which our children are reared, we have no real choice. And until we have choices, we are not free.[19]

The legal system, which divorces the parents of 1.2 million children every year, and the welfare system which subsidizes the needs of 700,000 children born to unmarried mothers each year, are helping them to achieve this freedom—and passing the costs on to the shrinking numbers of patriarchal families. Only a fraction of those costs consists of immediate money payments. "The vast majority of neurotics," writes John MacArthur, "both children and adults, grew up in home where there was no father, or the father was absent or weak, and the mother was domineering."[20] A disproportionate amount of child abuse takes place in female-headed families.[21] According to Neal R. Peirce, "there is a strong correlation between the single-parent family and child

---

18. *Of Woman Born* (New York: W. W. Norton, 1976), p. 183.
19. Barbara Love and Elizabeth Shanklin, "The Answer is Matriarchy," in Giny Vida (ed.), *Our Right to Love* [Englewood Cliffs, N.J., 1978), p. 184.
20. *Family Feuding: How To End It*, p. 93.
21. *Persuasion at Work*, August, 1985. See Annex to Chapter 1, pp.283ff.

abuse, truancy, substandard achievement in school and high unemployment and juvenile delinquency."[22] Most victims of child molestation come from single parent households or are the children of drug ring members.[23] The pattern among victims parallels that among offenders. Researchers at North Florida Evaluation and Treatment Center report that "the pattern of the child molester is characterized by a singular degree of closeness and attachment to the mother."[24]

Feminist Carolyn Shaw Bell proposes "a special tax to pay for the total welfare benefits of families headed by women, and sufficient to increase these benefits so as to wipe out the income differential between poor children with only a mother and well-off children with two parents. The tax would be levied on all men."[25] In other words the patriarchy ought to subsidize its own destruction by paying women to create fatherless families. According to Martha Sawyer, a Ph.D candidate at Howard University, the costs of these fatherless families should be paid by "the most advantaged category, monied white men."[26] Paid, that is, by men who retain a niche in the patriarchal system which creates the wealth.

"What would it have been like," ask feminists Monica Sjoo and Barbara Mor,

> if patriarchy had never happened? To get an idea, we have to comprehend the first law of matriarchy: Women control our own bodies. This would seem a basic premise of any fully evolved human culture; which is why primate patriarchy is based on its denial.
>
> ....
>
> The process of redefinition begins with women reclaiming total sexual and reproductive autonomy; for if the female body can be controlled or used, in any way, from the outside—via exploitive definitions or systems—

22. *Los Angeles Times*, 30 June, 1982. See the quote in Annex to Chapter 1, p. 225.

23. *Los Angeles Times*, 16 September, 1985. See Annex to Chapter 1, p.283.

24. *Los Angeles Times*, 16 December, 1986. See Annex to Chapter 1, p.283.

25. Carolyn Shaw Bell, "Alternatives for Social Change: The Future Status of Women," in *Women in the Professions*, Papers from a conference held at Washington University, St. Louis, April, 1975 (Toronto: D.C. Heath and Company, 1975), p. 133.

26. Cited in *off our backs*, December, 1983.

then so, it follows, can everything else. (The definition and use of the female body is the paradigm for the definition and use of all things; if the autonomy of the female body is defined as sacred, then so will be the autonomy of all things.) Patriarchal men have tried to pretend that males can be "free" while females can be dominated and enslaved; just as white imperialists have pretended that they can be "independent and soulful" beings in private life, while publicly colonizing and brutalizing darker peoples.[27]

The most significant thing about this statement of "the first law of matriarchy" is that it is asserted categorically, without reference to the marriage contract. It assumes without even bothering to assert it that marriage confers no rights on husbands. It must be obvious to most men—though it is clearly not obvious to these women—that this female sexual autonomy rules out the possibility of using the family as a system for motivating males. Such is the state of things said (correctly) by Sjoo and Mor to have existed prior to the creation of patriarchy a few thousand years ago, and such is again becoming the state of things as patriarchy melts away. It was to prevent this state of things that patriarchy was created, a central feature of it being society's guarantee of the Legitimacy Principle—every child must have a father. The present situation, which has created the Garbage Generation, results from society's delinquency in refusing to implement this guarantee.

"It would not be far-fetched," writes Evelyn Ackworth, "to describe the whole conception of the Welfare State as a matriarchal approach to a problem of social life."[28] Exactly. The Welfare State has teamed with the feminist/sexual revolution to replace the patriarchal family with the older matrilineal unit. The ghettos provide the textbook example:

---

27. *The Great Cosmic Mother* (San Francisco: Harper and Row, 1987). pp. 200, 384.

28. *The New Matriarchy*, p. 165.

Now here's how it is [writes black feminist Patricia Robinson]. Poor black men won't support their families, won't stick by their women—all they think about is the street, dope and liquor, women, a piece of ass, and their cars. That's all that counts. Poor black women would be fools to sit up in the house with a whole lot of children and eventually go crazy, sick, heartbroken, no place to go, no sign of affection—nothing.[29]

Ms. Robinson's complaint is that men won't love, honor and protect their families—which is patriarchy. She cannot see that the first law of matriarchy ("Women control our own bodies") has deprived these men of families and therefore of the motivation which would keep them working. When Othello becomes convinced of his wife's unchastity he bids farewell to his profession: "Othello's *occupation's* gone!"[30]

Here's an example of how the Promiscuity Principle [identical with the first law of matriarchy] works, from Ann Landers' advice column in the *Los Angeles Times* of 1 November, 1988:

DEAR ANN: I'm writing this letter in the hope that you can help me. You have access to the best doctors and I am ashamed to talk to anybody I know.

I recently had a baby but I don't know who the father is. She looks like me. I had sex with Guy No. 1 on May 7, Guy No. 2 on May 14 and 15 and Guy No. 3 on May 27. I had my last period on May 1. I never had any problem with my pregnancy and the baby came right on my due date, which was Feb. 7. She is adorable and I don't regret having her, but I would sure like to know who the father is.

My friends tell me I'm entitled to support money but I can't bring a guy into court unless I'm pretty sure I know what I'm talking about. Thanks for your help, Ann.

The Promiscuity Principle entitles her to paternity suit income. It is her right to control her own sexual behavior—

29. *Black Sisters*, cited in Betty and Theodore Roszak, *Masculine/Feminine: Readings in Sexual Mythology and the Liberation of Women* (New York: Harper and Row, 1969), p. 212.
30. *Othello* III, iii, 357.

including the right not to use contraceptives—and to impose the economic costs upon one of her sex partners—if the District Attorney can round up her playmates, compel them to take blood tests, and identify the lucky one. Then her sexual irresponsibility will pay off and reinforce society's acceptance of the first law of matriarchy, otherwise known as the Promiscuity Principle. The identified boyfriend will be reduced to years of involuntary servitude for the benefit of another person—slavery.

The feminist will insist that the boyfriend is equally responsible with the mother for the procreation of the illegitimate child and therefore equally bound to pay for its costs. Not so in the patriarchal system. Patriarchy divides women into good and bad, those who accept the Sexual Constitution (sexual law-and order, monogamy, the Legitimacy Principle, the double standard, etc.) and those who reject it. This woman rejects it, and she is "bad" because she denies to a man the possibility of having responsible sex with her even if he wants to. Her unchastity deprives her child of a father and deprives men of the possibility of *being* a father to her children. She can have a sexual relationship only with a man as irresponsible as herself. She is a sexual Typhoid Mary who has inflicted illegitimacy upon a child and seeks to ameliorate what she has done by demanding to be paid for it. She will plead as justification that "there is no such thing as an illegitimate child," signifying there is no such thing as an unchaste woman.

Ramsey Clark assures us that "Women are not a threat to the public."[31] This woman is. She has procreated a fatherless child several times more likely to become a delinquent.[32] If the courts adopt the proposals of Senator Moynihan and Professor Barbara Bergmann and other feminists to garnish the paycheck of her child's father, he will become a less employable, less motivated, less marriageable, less productive member of society. He may drop out of the taxable/garnishable economy altogether and enter the underground economy, or become parasitic upon a female AFDC recipient—the pattern found in millions of ghetto households. The program for making men economically

---

31. Cited in Chapter 1, footnote 1.
32. This statistic is discussed on page 178.

responsible for procreation *outside* of the Sexual Constitution has the effect of making them irresponsible *within* it. (Also it doesn't work—most men will evade its sanctions.)

The workability of the patriarchal system requires the regulation of female sexuality, including the enforcing of the double standard. In no other way can men participate meaningfully in reproduction. A woman violates the Sexual Constitution by being promiscuous. A man violates it by refusing to provide for his *family*. The new feminist sexual order proposes that women shall be free to be promiscuous and that the social disruption . thereby created shall be made tolerable by compelling men to provide for *non*-families. But men cannot be held responsible for female irresponsibility if this irresponsibility prevents them from having families to begin with; and it is for this reason that patriarchy holds a man responsible only for the subsidization of a *wife*, a "good" woman who accepts the Sexual Constitution and her obligation under it to bear only legitimate children. The historical development of this arrangement in the second millennium B. C. is thus described by Dr. Gerda Lerner:

> As we compare the legal and social position of women in Mesopotamian and Hebrew societies, we note similarities in the strict regulation of women's sexuality and in the institutionalization of a sexual double standard in the law codes. In general, the married Jewish woman occupied an inferior position to that of her counterpart in Mesopotamian societies. Babylonian women could own property, sign contracts, take legal action, and they were entitled to a share in the husband's inheritance. But we must also note a strong upgrading of the role of women as mothers in the Old Testament....This is quite in line with the general stress on the family as the basic unit of society, which we have also noted in Mesopotamian society at the time of state formation.[33]

The more important point is the upgrading of the role of men as fathers—which is to say the strengthening of the family's weakest link, the father's role, which depends in turn upon "the

---

33. *The Creation of Patriarchy* (New York: Oxford University Press, 1986), p. 171.

22

strict regulation of women's sexuality" which today's feminists seek to get rid of. The "time of state formation" [read: the creation of civilization] was the time which stressed the family as the basic unit of society, just as today's social and sexual anarchy is the time which stresses women's desire to wreck the family and return to "beena marriage,...a form of marriage which allows the woman greater autonomy and which makes divorce easier for her."[34] This is the arrangement Ann Landers' correspondent is interested in, one with sexual freedom and no responsibilities—plus the advantage of having bill-paying men around as long as they behave themselves and accept second class status.

"The various laws against rape," says Dr. Lerner, "all incorporated the principle that the injured party is the husband or the father of the raped woman."[35] Feminists think this is outrageous. What it signifies is that the protection of female chastity is normally the function of the husband or the father—in contrast to the feminist Promiscuity Principle which declares that a woman's reproductive life is entirely her own business. The ancient Mesopotamian and Hebrew societies Dr. Lerner refers to stipulated that the law would interfere when the husband or father could not handle his own family matters, and when he delegated the responsibility to the state. The underlying difference of opinion between the feminist view and the Mesopotamian/Hebrew/patriarchal view is whether society should be understood as composed of families or of individuals. Those who today believe the latter might be asked whether sexual behavior is better regulated in the ghettos on the basis of the Promiscuity Principle than it was in the Kingdom of Hammurabi on the basis of the Legitimacy Principle. The Legitimacy Principle can only operate if its implementation is in the hands of *men* who conceive of it as operating to preserve *their* families and *their* meaningful role within them. It is the purpose of feminism to deny men this role.

Nothing has changed in four thousand years. In ancient Mesopotamia, as in the United States today, women were more concerned with maintaining their sexual autonomy, men more

---

34. Lerner, p. 109.
35. Lerner, p. 116.

concerned with maintaining the integrity of families, and per corollary the regulation of female chastity upon which the family depends. What Hammurabi's legislation shows is what contemporary lawmakers fail to see—that the Sexual Constitution is a male creation and must be supported by males. Men, not women, are the ultimate guardians of morality; and while men may delegate the responsibility to women (as in the Victorian age), when women subvert the moral order, men must reassert their responsibility to restore it.

"The discoverers of the matrikinship system," says Evelyn Reed,

> correctly inferred it to be a survival from a prefamily period when, as some put it, "fathers were unknown." They reasoned that cases where kinship ties and the line of descent passed through the mothers, without recognizing fathers, were evidence that the matriclan had existed before the father-family. The matrikinship system persists up to our times in many primitive regions, even where fathers have become known.[36]

This persistence is, of course, the chief reason why these regions are primitive.

Jamaica is a another textbook case. "Many Jamaican women live alone," says Honor Ford Smith, artistic director of Sistren, a women's cultural organization there:

> When I say alone, what I mean is live without a man. It's often one woman with a lot of children in the house. But unlike many societies there has been a tradition of women being able to live without men and without living within the bosom of the extended family. So that there's been a tradition of independent women living on their own, but the price that traditionally women have paid for that is that they then have to become the sole supporters of their children....But it brings with it certain benefits in the sense that unlike in the Middle East, or say Asia, some other countries, it's possible to not be

---

36. *Woman's Evolution*, p. 132.

ostracized for having many sexual partners, it's possible to live a little independently, to dress in certain ways, to move differently than has been traditionally possible in European or Asian societies. [37]

Jamaican women practice the first law of matriarchy and thereby deny a meaningful role to males, many of whom become anti-social:

The situation of women has gotten worse in many ways. If you look at some of the so-called traditional indicators of progress, which is employment, etc., the situation of women hasn't gotten any better. It's got worse....In terms of the streets, in times gone by, in days of yore, women controlled the streets. Now the streets is not a woman's domain. Violence of Jamaican society which is virtually taken for granted by everybody. I myself am looking for a place to live with grills [iron bars over the windows for security] everywhere at the moment....For a lot of women it is a matter of you can't go out of the house after six o'clock, you must get home before dark, if you go to the theatre they have a special six o'clock matinee which is almost completely attended by women because that is the time when they have to go out. So that is a situation which has gotten much worse, too....Of course the level of sexual violence has increased so much that now the streets are not the domain of women, certainly the docks aren't.[38]

The violence is male violence, a fact heavily emphasized is feminist propaganda, which calls it *patriarchal* violence. But these violent males are not patriarchs; they are exiles from the patriarchal system, males denied a meaningful role by the first law of matriarchy.

"The role of the male," says George Gilder, "is the Achilles' heel of civilized society....The man still needs to be tamed."[39] The man's violence needs to be tamed, no doubt, so that his energies

---

37. *off our backs*, March, 1987.
38. *Ibid.*
39. *Men and Marriage* (Gretna, LA: Pelican Publishing Company, 1986), pp. 45, 47.

may channeled into a useful direction rather than becoming destructive. But the taming and channeling are impossible without a meaningful male role; and since the first law of matriarchy denies men that meaningful role, the female is as much in need of taming as the male.

According to Carl Williams, head of California's Workfare program, the unmarried teen-age motherhood resulting from the first law of matriarchy burdens the welfare system and contributes to illiteracy. 60 percent of California women under 30 who are now on public assistance began receiving welfare as teen-agers.[40] 57 percent of them cannot read, write, add or subtract well enough to get a job or train for one.[41]

The males procreated by these sexually liberated females, males exploited in feminist propaganda as illustrating male anti-sociality, could better be used as illustrations of female socialization. A survey of 108 rapists undertaken by Raymond A. Knight and Robert A. Prentky, revealed that 60 percent came from female-headed homes, that 70 percent of those describable as "violent" came from female-headed homes, that 80 percent of those motivated by "displaced anger" came from female-headed homes.[42]

The first law of matriarchy implies the right of one woman to undermine the marriage of another woman. According to Laurel Richardson, a Professor of Sociology at Ohio State University, many liberated professional women prefer affairs with married men—they're less time-consuming. Unfortunately for them, however, they usually get so involved that they "lose control" over the relationships, which "end up benefiting the men more than the women,"[43] surely no part of any feminist's intention.

The first law of matriarchy is good for the abortion business. It is projected that 46 percent of today's teen-age girls will have had an abortion by the age of 45.[44]

---

40. *Los Angeles Times*, 3 May, 1987.
41. *Los Angeles Times*, 30 April, 1987
42. "The Development Antecedents and Adult Adaptations of Rapist Subtypes," *Criminal Justice and Behavior*, December, 1987, pp. 403-426. See Annex to Chapter 1, p. 237.
43. *Los Angeles Times*, 12 January, 1986.
44. *Los Angeles Times*, 7 June, 1987.

Thanks to the first law of matriarchy, births out of wedlock have increased more than 450 percent in thirty years, with obvious consequences for the welfare system. According to Gary L. Bauer,

> We know that women who receive Aid to Families with Dependent Children (AFDC) benefits when they are less than 25 years old remain dependent on AFDC for long periods of time. In fact, 70 percent received AFDC for at least five years; more than one-third got it for at least 10 years.
>
> Raised in an environment in which fathers don't provide for their young and dependency on government is assumed, few children will develop the skills of self-sufficiency, or even the concept of personal responsibility. Young men will not strive to be good providers and young women will not expect it of their men. Family breakdown becomes cyclical, out-of-wedlock births become cyclical, poverty and dependence becomes cyclical. And the culture of poverty grows.[45]

Bauer quotes Charles Murray:

> For the young woman who is not pregnant, "enabling" means she does not ask, "Do I want a welfare check badly enough to get pregnant?" but rather, "If I happen to get pregnant, will the consequences really be so bad?"
>
> ....
>
> The existence of an extensive welfare system permits the woman to put less pressure on the man to behave responsibly, which facilitates irresponsible behavior on his part, which in turn leads the woman to put less reliance on the man, which exacerbates his sense of superfluity and his search for alternative definitions of manliness.[46]

---

45. *Human Events*, 24 January, 1987.
46. *Ibid.*

The pattern is not confined to the lower orders. It underlies equally the reluctance of educated men to marry educated women, producing feminist complaints about the refusal of males to make stable and reliable commitments to women. The same male reluctance underlay the flurry of panicky articles appearing in 1986 on the subject of the "marriage crunch," the unmarriageability of educated women in their thirties. These educated women enjoy the freedoms, economic and sexual, coveted for them by the feminist movement, but they find themselves (as men too find themselves) without marriages and families. At the time, feminist Georgie Anne Geyer wrote a piece under the title "'Why Don't You Get Married?': Shorthand for Curbing Woman's Function."[47] Ms. Geyer describes herself as enraged by the pressures put on women to marry:

> We are talking here about woman as function. We are talking here about fulfilling others' ideas about what one should be fitted for and for what one exists. Worse, we are talking here not about love, faith or goodness, but about fitting into the structures that others decide for you. We are talking about control.
> To put it frankly, this kind of "concern" about one's chances at marriage is about ways of controlling women.
>
> ....
>
> Marriage can be one kind of love, and at best it certainly is one of the two or three greatest kinds. But when dealt with in terms of controlling a woman, it becomes the antithesis of love and fulfillment.

Controlling a *woman*, she says. But the man equally submits to control; and one of the persistent demands of feminists is that the woman's emancipation from control by divorce shall not emancipate the man, but obligate him to make her "independent" of him by giving her alimony and child support money.

The statistics on the unmarriageability of educated and economically independent women are factual.[48] Ms. Geyer resents them because they suggest the advisability of women

---

47. *Los Angeles Times*, 11 June, 1986.
48. See note 10.

accepting a degree of sexual regulation. She wants female behavior thought of "in positive and freeing terms rather than in negative and controlling terms." One might describe a train which jumps its tracks as behaving in a "positive and freeing" way and a train which remains on the tracks as behaving in a "negative and controlling" way. The feminist would respond that women are not machines, but the comparison will stand for all that. Women (and men) require socialization as much as trains require rails if they are to avoid catastrophe. Controlling women (and men) is not the "antithesis" but the precondition of "love and fulfillment" as well as of social stability and civilization.

Let's consider a specific case. Brandon Tholmer, 29, killer of four women, suspected killer of eight others. Tholmer is illegitimate, but that's OK, because, as Ms. Phyllis Chesler says, "every child has the right to be wanted." It doesn't occur to Ms. Chesler that the best way of insuring this right is for him to have a father who would want him, protect him and provide for him. Anyway, Tholmer's Mom practices the first law of matriarchy and her kid. is a killer. The jury which convicts him takes only an hour to decide that he should not go to the gas chamber, because of his "upbringing." According to a juror "there was nobody who took any interest in him. He had suffered most of his life."[49] He came from a broken home and from the age of 8 was kicked out into the street at night. At age 11, he was put in a juvenile detention home by Mom, later sent to a state industrial school for stealing and loitering. He is "borderline retarded," a convicted mentally disordered sex offender, a rapist, a sodomite, an arsonist, a burglar. Blaming his "upbringing" signifies that the blame lies elsewhere, as indeed it does—with the acceptance by Tholmer's Mom and by society of the first law of matriarchy.

Another case. Dean Philip Carter is convicted of killing three women and suspected of killing two others. The evidence against him is overwhelming and his attorneys don't even try to refute it:

---

49. *Los Angeles Times*, 9 August, 1986.

Relying instead [says the *Los Angeles Times* of 29 January, 1990] on an atempt to save him from the death penalty, defense attorney Howard Gillingham called 21 witnesses to testify about Carter's troubled childhood.

21 witnesses show that he had a troubled childhood and therefore is less culpable. Quite so. But who, then, is responsible for having inflicted the troubled childhood upon him? Part of the answer is to be inferred from *The Los Angeles Times'* assertion that Carter was "born the illegitimate son of a half-Eskimo woman in Nome, Alaska, on Aug. 30, 1955." Mom accepted the Promiscuity Principle and exercised her right to impose illegitimacy upon her boy, which placed him at greater risk of becoming a criminal, as the evidence given in the Annex to Chapter I shows.

Another case. Arlene W. of Wisconsin. "In the summer of 1977," writes feminist Phyllis Chesler, "Arlene W. met Red E. Early in 1978 Arlene became pregnant."[50] Patriarchal socialization would have taught Arlene the importance of pre-nuptial chastity and would have prevented the tragedy which now unfolds. But patriarchal socialization is made inoperative by the first law of matriarchy.

> Early in 1979, Red's paternity was established by the Welfare Department....Visitation was allowed....Red was physically abusive to both Arlene and [their daughter] Andrea during several visits. Arlene decided to refuse further visitation.
>
> In the fall of 1980, Red legally demanded overnight visitation twice monthly. Judge John E. McCormick told Arlene to "give a man a second chance." He ordered visitation for one weekend day and one half weekday. Visitation began. At this point, Andrea started "acting out" behavior: aggressive hitting, crying, clinging, not sleeping, wetting herself, vomiting. Andrea complained of being hit by her father—and marks were detectable....The hospital report concluded that Andrea

---

50. Phyllis Chesler, *Mothers on Trial* (New York: McGraw-Hill Book Company, 1986), p. 251.

had been sexually abused....Arlene fled Wisconsin to her brother's home in the state of Washington....Police arrived with a warrant for Arlene's arrest. They separated her from her daughter, denied her bail and the use of the telephone, and jailed her for four days....Feminists, ministers, psychiatrists, incest victims, experts, academics, jurists, the department of social services—all launched a campaign against Arlene's extradition. Arlene's unedited "Chronology of Events" documents the profound isolation and vulnerability of a battered, unwed, and welfare dependent mother who has discovered paternal incest, and the state's absolute refusal to believe or assist her.[51]

What the events document is the importance of not being an unwed mother. They also document the damage inflicted upon Arlene and Andrea by the first law of matriarchy and the incapacity of the legal system to patch up the mess created by Arlene's and Red's unchastity. Arlene is represented throughout Ms. Chesler's account as a victim. In fact she created her own miseries and those of her daughter.

The enforcing of the patriarchal sexual constitution in 1978 would have guaranteed, not infringed Arlene's autonomy, would have clarified *her* responsibility for the consequences of her sexual behavior—those she later tried (with the help of Ms. Chesler, and the feminists, ministers, psychiatrists, etc.) to blame society for. The whole thrust of Ms. Chesler's argument is that society should bail her out, thus legitimizing her unchastity in 1978. Little Andrea, whose life has been blighted by her mother's irresponsibility in disregarding the Legitimacy Principle, is put on display and her sufferings lamented in order to assist Ms. Chesler's program to further undermine the sexual constitution and the Legitimacy Principle and to promote more single motherhood, more feminism, more Andreas.

Ms. Chesler's point that the legal system is incompetent to do much for Arlene and Andrea is valid enough; but she chooses not to see how the mess she describes is created not by patriarchy but

---

51. *Ibid.*, 251-3.

by the failure of patriarchy to regulate Arlene's behavior in 1978—by society's acquiescence in the first law of matriarchy.

The pattern being promoted by feminism is well summarized by a recent Canadian study of female offenders:

> Among its findings in a survey of 100 women arrested, the majority had early sexual involvements, with over 40 percent reporting their first intercourse to have occurred between the ages of 10 and 15. Two thirds had children, but almost as many had never been married, and less than one in 10 was married at the time of her arrest. The majority, then, were single or divorced mothers. Most came from broken homes, with 73 percent of the women reporting problems such as one parent being absent all the time, divorce, foster homes, alcohol problems and child abuse. Mentally disturbed parents were common—indeed, female criminals had psychiatric problems in their immediate family twice as often as did male criminals. The authors speculate that "for women to break out of the traditional female role of compliance and passivity and become criminal they have to be products of a more disturbed background."

> In response to suggestions that the feminist movement has brought "a new era of emancipated female offenders showing some of the same patterns as male offenders," the authors acknowledge many similarities. For example, about the same percentage of female criminals commit violent offenses as do males (although "women's victims more so than men's have trouble defending themselves—for example, children, intoxicated, asleep, infirm").

> The authors resist describing women criminals as "emancipated," but what their study *does* describe— sexual promiscuity, divorce, women who act increasingly like men—are familiar results of the sexual revolution.[52]

52. R. G. Robertson, *et al.*, "The Female Offender: A Canadian Study," *Canadian Journal of Psychiatry*, 32 (December, 1987), pp. 749-755; epitomized in *The Family in America: New Research*, April, 1988.

The problems created by the first law of matriarchy were predictable—female promiscuity and illegitimacy, male roleless-ness and anti-sociality. With more illegitimacy,[53] come more second generation crime, more educational failure, more demor-alization, less motivation, less productivity, reduced self-es-teem, less commitment to the future as evidenced by reduced accumulation of stabilizing (and garnishable) assets such as real estate, annuities, pensions, stock portfolios, savings accounts, insurance. More sexual confusion, more hedonism, more infan-tilism (of which non-commitment is a variety), more emotional shallowness. And, of course, in consequence of all of these, more family breakdown, more family non-formation, more demands for freebies from the government's Backup System (welfare, day care, workfare, wage-garnishment as a means of financing fami-lies—with the consequence of yet further fear of commitment to family living). And so on, without end, each attempt by the Backup System to patch up the mess created by family break-down working to further undermine the male role, and with it the family.

"If women were really people," wrote Ms. Friedan in 1973, "—no more, no less—then all the things that kept them from being full people in our society would have to be changed."[54] "Full" means something like "without sex-role socialization." Along with the abandoning of this socialization for girls, there has been a complementary abandoning of the sex role socializa-tion of boys. The results can be witnessed by anyone who takes a stroll across one of today's high school campuses. Such a stroll reveals that a majority of girls have become shallow, sassy tarts,

---

53. Daughters in one-parent homes are much more likely to engage in premarital sex than are daughters in two-parent homes." (Susan Newcomer and J. Richard Udry, "Parental Marital Status Effects on Adolescent Sexual Behavior," *Journal of Marriage and the Family*, 49, No. 2 (May, 1987), pp. 235-40; cited in *The Family in America: New Research*, August, 1987.) See the fuller quote in Annex to Chapter 1, p. 248.

"Daughters from female-headed households are much more likely than daugh-ters from two-parent families to themselves become single parents and to rely on welfare for support as adults." (Sara S. McLanahan, "Family Structure and Dependency: Early Transitions to Female Household Headship," *Demography* 25 [Feb., 1988], 1-16; epitomized in *The Family in America: New Research*, May, 1988.) See the fuller quote in Annex to Chapter 1, p. 240.

54. Introduction to the 10th anniversary edition of *The Feminine Mystique* (New York: W. W. Norton, 1973), p. 4.

a majority of boys little better than slobs with little self-discipline, little frustration-tolerance, little character, little inner-direction.

Back in 1963, when Ms. Friedan unleashed feminism upon us with her book *The Feminine Mystique*, she said that her ideas "may disturb the experts and women alike, for they imply social change."[55] The change has gone on long enough to permit an evaluation. Are women happier? Are men? Are children better mannered, better socialized? Is there more premarital sexual activity? More venereal disease? More single motherhood? More shacking-up? More adultery? Is the family more stable? Is educational performance superior to what it was in the early 1960s? (Remember that the original "new life plan for women" was a program of education.) Are there fewer school dropouts? Is the level of public debate more civilized, more mature? Are better young people choosing teaching as a career and providing youth with better instruction and better role models? Are the streets safer? Do the media reflect a growing refinement of taste and morality? Are more or fewer women living in poverty? In substance abuse? Are the relationships between the sexes more refined and civilized or more cynical, trivial and exploitive? Is there more or less cheating in classrooms, business relationships and tax forms and everywhere else? Have the costs of welfare, police and government increased or decreased? Do we get more or less in services for our tax dollar? Is there more or less trash deposited on our beaches? Are public parks more or less inviting places of recreation? Does the legal profession eat up more or less of our earnings? Is service more or less courteous than it was a quarter of a century ago?

Social change indeed. There is no area in which the undermining of sex role socialization has not been disastrous.

Here is the way today's women are coming to perceive their responsibilities towards society and society's responsibilities to them. The speaker is Byllye Avery, Director of the National Black Women's Health Project: "I have a right to life, to a house, education, job, food, a good, high quality standard of living, and

---

55. *The Feminine Mystique*, p. 10.

a right to control my reproduction."[56] This is the fruition of Ms. Friedan's program to make women stand on their own feet—and make demands upon others.

Let us now turn from the two-hundred-million-year-old biologically based mammalian/matrilineal reproductive arrangement and examine the patriarchal system which succeeded it a few thousand years ago and made civilization possible—the artificial, fragile patriarchal arrangement designed to elevate male sperm-providers into *fathers* and to allow them an equal share in human reproduction. It is the purpose of the feminist/ sexual revolution to do away with this manmade superstructure built on the foundation of female reproductive biology and to restore the original mammalian/matrilineal arrangement—a purpose only vaguely perceived by a minority of radical feminists and as yet uncomprehended by the patriarchal males whose responsibility it must be to restore and stabilize it.

---

56. *off our backs*, April, 1986.

III

The Patriarchal System:

Putting Sex To Work

The matriarchy described in the previous chapter is perceived by feminists as a lost Golden Age—and also as the bright wave of the future. Women living in surviving Stone Age societies, such as exist on Indian reservations, are held up as exemplars for the liberated women of our own society. "There are parts of the world," writes feminist Elise Boulding,

> where women already feel the autonomy I am imagining for Western women in the future. For Americans, North and South, there is an alternative model for women close at hand, in the Native American communities...It doesn't take many encounters with women tribal leaders who have the quiet confidence of centuries of traditional knowledge behind them to realize that here are a set of teachers for European-stock American women right in our midst. Where does their serenity and self-confidence come from? What do they "know"?...This is a time for the rest of us, especially middle-class Western women, to "go to school" to those of our sisters who have the unacknowledged skills, the confidence, the serenity, and the knowledge required for creative social change.[1]

These Stone Age women, despite their squalor, ignorance and poverty, are contented. They fill the biological role of the mammalian female, heading the reproductive unit, enjoying the liberty of the first law of matriarchy. And today's feminists are coming to share their tranquility and placidity. They are, as

---

1. Elise Boulding, *The Underside of History* (Boulder, Colorado: Westview Press, 1976), pp. 790ff.

Helen Fisher says, "moving towards the kind of roles they had on the grasslands of Africa millions of years ago....Human society is now discovering its ancient roots."[2] As Betty Friedan puts it,

> For my generation and the generation that followed, the battle for women's rights came in the middle of life— after we'd started our families and were already living the feminine mystique. For us, the feminist movement meant the marvelous midlife discovery of a whole new identity, a new sense of self. The most notable result of this newfound identity was a dramatic improvement in the mental health of older women....Two decades ago mental hospitals were full of women suffering from involutional melancholia, a severe depression that afflicted women at the time of menopause when, according to the old feminine mystique, their life was over. But a few years ago the American Psychiatric Association stopped using the term because such acute depression was no longer considered age related.
> Today the mental health of women in their 40s, 50s and 60s is as good as that of women in their 20s and 30s. No such improvement has occurred in men, so it really is related to the women's movement toward equality.[3]

No such improvement has occurred in men because men have had to pay the costs. Men in the larger society are being ground down to the status of the men on Indian reservations—roleless, unmotivated, alcoholic and suicidal, because the first law of matriarchy deprives them of a stable family role.

It was the discovery a few thousand years ago of this connection between the regulation of female sexuality on the one hand and family and social stability, male productivity and social progress on the other which ended the Stone Age and began the era of patriarchal civilization. "Patriarchy's age," says lesbian-feminist Susan Cavin, "is approximately 3,000-5,000 years old.

---

2. *Supra*, p. 5.
3. Betty Friedan. "Not for Women Only." *Modern Maturity*, April-May, 1989, p. 70.

Compared to the millions of years human ancestors have populated the earth, patriarchy represents only a dot of human
time."[4]

True. The fact shows that the creation of patriarchy is the
greatest of human achievements, since each and every one of the
other achievements of civilization came into existence during
hat dot of time, whereas the preceding millions of years creat-
ednone of them. Patriarchy, says Adrienne Rich, "is the one
system which recorded civilization has never actively chal-
lenged."[5] That is because without patriarchy there can be no
recorded (or unrecorded) civilization.

The central fact about patriarchal civilization, besides its
recency and the magnitude of its accomplishments, is its artifi-
ciality and fragility, its dependence on women's willingness to
submit to sexual regulation. Women's de-regulation of themselves by achieving economic and sexual independence can
wreck the system. The ghettos show how easily this can happen.
The wrecking of the system is rapidly spreading from the ghettos
to the larger society, where the legal system has become
patriarchy's chief enemy, expelling half of society's fathers from
their homes.

Dr. Gerda Lerner describes how sexual regulation was imposed on women in ancient Mesopotamia, during the era in
which the patriarchal system was being developed: "While the
wife enjoyed considerable and specified rights in marriage, she
was *sexually* the man's property."[6] Her rights and her status
depended upon her acceptance of the patriarchal system—and
vice versa, the system depended upon her acceptance of regulation. "In Mesopotamian law, and even more strongly in Hebrew
law," continues Dr. Lerner, "all women are increasingly under
sexual dominance and regulation....The strict obligations by
husbands and sons toward mothers and wives in Hammurabic

---

4. Susan Cavin. *An Hystorical and Cross-Cultural Analysis of Sex Ratios, Female
Sexuality, and Homo-Sexual Segregation Versus Hetero-Sexual Integration Patterns
in Relation to the Liberation of Women.* Ph.D. dissertation. Rutgers. 1979, p. 4.
(Feminists affect spellings such as *hystorical, wimin,* and *herstory* in order to avoid
the hated masculine forms *his* and *man.*) There exists a lesbian organization called
"Wimmin" for Womyn.")

5. *Of Woman Born* (New York: W. W. Norton, 1976). p. 56.

6. *The Creation of Patriarchy* (New York: Oxford University Press, 1986). p. 114.
This is further discussed below. Chapter X, p. 193.

and Hebrew law can thus be seen as strengthening the patriarchal family, which depends on the willing cooperation of wives in
a system which offers them class advantages in exchange for
their subordination in sexual matters."[7]

Providing for a woman and placing her "under coverture" in
the honorable state of marriage is perceived by today's feminists
in wholly negative terms as dominance, regulation and oppression. Feminist Dr. Alice Rossi speaks of "an exchange" between
a husband and a wife in which the husband confers social status
on the wife and "in exchange...she assumes economic dependence on him"—permits *him* to pay *her* bills.[8] It doesn't occur to
feminists that "their subordination in sexual matters" benefits
women as much as it benefits men. It means law-and-order in
the sexual realm and the creation of wealth in the economic
realm. It means stable families which provide women with
security and status and in which children can be decently reared
and socialized.

As will be explained in detail in Chapter VII, Dr. Lerner's and
Dr. Rossi's view of sexual law-and-order as something imposed
by males is the opposite of George Gilder's. Gilder imagines that
women have a primal yearning to impose sexual law-and-order
on men and that civilization depends on men submitting themselves to women's higher ethic:

> She is the vessel of the ultimate values of the nation. The
> community is largely what she is and what she demands
> in men.[9]

He describes this imposition of female values on males as
"creating civilization." But if civilization is a female creation,
imposed by women upon men, why did not civilization precede
patriarchy? "The appropriation by men of women's sexual and
reproductive capacity," says Dr. Lerner, "occurred *prior* to the
formation of private property and class society."[10] It was the
precondition for the creation of the wealth upon which civiliza-

---

7. *Ibid.*, p. 113.
8. In Theodore Roszak, *The Masculine/Feminine: Readings in Sexual Mythology and the Liberation of Women* (New York, Harper and Row, 1969), p. 178.
9. Gilder, *Men and Marriage* (Gretna, LA: Pelican Publishing Company), p. 169.
10. *The Creation of Patriarchy*, p. 8.

tion depends. Without sexual law-and-order men cannot be motivated to create wealth or do anything else worth doing.

While Dr. Lerner is oblivious to the advantages for women of this patriarchal law-and-order, she is correct in insisting that the law-and-order is a male idea. In discussing the Garden of Eden story she writes:

> [T]he consequences of Adam and Eve's transgression fall with uneven weight upon the woman. The consequence of sexual knowledge is to sever female sexuality from procreation. God puts enmity between the snake and the woman (Gen. 3:15). In the historical context of the times of the writing of Genesis, the snake was clearly associated with the fertility goddess and symbolically represented her. Thus, by God's command, the free and open sexuality of the fertility-oddess was to be forbidden to fallen woman. The way her sexuality was to find expression was in motherhood.[11]

It is significant that a feminist like Dr. Lerner perceives "female sexuality" as female *promiscuity*. On page 198, she has this:

> To the question "Who brought sin and death into the world?" Genesis answers, "Woman, in her alliance with the snake, which stands for *free* female sexuality." [Emphasis added]

The Biblical view is not that "female sexuality" is *severed* from procreation but that it is *joined* to it, in other words that it must be regulated in accordance with the patriarchal Sexual Constitution which Gilder imagines as something which women try to impose on men, but which Genesis and Dr. Lerner more plausibly see as something men impose on women.

Dr. Lerner affects to believe (perhaps does believe) that sexual promiscuity signifies high status for women:

---

11. *The Creation of Patriarchy*, p. 196.

Further, women [in the Ancient Near East] seemed to have greatly different status in different aspects of their lives, so that, for example, in Babylon in the second millennium B.C. women's sexuality was totally controlled by men, while some women enjoyed great economic independence, many legal rights and privileges and held many important high status positions in society. I was puzzled to find that the historical evidence pertaining to women made little sense, when judged by traditional criteria. After a while I began to see that I needed to focus more on the control of women's sexuality and procreativity than on the usual economic questions, so I began to look for the causes and effects of such sexual control.[12]

Her views, paralleling those of promiscuity chic movie actresses and other anti-patriarchal groupies, are antithetical to those of Gilder. Much of the feminist struggle is one to displace the feminine mystique "image" of the weakly virtuous patriarchy-accepting doll-wife abominated by Betty Friedan (and lauded by George Gilder) by the image of a defiantly promiscuous hell-raiser who will destroy the patriarchy by re-instituting the first law of matriarchy.

"The sexual control of women," says Dr. Lerner, "has been an essential feature of patriarchal power. The sexual regulation of women underlies the formation of classes and is one of the foundations upon which the state rests."[13] Quite so. If you doubt it, ask yourself what kind of a state we will have when it is populated, as it is coming to be, by the fatherless offspring of today's promiscuous females—when the feminists on the campuses of our schools and colleges have convinced young women that the traditional patriarchal attempts to regulate their reproduction by imposing chastity and modesty upon them are a sexist plot to contravene the first law of matriarchy. The kind of state we will have is indicated by the evidence given in Chapter I, showing the high correlation between female-headed families and social pathology.

12. *Ibid.*, p. 8.
13. P. 140.

"The state," continues Dr. Lerner,

> during the process of the establishment of written law
> codes, increased the property rights of upper-class
> women, while it circumscribed their sexual rights and
> finally totally eroded them.[14]

By their "sexual rights" she means not their right to be loved,
honored and protected under coverture, not their right to enter
into a stable and binding—and highly advantageous—contract
to share their reproductive life with a man, but their right to be
promiscuous, and therefore of no value to a man interested in
having a family rather than a one-night stand. She does not even
consider (what Gilder supposes to be self-evident) that many
women covet the right to have a stable monogamous marriage,
and thereby acquire the economic and emotional security and
the status which the patriarchy offers women in exchange for
allowing men a meaningful reproductive role—the right to be
decently socialized in childhood, the right to the high status
patriarchy confers upon "good" women.

"Their sexual and reproductive capacities," continues Dr.
Lerner, "were commodified, traded, leased, or sold in the interest
of male family members."[15] What is the alternative? To have
men *not* interested in stable family arrangements—to leave
these arrangements instead to female improvisation of the sort
found in the ghettos and on Indian reservations?

> The Code of Hammurabi [continues Dr. Lerner] marks
> the beginning of the institutionalization of the patriar-
> chal family as an aspect of state power. It reflects a class
> society in which women's status depended on the male
> family head's social status and property. The wife of an
> impoverished burgher could by a change of his status,
> without her volition or action, be turned from a respect-
> able woman into a debt slave or a prostitute. On the
> other hand, a married woman's sexual behavior, such as

---

14. P. 141.
15. P. 141. The word "commodified," common in feminist literature, is not
defined in any dictionary I have consulted.

adultery or an unmarried woman's loss of chastity, could declass her in a way in which no man could be declassed by his sexual activity.[16]

Her status depended upon his status. Therefore she was motivated to make him achieve high status. And the success of the system in generating male overachievers who create wealth, social stability and progress—all beneficial to women—proves the arrangement to be desirable. Women would not have accepted it unless its benefits were greater than those offered by matriarchy. The wife of an impoverished burgher could have been de-classed by her husband's behavior, but she chose to be his wife because through marriage her status and income were more likely to be raised than lowered. This is the way the patriarchal system works, and it benefits everyone. It gives men motivation, makes them productive and thus helps their wives and children. It puts sex to work as a motivator, focusing on long-term (family) arrangements rather than on short term sexuality—promiscuity, the first law of matriarchy.

"Society asks so little of women," says Betty Friedan.[17] But that little must include the chastity and loyalty which makes patriarchal fatherhood and legitimate children possible.

"When Nigerian Muslim communities get richer through development," writes feminist sociologist Caroline Knowles, "women are increasingly confined in the home."[18] Is it not then other way round—that when women are increasingly confined to the home, the communities get richer because more stable families are better motivators of male achievement?

There exists a woman's organization called Single Mothers by Choice but there exists no comparable men's organization called Single Fathers by Choice. A man must choose to *marry* if he wants children. Only a woman can choose to be a single parent—but for every woman who makes that choice there exists a man who is denied the choice of marriage and family, and therefore patriarchal society must deter single women from choosing parenthood. If women were to become economically

---

16. P. 140.

17. *The Feminine Mystique* (New York: W. W. Norton, 1963), p. 338.

18. *off our backs*, November, 1987.

independent (as feminism wishes them to be) and if the feminist principle becomes accepted that "there is no such thing as an illegitimate child," then men have no bargaining power, no way of inducing women to enter a stable marriage (though they may be willing to enter an *un*stable one as long as, following divorce, they have assurance of custody of the children accompanied by economic advantages). Under such conditions society becomes a matriarchal ghetto.

"Woman, in precivilized society," writes Dr. Lerner, "must have been man's equal and may well have felt herself to be his superior."[19] Her superiority (which made males idle drones) is why it was "precivilized"—and why precivilization lasted a million years. Her superiority is why Elise Boulding holds up the squaws on Indian reservations as models for American middle-class women. Her superiority is why women would not be altogether reluctant to return to precivilization, why feminists like Mary Daly declare that "society is a male creation and serves male interests" and that "sisterhood means revolution,"[20] why Freud thought that woman was the enemy of civilization, why feminists like Adrienne Rich insist that patriarchal civilization has been imposed upon women over "an enormous potential counterforce."[21]

"In some places like Dahomey and among the Tlinkits of Alaska," writes feminist Marilyn French, "wealthy classes are patrilineal while poorer classes are matrilineal."[22] Let's put this the other way round: the patrilineal classes are wealthy—because their males are motivated to provide for stable families; the matrilineal classes are poor because their males are not. As she adds on the following page, "In matrilineal societies there are more sexually integrated activities and more sexual freedom for women." That is why they are poorer. Savage women and feminists *want* marriage to be unstable in order that they may point to its instability not only as justification for the first law of

19. *The Creation of Patriarchy*, p. 43.

20. *Beyond God the Father: Toward a Philosophy of Women's Liberation* (Boston: Beacon Press, 1973), p. 59.

21. "Compulsory Heterosexuality and Lesbian Existence," in *Feminist Frontiers: Rethinking Sex, Gender, and Society*, ed. Laurel Richardson and Verta Taylor (Reading, MA: Addison-Wesley Publishing Company, 1983), p. 222.

22. *Beyond Power* (New York: Summit Books, 1985), p. 56.

matriarchy but as proving the necessity for women to be subsidized by non-family arrangements which do not impose sexual law-and-order upon them. That the subsidization they demand must be paid for by taxing the shrinking numbers of patriarchal families who *do* submit to sexual law-and-order is no concern of theirs—except as it further undermines the patriarchy, which (they think) is good.

Men stabilize marriage by creating wealth. According to Emily Hahn, "Necessity, as well as instinct, sends the ladies pell-mell to the altar; it is only the secondary things, social pressure of conscience, that send the men."[23] (What sends the men is the desire to have families—which is not secondary, but never mind that.) What Ms. Hahn is acknowledging is that with women the economic motive is primary. Feminist Barbara Ehrenreich agrees:

> Women were, and to a large extent still are, economically dependent on men....So what was at stake for women in the battle of the sexes was, crudely put, a claim on some man's wage.
>
> ....
>
> The fact that, in a purely economic sense, women need men more than the other way round, gives marriage an inherent instability that predates the sexual revolution, the revival of feminism, the "me generation" or other well-worn explanations for what has come to be known as the "breakdown of the family."[24]

(The instability does not predate the feminist/sexual revolution but is a principal consequence of this revolution.)

> It is, in retrospect [continues Ms. Ehrenreich], frightening to think how much of our sense of social order and continuity has depended on the willingness of men to succumb in the battle of the sexes: to marry, to become wage-earners and to reliably share their wages with their dependents.

23. Quoted in Barbara Ehrenreich, *The Hearts of Men: American Dreams and the Flight from Commitment* (Garden City, NY: Anchor Books, 1984), p. 1.
24. P. 2; emphasis added.

45

(A man formerly—in the days of stable marriage contracts—did not "succumb"; he entered into what he believed to be a binding agreement which promised him the satisfactions of marriage and the right of procreating legitimate and inalienable offspring. It is the invalidating of these expectations which has turned men off from marriage or made them enter into it with the shallow commitment of which Ms. Ehrenreich complains.)

She continues:

> In fact, most of us require more comforting alternative descriptions of the bond between men and women. We romanticize it, as in the popular song lyrics of the fifties where love was an adventure culminating either in matrimony or premature death. Or we convince ourselves that there is really a fair and equal exchange at work so that the wages men offer to women are more than compensated for by the services women offer to men. Any other conclusion would be a grave embarrassment to both sexes. Women do not like to admit to a disproportionate dependence, just as men do not like to admit that they may have been conned into undertaking what one cynical male called "the lifelong support of the female unemployed."[25]

She shows that it is the man's paycheck which holds marriage together, and then she, most illogically, describes this paycheck as something causing *instability*. The least stable marriages are those in which the husband fails to earn the paycheck and those in which the wife earns a large enough paycheck to make her economically independent of the husband. "In the overwhelming majority of households today," says Lynne Segal, "men are no longer the sole breadwinners, and as their economic power has declined, domestic conflict and strain have increased...." [26] Segal regards it as self-evidently good that women should shake off male controls and that the relative decline in men's economic

---

25. P. 2-3.
26. *Is The Future Female? Troubled Thoughts on Contemporary Feminism* (New York: Peter Bedrick Books, 1988), p. 106. For confirmation of what Ms. Segal says, see Chapter II, note 10.

power facilitates this shaking-off. She speaks for most women. Besides economic emancipation, there is an emancipation from traditional mores. The increase in illegitimate births among white teenagers from 6.6 percent in 1955 to 40 percent today follows from the removal of the controls (shame, guilt, etc.) which feminists have been working to remove, and their replacement by "a woman's right to control her own sexuality."

Popular songs such as "Papa, Don't Preach" and "Thanks for My Child" illustrate the failure to comprehend the Legitimacy Principle as essential to the working of the patriarchal system. Mrs. E. M. Anderson of Compton's Teen Mothers Program comments thus concerning the message of "Thanks for My Child," dealing with the woes (but also the noble inner strength) of a poor female who meets the father of her child four years after it is born:

> These guys [i.e., the unwed fathers] are dumb—dumb. All they think about is themselves. *Responsibility?* Forget it. They cause a lot of pain and are too dumb to care.[27]

"The song," says Mrs. Anderson, "does a service if it exposes the problem of these young kids getting pregnant out of wedlock by these guys who don't want any part of being fathers." A better service would be to explain to the dumb guys how they might *claim* the responsibilities of fatherhood if they wished to do so. What inducement would she have society offer the guys who *want* to be fathers and have families?[28] The larger society offers white males a fifty percent chance of having and keeping children and a fifty percent chance of losing them to their ex-wives. In the ghettos society offers virtually nothing to males who accept the responsibilities of fatherhood—and it attempts to compensate for its failure to provide the props needed by respon-

---

27. *Los Angeles Times*, 24 November, 1988.

28. See the quotation from Beverly Beyette, *Los Angeles Times*, 10 April, 1986 in Annex to Chapter I, p. 242: "They are rather casual about pregnancy--no, they would not choose *not* to be pregnant. And, no, they do not expect, nor do they want, to marry their babies' fathers. Camilla, a sophomore, said, 'I tell him it isn't his baby so he won't call.'"

What could Camilla's boyfriend do if he *wanted* to behave "responsibly"?

sible fathers by showering rewards upon single mothers (non-ghetto and ghetto) in the form of AFDC, food stamps, subsidized housing, free medical care and the rest.

Besides these material rewards, there are status rewards. According to Jeff Wyatt, program director of a radio station which plays "Thanks for my Child" every day on the demand of enthusiastic female listeners,

> The message really touches them—the mother-child aspect of it. Women identify with the woman in the song. Maybe some of them know young ladies who have been in that situation. Maybe some of them have been in that situation themselves.[29]

According to Mike Archie, music director of WHUR-FM in Washington, D. C., women, especially black women, are responding strongly to the record, which has been the most requested single at his station:

> The single focuses on the inner strength of black women, which makes it appeal strongly to black women. I find that it really touches single female parents—or women with children in general. In the song this woman is saying how much she really loves her child and that love can carry her through anything.

This is the old "feminine mystique" again—which feminism was created to get rid of. Women were told by Ms. Friedan to make less of a fuss about their maternal functions ("Don't you want to be more than an animal?"[31]) and participate instead in

29. *Ibid.*
30. *Ibid.*
31. *The Feminine Mystique*, p. 339. Cf. p. 289: "These mothers have themselves become more infantile, and because they are forced to seek more and more gratification through the child, they are incapable of finally separating themselves from the child. Thus, it would seem, it is the child who supports life in the mother in that 'symbiotic' relationship, and the child is virtually destroyed in the process."

It is these destroyed children who have become today's Garbage Generation. Their problem is not so much the mother's infantilism as her power to deprive the children of fathers. Ms. Friedan can thnk only of *Mom*, what *Mom* wants or should want if she is the achieve the "growth" of which she writes so interminably. She says:

> By permitting girls to evade tests of reality, and real commitments, in school and the world [by "real" Ms. Friedan means male-style achievement, not mere maternity], by the promise of magical fulfillment through marriage [today read: marriage or promiscuity], the feminine mystique arrests their development at an infantile level, short of personal identity, with an inevitably weak core of self. [p. 290]

the arena of male achievement. "Thanks for My Child" reverts
to Mom's maternal functions as the true source of woman's glory.
The miserable consequences of female unchastity are celebrated
as proving "the inner strength of black women." And the same
wonderful inner strength is illustrated by comparison with the
irresponsibility of the dumb male. *The Los Angeles Times* article
describing the popularity of the song quotes Wes Hall, dean of
students at Compton High School, in the Los Angeles ghetto:

> The guys who father these kids have all the excuses for
> ignoring their responsibilities. If no one makes the
> young man see his responsibility, he'll go scot-free and
> father more kids. The burden falls on the teen-age girls
> who are too young to handle it. Maybe this song will get
> a message to some of these young men—that what
> they're doing is very wrong.[32]

The girls are too young to handle it—and therefore they need
to be taught what nobody teaches them, the necessity of chastity
and conformity to the Sexual Constitution, the necessity of
rejecting the Promiscuity Principle which tells them they alone
have the right to control their sexuality—without interference
from the irresponsible males whom Wes Hall would like to make
responsible but who are discouraged—or prevented—from responsibility by the Promiscuity Principle which allows females
to be mothers while preventing males from being fathers. Instead of teaching these girls chastity, the song teaches them
about their wonderful inner strength (which nobody would have
known about if they hadn't been promiscuous), about the moral
inferiority of the dumb male, equally responsible but lacking
their inner strength—as though unchaste females might protect
their virtue by surrounding themselves with chaste Parsifal-like
males. They are taught that there is no such thing as an
illegitimate child, that society must not be judgmental of them,
meaning that it must not use shame and guilt to regulate their
anti-social behavior. And so forth. Wes Hall simply refuses to
see the fact that males cannot be responsible heads of families
unless society insists upon female chastity and loyalty and

32. *Ibid.*

implements its insistence by guaranteeing to males the rewards of family life which justify imposing upon them the obligations of paternal responsibility. For males to accept the responsibility which Wes Hall wishes them to accept there must exist some reasonably dependable way for them to *assume* responsibility—and there is no way, because Mom and society want no part of them except their paychecks.

Here's Edward McNamara, who wants to do what Wes Hall is urging the young black teenagers to do—accept the responsibilities of fatherhood. The law won't let him. He has had six court appearances to gain custody of an illegitimate daughter, and, after giving up on custody, more court appearances to gain visitation rights. According to the *Los Angeles Times,*

> McNamara, 41, maintains that his constitutional rights were violated when San Diego County social workers—acting at the behest of the baby's mother—placed the girl with an adoptive family four weeks after her birth.
>
> But in sharp questioning in a high court [U.S. Supreme Court] hearing on the case, the justices disputed the notion that the U. S. Constitution gives an unwed father rights that outweigh those of the child.
>
> "Why can't the state of California decide it wants to follow this polity" of acting in the best interest of the child? asked Chief Justice William H. Rehnquist. State law directs social workers to consider the child's welfare foremost in custody cases, and the courts have agreed that McNamara's daughter would be better served in the care of the adopting family.
>
> Justice Sandra Day O'Connor said she wondered why someone who engages "in a so-called one-night stand" would have a constitutional right to control the fate of the child who accidentally results from the affair.[33]

The right of "someone" is unquestioned if "someone" is the *female* who engages in the one-night stand. And if McNamara were not a participant in a one-night stand but a husband or ex-husband he would stand little better with the law. According to the *Los Angeles Daily News,*

---

33. *Los Angeles Times,* 29 November, 1988.

In 1976, the Supreme Court ruled that a husband did not have the power to impose an "absolute veto" over his wife's decision to have an abortion....Women's groups reject out of hand the argument that men have a right to a legal say in the decisionmaking process...and insist that the abortion decision should belong solely to the woman.[34]

The point is equally relevant to McNamara and to the black youths scolded by Wes Hall: Women's (and girls') refusal to grant men a significant role in reproduction means that they are denying to *themselves* the right to make a dependable commitment to bear a husband's children. The Promiscuity Principle (a woman's right to control her own sexuality) makes women moral minors who cannot enter into an enforceable contract to share reproduction with a man. A contract with a woman is worthless if she insists on her right to break it—and has the law on her side in doing so. No matter what a man does, a promiscuous woman excludes him from responsible reproduction. It is for this reason that the civilizations of antiquity found it necessary to divide women into "good" and "bad," those with whom a binding contract of marriage was possible and those with whom it was not. Only with society's enforcement of the man's rights under the contract is it possible for him to accept the kind of responsibility Wes Hall wants black teenage youths to accept. The entire fabric of patriarchal civilization rests upon female chastity. It would be ridiculous to refer to a man's chastity as his *virtue* because his *un*chastity does not destroy his family and his wife's reproductive role. But a woman's chastity is her virtue because her unchastity destroys her family and her husband's reproductive role—and civilized society along with them, because civilized society is built on the patriarchal, nuclear, two-parent family.

Feminist Hazel Henderson writes a piece titled "Thinking Globally, Acting Locally," in which she complains of "fathers who refuse to pay their child support payments ordered by courts." In the same column of the same page she rejoices thus over the success of the sexual/feminist revolution:

---

34. *Los Angeles Daily News*, 13 November, 1988.

Yet the genie will not go back in the bottle—the cultural revolution has already occurred. Politics only ratifies social change after at least a ten year lag. Even more terrifying for the old patriarchs and their female dupes is the knowledge that the whole culture is "up for grabs." For example, it could shift fundamentally in less than a generation IF women simply took back their reproductive rights, endowed by biology and Nature. All that women would need to do to create a quiet revolution is to resume the old practice of keeping the paternity of their children a secret.[35]

She cherishes the Promiscuity Principle—but also men's money. Men must teach women that the money will not be forthcoming unless they submit to the patriarchal Sexual Constitution and allow fathers to have legitimate and inalienable children. Society wants males to earn money. It is the labor of males which creates the prosperity of society, as the poverty of the surviving Stone Age societies, the ghettos, and the Indian reservations amply shows. There is one way, and only one, of motivating males to earn that money, and that is to make them heads of families. Wes Hall may condemn the young black males who procreate illegitimate children and go "scot-free" of the responsibility which ought to accompany fatherhood. These young black males ought to be taught in their sex education classes that they aren't so much getting something for nothing, as they are being *deprived* of the possibility of real fatherhood because of the unchastity of the females who consent to cohabit with them and because of society's unwillingness to supply the props (in addition to demanding the complementary responsibilities) which fatherhood must have because of its biological marginality.

The black matriarchs who, like Mrs. E. M. Anderson, view "Thanks for My Child" as "a positive statement of a mother's love for her child" no doubt also perceive it as a reaffirmation of female moral superiority, paralleling the one-upmanship of their Latin American sisters who encourage their men in childish displays of machismo in order to cast themselves in the

---

35. *Woman of Power,* Fall, 1988, p. 16.

complementary role ("marianismo") of morally superior, spiritually strong, understanding but forbearing "Mamacitas." It is *men* who must put an end to this *feminine mystique*. The male reply to the condescension of "Thanks for My Child" ought to be an indignantly ironic "Thanks for reducing me to the status of a stud. Thanks for preventing me from being a real father, from having a real family."

The male is not equally responsible with the female for inflicting illegitimacy on a child. In the patriarchal system a man can only be held responsible to a "good" woman, one who accepts the Sexual Constitution. The bad women are an essential part of the system, but they must be de-classed and regarded as unfit for marriage, since husbands can have no assurance of their chastity and loyalty, no assurance of having legitimate children by them. The feminist campaign to do away with the double standard is an attempt to remove this class distinction and make all women "good." Instead, it is making all women "bad," creating the Garbage Generation in the process. The predicament lamented in "Thanks for My Child" has the consequence that women can no longer trust men and men can no longer trust women.

77 percent of the women readers of *Glamour* magazine responded "yes" to a survey (Nov., 1985) asking whether they approved of single women having children. 40 percent of girls in school today will be heads of households—signifying that 40 percent of boys will not be. These females will deem themselves to be leading meaningful and (now that their sexuality is deregulated) socially acceptable lives. The displaced males will be leading roleless, often disruptive lives. If the fathers of illegitimate children can be coerced into supporting the mothers, the mothers will believe that a paternity suit (or a divorce decree) is as good as a marriage contract—or rather better, since it involves no reciprocal responsibilities, not even temporarily. Such sexual de-regulation of females means the destruction of the family and the ghettoizing of society.

The Prophet Mohammed emphasized the importance of regulating female sexuality. According to Dr. Fatima Mernissi, he saw the establishment of the male-dominated Muslim family as crucial to the establishment of Islam. He bitterly fought existing sexual practices where marital unions for both men and women were numerous and lax.[37]

In Saudi Arabia there exists a Committee for the Protection of Virtue and Prevention of Vice, whose executive arm is the *Mutatawa* or religious police. According to Kim Murphy,

> Nearly every woman has an unpleasant encounter with the Mutatawa to report, an incident when she was observed talking to an unrelated man in public, or shopping without the proper headgear or *abaya*, and subjected to a public tongue-lashing, or worse.
>
> "In the *souq* [market], they'll come up to you and say, Aren't you ashamed of yourself?' Or worse yet, they go up to your husband and say, 'Aren't you a man? Why are you dragging this hussy around with you?'" Raslan said. "You've embarrassed yourself, you've embarrassed your husband, and for what? For what reason?"
>
> "Officially," she said, "they say, 'We don't want the ladies having to face the hazards [of being part of the working world], we want to protect them.' But unofficially, what the women see is they are apprehensive of women finding their own feet."[38]

Apprehensive that women will sexually de-regulate themselves, restore the first law of matriarchy, replace the two-parent family with the "rotational" family, destroy the male role and ghettoize society. The Matatawa themselves may be ridiculous, but their apprehension is not. Take another look at the words of Hazel Henderson or those of Helen Fisher on page 5. What the Matatawa are afraid of has already happened in the ghettos and is happening before our eyes in the larger society. The ridiculousness of the religious police, like the ridiculousness

---

37. Fatima Mernissi, *Beyond the Veil: Male and Female Dynamics in a Modern Muslim Society*, cited in Phyllis Chesler, *Mothers on Trial: The Battle for Children and Custody* (New York: McGraw-Hill, 1986), p. 569.

38. *Los Angeles Times*, 24 November, 1989.

of Victorian puritanism, proves not the silliness of the patriarchal system but its shakiness and the marginality of the male role within it—and its need for social props to sustain it. Female promiscuity can wreck it, as Hazel Henderson and Sjoo and Mor and other feminists clearly perceive.

"The women's libbers," says Samuel Blumenfeld,

> object to the moral codes that the patriarchal system evolved as aids in the subjugation of women. But we must marvel at man's intellectual genius in creating such effective cultural and social devices to maintain the integrity of the family, as well as his control over women with a minimum of physical force.[39]

Blumenfeld sees "the moral codes crumbling all around us," and says

> Whoever sold teen-agers on the idea that there is such a thing as premarital "recreational sex" ought to be shot. Unless one understands that sexual pleasure was created by nature as bait for the more painful responsibilities of existence, one cannot understand sex, one cannot understand love, one cannot understand life. Unless sexual pleasure leads to human responsibility, it then becomes the shallowest and most depressing of pursuits.[40]

It is not "nature" but the patriarchal system which puts sex to work as the great stabilizer and motivator of society, and the central feature of this system is society's guarantee to the *father* of the legitimacy and inalienability of his offspring. "Everywhere *as society advances*," says W. Robertson Smith, "a stage is reached when the child ceases to belong to the mother's kin and follows the father."[41] "Everywhere" except in contemporary America, where society is reverting to the matriarchal pattern, with consequent social deterioration.

---

39. *The Retreat from Motherhood* (New Rochelle, N.Y.: Arlington House, 1975), p. 95.
40. P. 96.
41. *Kinship and Marriage in Early Arabia* (London: A. and C. Black, 1903), p. 37; emphasis added.

Freiherr F. von Reitzenstein, writing of early Roman antiquity, says

> We cannot doubt the existence of matriarchy, which was constantly encouraged by the Etruscans...Marriage as a binding union was certainly unknown to the plebeians; accordingly their children belonged to the mother's family. This agamous or marriageless relationship still existed at Rome in later times, and was the basis of a widely developed system of free love, which soon changed into different kinds of prostitution.[42]

Otto Kiefer's *Sexual Life in Ancient Rome* informs us that the celebrated Swiss jurist J. J. Bachofen

> sought to prove that in ancient Italy the reign of strong paternal authority had been preceded by a state of exclusive matriarchy, chiefly represented by the Etruscans. He considered that the development of exclusive patriarchy, which we find to be the prevailing type of legitimate relation in historic times, was a universal reform, a vast and incomparable advance in civilization.[43]

"We understand," writes lesbian-feminist Charlotte Bunch, "that the demand by some for control over our intimate lives—denying each person's right to control and express her or his own sexuality and denying women the right to control over the reproductive process in our bodies—creates an atmosphere in which domination over others and militarism are seen as acceptable."[44]

She makes no reference to the contract of marriage, which is intended to allow men to share in women's reproductive lives. She would have the marriage contract place no obligations on the woman, and allow her to exercise her reproductive freedom as though there were no contract.

---

42. Freiherr F. von Reitzenstein, *Love and Marriage in Ancient Europe*, p. 28; quoted in Otto Kiefer, *Sexual Life in Ancient Rome* (London: Abbey Library, 1934), p. 8.
43. Kiefer, pp. 8f.
44. Charlotte Bunch, *Passionate Politics* (New York: St. Martin's Press, 1987) p. 208.

She continues:

> We know that priorities are amiss in the world when children are not protected from parents who abuse them sexually while a lesbian mother is denied custody of her child and labeled immoral simply because she loves women.[45]

She is labeled immoral because she denies her child a father and wishes to transform society in order to make her lifestyle normative and thus make it unnecessary for *any* child to have a father. In other words, while she considers child abuse bad, she considers destruction of the patriarchal Sexual Constitution good, even though child abuse is commoner in the female-headed homes she wishes to create by destroying the Sexual Constitution.[46]

Let's look as a concrete example. Charles Rothenberg was divorced by his wife and confronted with the loss of the one love object of his life, his 6 year old son David. He kidnapped the boy and then, realizing the futility of his one-man revolt against the legal system which was about to take the boy back, made the desperate resolve to kill the boy and himself. He doused David with kerosene and set him afire but lost his nerve when it came his own turn. He fled and was captured. The fire left David disfigured with burns over his face and most of his body. The righteously indignant judge, James R. Franks, who sentenced Charles to 13 years in prison wept in his chambers over the fact that this was the maximum allowed by the law.

A hideous crime. It might not have happened if Charles had not been goaded and crazed by the knowledge that he had no chance of getting a fair custody shake from the court.

---

45. P. 209.

46. Henry Biller and Richard Solomon. *Child Maltreatment and Paternal Deprivation: A Manifesto for Research, Prevention, and Treatment* (Lexington, MA: D.C. Heath, 1986). pp. 21f: "Upwards of 25 percent of children in our society do not have a father living at home. Children in such families are overrepresented in terms of reported cases of physical abuse and other forms of child maltreatment."

According to *The Family in America: New Research*, December, 1989, citing a Milwaukee County inter-office memo, "of all 1,050 ongoing substantiated child abuse and neglect cases in Milwaukee County in May 1989, 83 percent involved households receiving Aid to Families with Dependent Children (AFDC) [read: female-headed households]. See Annex to Chapter I, p. 000.

Aside from this, is there anything to be learned from what Rothenberg did? This mixed-up man was, like Charles Manson, the offspring of an unmarried teen-age prostitute and a father he never saw. Presumably he got messed up because his socialization was messed-up. The sins of the father were visited upon the son, David. But also the sins of the grandmother, who brought Charles into the world in violation of the Legitimacy Principle. Grandma is unpunished because her sins are non-violent, merely sexual, merely sins against the Sexual Constitution which Ms. Bunch wants to do away with.

"There is no such thing as an illegitimate child"—no such thing as an unchaste woman, no need to regulate sexual behavior.[47] But there are unchaste women and Charles's mother was one of them, and unchaste women do bring illegitimate children into the world, and Charles was one of them, and illegitimate children are responsible for a disproportionate amount of social pathology, a fact which will not be changed by passing as law (as has been done in Sweden) that there are no illegitimate children.

Harriet Taylor, friend, and later wife, of the 19th century feminist John Stuart Mill, expressed the feminist view about regulating women:

> that if men are so sure that nature intended women for marriage, motherhood and servitude, why then do they find it necessary to erect so many barriers to other options, why are they required to force women to be restricted to this role? For if women's preference be natural there can be no necessity for enforcing it by law, and it has never been considered necessary in any other area to make laws compelling people to follow their inclination.[48]

Women aren't drawn into marriage by their "nature." They accept it because it is advantageous and because its advantages cannot be obtained without submitting to the patriarchal con-

---

47. Feminists would like to say (as Wes Hall does) there *is* fault in male unchastity—but that would give the whole argument away, wouldn't it?

48. Cited in Dale Spender, *Women of Ideas and What Men Have Done to Them from Aphra Behn to Adrienne Rich* (London: ARK Paperbacks, 1982), p. 193.

straints whose purpose is to channel procreation through families. The present disruption of sexual law-and-order is produced by women's trying to retain the advantages while rejecting the constraints.

We read in the book of Hosea in the Bible that Gomer, wife of the prophet, dressed herself in fine raiment and had sex with strangers at the Temple in Jerusalem. According to feminist Merlin Stone,

> She took part in the sexual customs of her own free will and...viewed them not as an obligatory or compulsory duty but as pleasant occasions, rather like festive parties. This situation was clearly unacceptable to the men who espoused the patrilineal Hebrew system, as Hosea did, but it does reveal that for those who belonged to other religious systems it was quite typical behavior.
>
> For thousands of years these sexual customs had been accepted as natural among the people of the Near and Middle East. They may have permitted and even encouraged matrilineal descent patterns to continue and a female-kinship system to survive. Inherent within the very practice of the sexual customs was the lack of concern for the *paternity* of children—and it is only with a certain knowledge of paternity that a patrilineal system can be maintained.[49]

Hosea was a spokesman for the newer patriarchal religion of Jahweh, Gomer a representative of the older worship of the Great Goddess. "The male and female religions existed side by side for thousands of years," reads a publisher's flyer advertising Merlin Stone's book:

> Goddess worship continued throughout the periods of Abraham, Moses, David and Solomon and as late as St. Paul. It appears that the worship of the Goddess did not naturally give way to the new masculine religions, but was the victim of centuries of continual persecution and suppression by the

---

49. *When God Was a Woman* (New York: Dial Press, 1976), p. 161.

more aggressive, war-like invaders....Merlin Stone believes that the persecution of Goddess worshippers had
a political and economic basis. The invaders had a
patrilineal system whereby men controlled paternity,
property and the right to rule. If Goddess worship was
destroyed, the indigenous, matrilineal system would
also be destroyed. *It was only by denying women the
sexual freedom they had under the Goddess that men
could control paternity.* Therefore, moral imperatives,
such as premarital virginity and marriage fidelity for
women reflected and reinforced politically inspired religion. Stone's research has shown her that this integral
Biblical story [the Garden of Eden story] which is used
theologically to explain male dominance in all things,
has been used through the ages to justify the continual
oppression and subjugation of women. Ms. Stone believes that the story symbolically describes the eradica-
tion of Goddess worship and the damning of its religious
trappings and institutions, i.e., wise, prophetic serpents
as adjuncts of the Goddess, holy fruit trees, sexually
active and free women. [Emphasis added.]

The male and female religions existed side by side for thousands of years. In other words, it required thousands of years of
struggle to establish the patriarchal system and to do away with
forms of religious worship which W. Robertson Smith describes
as "horrible orgies of unrestrained sensuality, of which we no
longer dare to speak in unveiled words."[50]
The single generation following the publishing of *The Feminine Mystique* has produced a catastrophic subversion of the
fragile and artificial patriarchal system and a more-than-partial
return to the older matriarchal system, including even some
tentative attempts in books like Stone's *When God Was a Woman*
and Sjoo and Mor's *The Great Cosmic Mother* to provide it with
a theological superstructure. The central issue, however, is not
theological but familial: whether or not males shall participate

---

50. W. Roberston Smith. *The Old Testament in the Jewish Church: A Course of
Lectures on Biblical Criticism,* 2d ed. (London: Adam and Charles Black, 1892) p.
350.

equally with females in human reproduction. Equal male participation is possible only on the basis of stable families—on assurance of father custody in cases of divorce.

"Women by nature," writes Hendrik DeLeeuw,

> are no more monogamous than men and no less polyga-mous. Women's sexual tendencies, biologically, are no less variational than those of the male gender. Best historical proof lies in the case of some of the primitive communities where conditions of life did not hamper sex expression of women any more than of men. Among the natives of Victoria, for example, the women have so many lovers that it becomes almost impossible to guess the paternity of children. Brazilian historians relate that among the Guyacurus and the Guyanas Indians of South America, the women, and especially the nobler ones, have one or more lovers who remain at their side day and night to attend to their sexual requirements. And so it becomes obvious that wherever conditions permitted, women have rejected the monogamous rela-tionships as often as men. What it also implies is that, if granted equal freedom, women tend to be equally variational and multiple in their sex expression.[51]

This promiscuity is why these societies are "primitive." It is to prevent civilized society from relapsing into this primitivism that the Legitimacy Principle—every child must have a father—is enforced.

Here, from Dear Abby, 27 December, 1985, is an illustration of how easily the Legitimacy Principle is undermined:

> DEAR ABBY: I'll bet you never heard anything like this before. Our son, "Mike," has been living with his girlfriend, "Libby," for three years. They have a 2-year-old son whom we love like a grandson.

---

51. Hendrik de Leeuw, *Woman: The Dominant Sex* (New York: Thomas Yoseloff, 1957), p. 110.

Last year, money got tight, so to help out with the expenses, Libby and Mike rented their spare room to a friend of Mike's. (I'll call him Gary.)

As it turned out, Libby carried on a secret affair with Gary, and now she has a child by him, too. Our son wants to forgive Libby, marry her and adopt her new baby. We, his parents, cannot forgive her for what she did to Mike.

We love our son and the grandson he and Libby gave us, but we do not want to accept Libby as our daughter-in-law knowing she had an illegitimate child by a guy who rented a room in their house.

How should we handle this?
—GRAMAW

Abby's reply:

DEAR GRAMAW: Regardless of how you feel about Libby, if you don't accept her as your daughter-in-law along with her children, you can say goodby to your son and the grandson you love. It's a package deal. Take it or leave it; the choice is yours.

It's a good example of the contrasting ways in which matriarchy and patriarchy handle the regulation of sexuality. Libby accepts the first law of matriarchy—whatever she decides is final—and Mike *and the legal system* go along. In consequence, seven people are at risk, the two babies, the three parents and the two grandparents. The son must either subsidize an adulteress and a bastard or lose his own child. The mother is at risk of being a single parent caught in the Custody Trap—as sole provider and sole custodian, with reduced resources and doubled responsibilities, de-classed in the eyes of conservative people, perhaps driven onto welfare. The two babies are at risk of being fatherless and therefore more likely to be impoverished and delinquent. The two grandparents will either lose their grandchild or be compelled to accept the adulteress's value system, accept an illegitimate child they don't want as their grandchild and pretend not to care about traditional family values.

Suppose that the legal system didn't go along. Suppose it behaved in accordance with the principles of the patriarchy which created it. Suppose it provided props for the *father's* role rather than for the mother's.

Then (1) there would probably be no shacking-up to begin with, no illegitimate child. Libby would be far less likely to have shacked up with Mike or to have had her secret affair with Gary, knowing that Mike, not she, was the legal custodian of the grandson and knowing that Mike had the authority to toss her out and keep his grandson for himself—and find himself a *wife* who would not introduce confusion of progeny into his household.

Then (2) if there had been an affair between Gary and Libby anyway, it would have been up to Mike to decide whether to legitimize Libby's illegitimate child and by doing so guarantee it a place within the patriarchal system, or to expel Libby and her illegitimate child and by so doing safeguard the proper rearing and socializing of his son and his relationships with the grandparents—while at the same time giving Libby, Gary and their child their best opportunity of forming a patriarchal family of their own. And of course giving himself his best opportunity of marrying another woman and creating a patriarchal family of his own and providing his son with a stepmother who shared his patriarchal values.

Here's another letter to Abby, illustrating the sexual confusion of the times:

DEAR ABBY: Our parents' anniversary is coming up soon. Some of us would like to make them a gift of a family portrait including their children, their children's spouses and their grandchildren.

We want to limit this portrait to legitimate family members only, which would exclude the mother of one of the grandchildren and her son from a previous relationship.

We would like to include our brother and his legitimate child without including the woman he lives with and her illegitimate son. Is it possible to do this without causing hard feelings?
—PROBLEMS

DEAR PROBLEMS: No. Abandon the idea. There are no illegitimate children; just illegitimate parents.

The writer and his or her siblings believe in the Legitimacy Principle. No matter, says Abby. There are new proprieties to which everyone must conform on pain of being disliked by feminists and believers in the first law of matriarchy. Since the feminist/sexual revolution the Promiscuity Principle has replaced the Legitimacy Principle and one sexual arrangement is as good as another. Nobody's feelings must ever be hurt—unless they happen to believe in the Legitimacy Principle.

Field direction (thinking the way everyone else thinks), shame and guilt have hitherto been means of maintaining sexual law-and-order, especially among females, who used to glory in their role as the guardians of morality and who formerly had no greater pleasure than in gossiping about the sexual transgressions of their less virtuous sisters.

No more. What Charlotte Bunch said of lesbianism ("it threatens male supremacy at its core") is trebly true of the first law of matriarchy, now that field direction works for, rather than against it, now that shame and guilt no longer function to promote legitimacy, now that the courts (and Abby) are on the side of the Promiscuity Principle. Women now control their own sexuality without interference from men. The Legitimacy Principle, the patriarchal family and the male role as its head are obsolete. These changes, striking at the foundation of the patriarchal system, have been accomplished without any examination of their portentous consequences for society.

According to feminists Barbara Love and Elizabeth Shanklin:

The matriarchal mode of child-rearing, in which each individual is nurtured rather than dominated from birth provides the rational basis for a genuinely healthy society, a society of self-regulating, positive individuals.[52]

Things are this way in the ghettos, where half of the young bear the surnames of their mothers, and where the proportion of such maternal surnames increases every year,[53] along with crime and the other accompaniments of matriarchy.

"You Frenchmen," said an Iroquois Indian three hundred years ago to the Jesuit Father Le Jeune, "love only your own children; we love all the children of the tribe."[54] In a promiscuous matriclan this is the best way to see that all children are cared for; but it will not create the deep family loyalties needed to usher a society out of the Stone Age. "At the core of patriarchy," says Adrienne Rich, "is the individual family unit which originated with the idea of property and the desire to see one's property transmitted to one's biological descendants."[55] This creation of wealth cannot be motivated by a desire to transmit it to an ex-wife or to a welfare system which undermines the families whose resources it feeds upon.

The patriarchal family, whose linchpin is female chastity and loyalty, makes men work. That is why civilization must be patriarchal and why it slides into chaos, as ours is doing, where family arrangements become matrilineal. What feminist Marie Richmond-Abbott says of men in general is especially true of men in capitalist patriarchy:

A man's life is defined by his work, his occupation. The first question a man is usually asked is, "What do you do?" People shape their perception of him according to his answer.[56]

---

52. "The Answer is Matriarchy," in G. Vida, *Our Right to Love: A Lesbian Resource Book* (Englewood Cliffs, New Jersey: Prentice-Hall, 1978), p. 185.

53. George Gilder, *Visible Man: A True Story of Post-racist America* (New York: Basic Books, 1978), p. 24.

54. Quoted in Robert Briffault, *The Mothers*, I, 597.

55. *Of Woman Born: Motherhood as Experience and Institution* (New York: W. W. Norton, 1976), p. 60.

56. *Masculine and Feminine: Sex Roles Over the Life Cycle* (Menlo Park, CA: Addison-Wesley Publishing Company, 1983), p. 355.

A man's life may be defined by his work even under matriarchy, but it is only loosely defined. Here, described by the 19th century German explorer, G. W. Schweinfurth, is the way males perform when females regard them as inessential. The tribe described is the Monbuttu:

> Whilst the women attend to the tillage of the soil and the gathering of the harvest, the men, except they are absent either for war or hunting, spend the entire day in idleness. In the early hours of the morning they may be found under the shade of the oil-palms, lounging at full length upon their carved benches and smoking tobacco. During the middle of the day they gossip with their friends in the cool halls.[57]

Similarly, under communism, the state's guarantee of economic security weakens the male's commitment to work and undermines his productivity. "The other day," writes Eric Hoffer,

> I happened to ask myself a routine question and stumbled on a surprising answer. The question was: What is the uppermost problem which confronts the leadership in a Communist regime? The answer: The chief preoccupation of every government between the Elbe and the China Sea is how to make people work—how to induce them to plow, sow, harvest, build, manufacture, work in the mines, and so forth. It is the most vital problem which confronts them day in day out, and it shapes not only their domestic policies but their relations with the outside world.[58]

Who wants to plow, sow, harvest, build, manufacture, work in the mines—unless the work, unsatisfying and unfulfilling in itself, is made meaningful by a man's knowledge that it must be done if he is to provide for his family?

---

57. Quoted in John Baker's *Race* (Athens, Georgia: Foundations for Human Understanding, 1974), p. 399.
58. *The Ordeal of Change* (New York: Harper and Row, 1963), p. 23.

In the occident [continues Hoffer] the chief problem is not how to induce people to work but how to find enough jobs for people who want to work. We seem to take the readiness to work almost as much for granted as the readiness to breathe. Yet the goings on inside the Communist world serve to remind us that the Occident's attitude toward work so far from being natural and normal, is strange and unprecedented. it was the relatively recent emergence of this attitude which, as much as anything else, gave modern Western civilization its unique character and marked it off from all its predecessors.[59]

George Gilder makes the same point, but with a different emphasis, indicating the significance of family arrangements:

The industrial revolution was perhaps the most cataclysmic event in history, changing every aspect of human society.[60]

He points out that while multiple causes are at work,

it may well be that economic growth is most essentially a problem of interrelated motivation and demography—that is, a problem of familial and sexual organization.

Once again we may find that the success and durability of a society is less dependent on how it organizes its money and resources on a grand scale, or how it produces its goods, than on how it induces men to subordinate their sexual rhythms to extended female perspectives.[61]

Patriarchy comes to its full flowering in capitalism:

"Pre-industrial men," as the British demographer E. A. Wrigley puts it, "lived their lives in a moving present; short-term prospects occupied much of their attention."

---

59. *Ibid.*, p. 23.
60. *Sexual Suicide* (New York: Quadrange/The New York Times Book Co., 1973), p. 89.
61. *Loc. cit.*

Wrigley believes that it was the presence of relatively isolated conjugal or nuclear families that made possible the emergence of the highly motivated industrial bourgeoisie and labor force.

There were major differences between the families of Eastern Europe and Asia ("economically stagnant") and those of England and precocious parts of Western Europe where the Industrial Revolution began and flourished, and where "a couple generally could not get married unless it was economically independent, with a separate household."

> Thus sexual energies were directly tied to economic growth, and since *strong sanctions were imposed on premarital sex,* population growth was directly connected to economic productivity.[62]

The italicized words signify that the Legitimacy Principle was enforced, the first law of matriarchy made inoperative. Chastity and monogamy became an essential part of capitalism. It was a stroke of genius: *Work became sexy*—but only for men, and only if women are chaste and loyal to their husbands.

Now dig this, from *Harper's Index* for March, 1987:[63]

> Average number of sperm per cubic millimeter of an American male's semen in 1929: 100 million.

Today: 60 million.

Work is no longer sexy. Alas, alas. What a universe of social disruption and suffering—demoralization, broken marriages, sexual confusion, female-headed families, underachievement, declining productivity, increased absenteeism, jobs travelling overseas, educational failure, crime, illegitimacy, drug addiction—is revealed by that cubic millimeter.

---

62. *Loc. cit.;* emphasis added.
63. Cited in *Los Angeles Times,* 1 March, 1987.

The Family in America: New Research, April, 1988 cites a study made by the William T. Grant Foundation Commission on Work, Family and Citizenship, titled *The Forgotten Half: Non-College Youth in America*:

> Millions of young men are marking time in low-paying jobs that make them poor marriage prospects. This problem in male marriage and work patterns recently attracted the attention of the William T. Grant Foundation Commission on Work, Family and Citizenship, comprising some of the leading sociologists and policy analysts in America. In its interim report, the Commission notes that between 1973 and 1986, the average earnings of American males aged 20 to 24 fell from 11,939 to $8,859 (in 1985 dollars). This drop meant that while 59 percent of all males in 1973 could support a three-member family at or above the official poverty line, only 44 percent could in 1985. "No wonder, then," observes the Commission, "that marriage rates among young males (ages 20-24) declined almost in half, from 39.1 percent in 1974 to 21.2 percent in 1985." Among black males, the drop has been an even sharper 60 percent, from 29.2 percent in 1974 to only 11.1 percent in 1985. Understandably, as marriage rates have fallen, the proportion of children born out of wedlock has risen, stranding millions of children in impoverished female-headed households.

"There is," writes Gilder,

> considerable evidence of a sexual crisis among young men, marked by sexual fragility and retreat. Greater female availability and aggressiveness often seem to decrease male confidence and initiative. A large survey of college students indicated that while virginity among girls was rapidly diminishing, virginity among boys was actually increasing, and at an equal rate. Impotence has for some time been the leading complaint at most college psychiatric clinics. Citing evidence from "my patients,

both male and female, articles in medical journals, and conversations with my colleagues," one psychiatrist called it "the least publicized epidemic of the 1970s."[64]

Therapists have coined a new term for this, Inhibited Sexual Desire, ISD. According to *Newsweek,*

psychiatrists and psychologists say they are seeing a growing proportion of patients with such complaints—people whose main response to the sexual revolution has been some equivalent of "not tonight, dear." Clinically, their problem is known as Inhibited Sexual Desire (ISD), a condition marked by the inability to muster any interest in the great obsession. "The person with low sexual desire will not feel 'horny'....He will not be moved to seek out sexual activity, nor will he fantasize about sex," wrote psychiatrist Helen Singer Kaplan in a 1979 book that first called wide attention to the problem.
    Over the past decade ISD has emerged as the most common of all sexual complaints.[65]

Here is Gilder's explanation of how the patriarchal system works and why chastity and monogamy are essential to it:

The virtues of this arrangement, which also prevailed in the United States, go beyond the effective harnessing of male sexual and economic energies to the creation of family units. By concentrating rewards and penalties, the conjugal household set a pattern of incentives that applied for a lifetime. Benefits of special effort or initiative were not diffused among a large number of relatives, as in the extended family; and the effects of sloth or failure would not be mitigated by the success of the larger unit. In general, the man stood alone as provider for his wife and children. He was fully respon-

64. *Men and Marriage* (Gretna, LA: Pelican Publishing Co., 1986), p. 64.
65. *Newsweek,* 26 October, 1987.

sible for the rest of his life. Such responsibility transformed large numbers of pre-industrial men, living in "a moving present," into relatively long-term planners, preparing for an extended future.[66]

The alternative was shown in a 1986 T.V. film, *Man Made Famine*, which made the point that African women did most of the continent's agricultural work, a fact interpreted by the filmmakers as proving that "institutionalized male chauvinism is at the core of many of Africa's agricultural problems." These hard-working African women want independence from men and yet they complain of abandonment by men. Their problem is that their societies have failed to channel male energies into socially useful and economically productive directions. This is not institutionalized male chauvinism; it is the failure to impose patriarchy. The males will never be productive as long as women's sexual autonomy (the first law of matriarchy) cuts men off from families. They are in the same situation as millions of their American brothers, concerning whom Success magazine writes:

> The alienated poor. Some see their very existence as an indictment of capitalism. These are not the striving, ambitious immigrants who battle hardship and discrimination in order to ascend the economic ladder. These are the cut-off poor, whether in Harlem or Appalachia, who lack the conviction that they can succeed by dint of their own efforts. They are without skills, motivation, self-esteem, and awareness of opportunity. They are nonfunctional in a free-enterprise society, where effective work requires, to use [George] Gilder's words, "alertness and emotional commitment"—in short, a positive mental attitude.[67]

They hate capitalism, and capitalism does nothing for them because they have been deprived of the cornerstone of capitalism, a patriarchal family, without which most males remain unmotivated.

---

66. *Sexual Suicide*, p. 90f.
67. *Success!* Jan/Feb. 1987. The article is unsigned.

A famous 1965 study by Mattina Horner showed that women commonly feared success. The study was repeated in 1971 by Lois Hoffman, with surprising differences of result. According to Marie Richmond-Abbott,

> The group that had changed in their perceptions since Horner's (1965) study were the men! Horner reported only 8 percent of the males tried to avoid success, and Hoffman's (1971) study showed 77 percent of the men tried to do so. They were equally likely to show fear of success in all-male settings as in settings where both sexes functioned professionally.
>
> For both men and women, mean scores of "desire to achieve" had gone down significantly between 1965 and 1971. However, women's reasons for fear of success remained much as they had been earlier, whereas men's reasons seemed linked to a diminished desire to achieve at all. Hoffman points out that the content of the men's stories was different from that of the women's. The men seemed to question the value of success itself.[68]

"By age 30," says medical writer Janny Scott, "only 3% of those born before 1910 had experienced depression—compared to nearly 60% of those born around 1950."[69] The suicide rate of white males age 15-24 rose almost 50 percent between 1970 and 1983.

"Somewhere at the dawn of human history," says Margaret Mead, "some social invention was made under which males started nurturing females and their young."[71] Aside from a few tramps, she thinks, most men will accept their responsibilities to provide for their families. But there exists a male responsibility only if there exists a complementary female need. The goal of feminism is to remove this need. Hear Betty Friedan:

---

68. Marie Richmond-Abbott, *Masculine and Feminine: Sex Roles over the Life Cycle* (Reading, MA: Addison-Wesley, 1983), p. 168.

69. *Los Angeles Times*, 9 October, 1988.

70. *The Family in America*, October, 1988.

71. *Male and Female* (New York: William Morrow and Company, 1949), p. 195.

I've suspected that the men who really feel threatened
by the women's movement in general or by their own
wives' moves toward some independent activity are the
ones who are most unsure of their women's love. Such
a man often worries that his wife has married him only
for economic security or the status and vicarious power
he provides. If she can get these things for herself, what
does she need him for? Why will she continue to love
him? In his anger is also the fear she will surely leave
him.[72]

Of course. If she can get these things for herself she doesn't
need him and they both know it, even if they haven't read Nickles
and Ashcraft's *The Coming Matriarchy* and found out about the
divorce rates of economically independent women[73]—women
like Ms. Friedan herself, who put her husband's name on the
dedication page of *The Feminine Mystique,* but later, after she
discovered she could make it alone on her royalties and lecture
fees, tossed him out, took his children from him and removed his
name from the dedication page. (Not that she didn't complain
about his failure to provide her with child support money for the
children she took from him.[74])

A man who supposed his wife married him only out of love, the
motive proposed by Ms. Friedan as sufficient to hold marriages
together, would be a ruddy fool and—what is really bad from
society's point of view—an unmotivated fool, for society needs
the man's work and wealth, and if his family no longer expect
him to be a provider he won't work too hard—which is why single
men earn so much less than married men earn.[75]

72. *The Second Stage* (New York: Summit Books, 1981), p. 155.

73. See Chapter II, note 10.

74. Betty Friedan, *It Changed My Life: Writings on the Women's Movement* (New
York: Random House, 1976), p. 328.

75. George Gilder, *Men and Marriage* (Gretna, LA: Pelican Publishing Co., 1986),
p. 62: "One striking result of the bachelor pattern is low income. With the same age
and qualifications, single men have long earned about the same as single women.
As early as 1966, a Labor Department study found both earned about the same
hourly wages. Single college graduates over age twenty-five earned about the same
amount in 1969, whether male or female. Single men currently have median
incomes less than 10 percent higher than those of single women, who are alleged
to be hobbled by discrimination, even though single men work longer hours and in
general tend to use their earning capacity more. Yet they are 30 percent more likely
to be unemployed.

"Married men, however, earn some 70 percent more than singles of either sex."

Ms. Friedan cites a family therapist from Philadelphia, who is worried about his stake in his family:

"I was working at one of the big family-training centers in the country," he said. "There was constant theoretical discussion about getting the father back into the family. But the way our own jobs were set up, you had to work fifty to sixty hours a week. To really get anywhere you had to put in seventy hours, work nights, weekends. You didn't have time for your own family. You were supposed to make the job Number One in your life, and I wouldn't do that. My life is Number One, and my family—my job is only to be a good therapist. To play the office politics and be one of the big guns you had to devote your whole life to it. I started my own practice where I keep my own hours. Most of the other family therapists at the center are now divorced.[76]

They are divorced—and have lost their children and their homes. They were "unsure of their women's love" because they were economically superfluous. The man with whom Ms. Friedan spoke knows his wife may toss him out as his fellow-therapists were tossed out by their wives, and he is in a panic. A generation ago, a man's attachment to his family gave him the motivation to be a high achiever; today, the feminist/sexual revolution has made this attachment to his family the cause of his becoming a panicky underachiever.

Lesbian feminist Susan Cavin proposes using the first law of matriarchy as a means of destroying patriarchy and liberating women:

Collective refusal of women to tell men who is the "father" of their children; this could be accomplished by the simple method of hetero-females never sleeping with only one man for any length of time, but always having two or more male lovers. This method is based on the

---

76. Betty Friedan, *The Second Stage* (New York: Summit Books, 1981), pp. 157f.

assumption that mass high rates of "illegitimacy" will destroy the patrilineal family, especially its monogamian form.[77]

It would work if men refuseto enforce the Legitimacy Principle. Which is why they must enforce it—and why they must regain control over their paychecks in order to do so.

---

77. Cavin, *An Hystorical and Cross-Cultural Analysis Of Sex Ratios, Female Sexuality, and Homo-Sexual Segregation Versus Hetero-Sexual Integration.* Ph.D dissertation, Rutgers, 1978, p. 294.

IV

Sleeping Beauty Feminism Vs.
Slaughtered Saints Feminism

In 1963 Betty Friedan told American women they were childlike weaklings who should grow up and stand on their own feet like men. They "never feel that they are really exerting sufficient effort." The American housewife "feels 'lazy, neglectful, haunted by guilt feelings' because she doesn't have enough work to do."[1] "At one of the major women's magazines," she recalls,

> a woman editor, sensing that American housewives might be desperately in need of something to enlarge their world, tried for some months to convince her male colleagues to introduce a few ideas outside the home into the magazine. "We decided against it," the man who makes the final decisions said. "Women are so completely divorced from the world of ideas in their lives now, they couldn't take it." Perhaps it is irrelevant to ask, who divorced them? Perhaps these Frankensteins no longer have the power to stop the feminine monster they have created.

> I helped create this image. I have watched American women for fifteen years try to conform to it. But I can no longer deny my own knowledge of its terrible implications. It is not a harmless image. There may be no psychological terms for the harm it is doing. But what happens when women try to live according to an image that makes them deny their minds?[2]

---

1. Betty Friedan, *The Feminine Mystique* (New York: W. W. Norton, 1963), p. 213.
2. P. 66.

By giving an absolute meaning and a sanctimonious
value to the generic term "woman's role," functionalism
put American women into a kind of deep freeze—like
Sleeping Beauties, waiting for a Prince Charming to
waken them, while all around the magic circle the world
moved on.[3]

"Where will it end?" Ms. Friedan asks:

I think it will not end, as long as the feminine mystique
masks the emptiness of the housewife role, encouraging girls
to evade their own growth by vicarious living, by non-
commitment. We have gone on too long blaming or pitying
the mothers who devour their children, who sow the seeds of
progressive dehumanization, because they have never grown
to full humanity themselves. If the mother is at fault, why
isn't it time to break the pattern by urging all these Sleeping
Beauties to grow up and live their own lives? There never
will be enough Prince Charmings, or enough therapists to
break that pattern now. It is society's job, and finally that of
each woman alone. For it is not the strength of the mothers
that is at fault but their weakness, their passive childlike
dependency and immaturity that is mistaken for "femininity." Our society forces boys, insofar as it can, to grow up, to
endure the pains of growth, to educate themselves to work,
to move on. Why aren't girls forced to grow up—to achieve
somehow the core of self that will end the unnecessary
dilemma, the mistaken choice between femaleness and
humanness that is implied in the feminine mystique?[4]

Here is how Ms. Friedan told the women of 1963 to see
themselves:

For the women I interviewed, the problem seemed to be
not that too much was asked of them but too little.[5]

---

3. P. 127.
4. P. 304.
5. P. 252.

Society asks so little of women.[6]

You'd find them drinking, or sitting around talking to other women and watching children play because they can't bear to be alone or watching TV or reading a book.[7]

I have suggested that the real cause both of feminism and of women's frustration was the emptiness of the housewife's role.[8]

"Occupation: housewife" is not an adequate substitute for truly challenging work, important enough to society to be paid for in its coin....[9]

Most of the energy expended in housework is superfluous.[10]

Ms. Friedan's Sleeping Beauty feminism was an unwelcome derogation to American women because it came close to the truth, still more unwelcome because it threatened the free ride they had no intention of giving up. Many perceived that Ms. Friedan was making the same point to women that Playboy made in the same year to men with its mock ad:

TIRED OF THE RAT RACE?
FED UP WITH JOB ROUTINE?

Well, then...how would you like to make $8,000, $20,000—*as much as $50,000 and More*—working at Home in Your Spare Time? No selling! No commuting! No time clocks to punch!

BE YOUR OWN BOSS!!!!

---

6. P. 338.
7. P. 344.
8. P. 240.
9. P. 248.
10. P. 249.

Yes, an Assured Lifetime Income can be yours now, in an easy, low-pressure, part-time job that will permit you to spend most of each and every day as *you please!—* relaxing, watching TV, playing cards, socializing with friends!...

Incredible though it may seem, the above offer is completely legitimate. More than 40,000,000 Americans are already so employed.

These 40,000,000 Americans were the housewives referred to by Ms. Friedan when she said "Society asks so little of women."

Small wonder that the *Playboy / Feminine Mystique / Sleeping Beauty* pitch was discarded by feminists as an unsuitable basis for a popular movement and that is today as extinct as the trilobite. The idle sex-toy doll-housewife pampered by an over-worked husband is unmentioned in the literature of post-1960s feminism. The Sleeping Beauty has been replaced by the Slaughtered Saint, tyrannized over, oppressed, brainwashed, beaten, enslaved, exploited, crucified, impaled, racked and harrowed, flayed, trampled and hung in chains by remorseless, inhuman, fierce, sadistic, exploitive, brutal alcoholic male despots, beasts, marital rapists and so forth.

It is useful, though, to remember that the initial thrust of feminism was that "The problem seemed to be not that too much was asked of [women] but too little." In 1963 the subsidization of ex-wives by ex-husbands was said to be contemptible; today the feminist party line is a demand for "support rules that aim at equalizing the standards of living of the two parties after divorce"[11] and that divorced women "have earned the right to

---

11. Lenore Weitzman, *The Divorce Revolution: The Unexpected Social and Economic Conusequences for Women and Children in America* (New York: The Free Press, 1985), p. 390.

Daniel G. Saunders describes women's economic predicament thus:

Most researchers, includng [Murray] Straus, list women's economic entrapment in intimate relationships as one of the reasons to aid battered women more than abused men. [Daniel G. Saunders, 'Other Truths' about Domestic Violence A Reply to McNeely and Robinson-Simpson," *Social Work,* March/ April, 1988, p. 180.]

"Economic entrapment" signifies that marriage benefits women economically and therefore entitles them to *other* one-sided benefits.

share their *husbands'* income for the rest of their lives and to maintain a standard of living that is equal to theirs"[12]—so that even though the man is no longer a husband, and even though Betty Friedan had told wives to be ashamed of themselves for expecting to be subsidized for the trifling services they perform, the man deprived of these services should continue to subsidize the woman who withdraws them.

In Sleeping Beauty agitprop, contempt for women who accepted alimony was conspicuous. In Slaughtered Saints feminism, contempt for alimony is replaced by contempt for the *word* alimony: "Alimony?" wrote Betty Friedan in 1974, "Forget it— it's a sexist concept, and doesn't belong in a women's movement for equality."[13] But on the preceding page she wrote this:

> At that time, *we were so concerned with principle*—that equality of right and opportunity had to mean equality of responsibility, and therefore alimony was out—that we did not realize the trap we were falling into. It is a trap for thousands, hundreds of thousands, if not millions of women, when they face a no-fault divorce law— in which a separation begun before the law was even envisaged becomes de facto divorce—*with no provision for economic support* [read: no alimony] or division of property....She should be insured in her own right for Social Security in old age and *severance pay in divorce* [read: alimony]...*Maintenance, rehabilitation, severance pay—whatever you want to call it* [read: alimony]—is a necessity for many divorced women, as is child support.[14]

Under Sleeping Beauty feminism it was common for feminists like Gloria Steinem to sneer at marriage as "prostitution." Slaughtered Saints feminist Flo Kennedy disagreed:

---

12. *Ibid.*; emphasis added.
13. *It Changed My Life: Writings on the Women's Movement* (New York: Random House, 1976), p. 326.
14. *Ibid.*, pp. 325f.; emphasis added.

Prostitutes don't sell their bodies, they rent their bodies. Housewives sell their bodies when they get married— they cannot take them back—and most courts do not regard the taking of a woman's body by her husband against her will as rape.[15]

Now they can take their bodies back—and still get a free ride. Taking someone's money in exchange for nothing used to be called robbery, but Slaughtered Saints feminists regard it as a means of restoring women's dignity. As long as the money flows from the male to the female, as long as Steinem's "prostitution" is retroactive and requires no services, they are willing—they insist—that it be called something other than alimony and will affect to despise those women who take men's money and call what they do by its proper name. Like exophagic cannibals denouncing the barbarousness of endophagic cannibalism, like the Mayor of Gomorrah condemning the moral depravity of Sodom and San Francisco, like two-dollar hookers sneering at twenty-five cent hookers who are lowering the dignity of the profession, they have risen above that sort of thing.

"Society asks so little of women." That was Sleeping Beauty feminism, shaming women, telling them to stop filing their fingernails and get out and work like men. A decade later Slaughtered Saints feminists, seeking self-actualization and true humanity, claimed victimhood for themselves and affected to be the wretched of the earth—adorning themselves with crucifixes bearing a naked woman, telling men how oppressive it was for them not to do half of the "little" housework at which Ms. Friedan sneered. *Bwana fimbo!*—bad white man! By then the admired, achieving male of 1963, hobbled with his parasitic female, had become a gynocidal maniac, a wild beast:

Wife abuse is deeply rooted in our culture.[16]

[T]he Old Testament patriarchs quite intentionally set themselves against the lunar psyche in women (and in

---

15. *Syracuse New Times*, 10 October, 1976.
16. Ruth Sidel, *Women and Children Last: The Plight of Poor Women in Affluent America* (New York: Viking, 1986), p. 45

men, who are half-female), in their desire to destroy the Goddess religion, and the Goddess within us all. Because of this, the menstruating womb became the Devil of patriarchy—"the only good woman is a pregnant woman," etc.—and the three-hundred-plus years of European Christian witch-hunting has been accurately called "9 million menstrual murders." Women were burned for practicing our natural moon-crafts of midwifery, hypnotism, healing, dowsing, herbal and drug use, dream study, and sexual pleasure.[17]

Perhaps what is most galling is that while the housewife's duties resemble those of a servant, the financial arrangements she has with her husband somewhat resemble those of someone even lower down on the status ladder—namely, the slave.[18]

If we read the Bible as normative social literature, the absence of the Goddess is the single most important statement about the kind of social order that the men who over many centuries wrote and rewrote this religious document strove to establish and uphold. For symbolically the absence of the Goddess from the officially sanctioned Holy Scriptures was the absence of a divine power to protect women and avenge the wrongs inflicted upon them by men.[19]

As we have seen, it was not coincidental that everywhere in the ancient world the imposition of male dominance was part of the shift from a peaceful and equalitarian way of organizing human society to a hierarchic and

---

17. Monica Sjoo and Barbara Mor. *The Great Cosmic Mother: Rediscovering the Religion of the Earth* (San Francisco: Harper and Row, 1987), p. 192.
The bit about the nine million burnt witches has been passed on from one feminist writer to another until it has become part of the accepted folklore of feminism. Disbelieving it is one more proof (is more proof needed?) of male heartlessness.
18. Barbara Bergmann, *The Economic Emergence of Women* (New York: Basic Books, 1986), p. 209.
19. Riane Eisler, *The Chalice and the Blade: Our History, Our Future* (San Francisco: Harper and Row, 1987), p. 94.

violent order ruled by brutal and greedy men....At the same time that shedding blood by killing and injuring other human beings—in wars, in brutal punishments, and in the exercise of the male's practically absolute authority over women and children—becomes the norm, the act of giving life now becomes tainted and unclean....And so, first in Mesopotamia and Canaan and later in the theocracies of Judaea and Israel, warfare, authoritarian rule, and the subjugation of women became integral parts of the new dominator morality and society.[20]

What kind of society is it that calls love and affection between two women perverse, while male brutality to women is made profitable....What kind of society is it where the lifelong partnership of two women has no standing in court, while a husband can batter and rape his wife without interference?...It is a pornographic society; America is a pornographic patriarchy.[21]

Capitalism finds it expedient to reduce women to a state of enslavement.[22]

Is it any wonder then that men hate women so? Is it any wonder that they beat us and tear us apart and stomp us to death?...I suspect that they cannot forgive us for reminding them, by our stubborn survival, how they have raped and beaten and cheated and deceived and maimed and killed us for 5000 years.[23]

---

20. *Ibid.*, pp. 100ff.

21. Charlotte Bunch, *Passionate Politics: Feminist Theory in Action* (New York: St. Martin's Press, 1987), p. 206.

22. Joanne Cooke, Charlotte Bunch-Weeks and Robin Morgan, eds., *The New Woman: A Motive Anthology on Women's Liberation* (Greenwich, Conn.: Fawcett Publications, 1970), p. 68.

23. Sonia Johnson, *Going Out of Our Minds: The Metaphysics of Liberation* (Freedom, California: The Crossing Press, 1987), p. 286.

One of the accusations against the male is his refusal to believe in his own beastliness. Hear Irene Greene, Program Director of the University of Minnesota's Sexual Violence Program, explain why accusations made by females against males ought always to be believed:

> We respect that a woman's reality is her truth. In a society where far too often women are disbelieved, unsupported and blamed for their own victimization, it is important that they have at least one safe place where they will be believed....Because a fundamental anchor of our philosophy is to support and thus believe in each woman's reality, we may come upon the one-in-a-hundred situation where a story or parts of a story may be questionable. Since the occurrence of a false report is so rare, it is far more respectful, professional and necessary to err on the side of belief than to risk the slim chance that a story may not be totally accurate. It is important to support the individual and her reality rather than to deny and disbelieve her.[24]

Slaughtered Saints feminism is thus epitomized by feminist Mary Daly:

> ...feeding on the bodies and minds of women, sapping energy at the expense of female deaths. Like Dracula, the he-male has lived on women's blood....The priests of patriarchy have eaten the body and have drunk the blood of the Sacrificial Victim in their Mass, but they have not wished to know who has really been the Victim whose blood supported this parasitic life.
> The insatiable lust of males for female blood has resulted in a perpetual blood transfusion throughout the millennia—a one-way outpouring into the veins and arteries of the bloodthirsty monster, the Male Machine that now can continue its obscene life only by genocide. If the Machine dreams, it is of a future filled with megadeaths. The total vampire no longer needs even to

---

24. "All Violence Victims Deserve to be Believed," *Minnesota Daily*, 3 June, 1988.

speak of blood, which is after all visible, measurable. It drinks instead in quantities calculable only through the highest mathematics....It is men who have sapped the life-force of women.[25]

This horror over male atrocity, like feminist candlelight processions to "take back the night," is a public relations exercise. According to Dr. Karl Menninger, for every woman who complains to her psychiatrist about the brutality of her man there are a dozen who complain about his weakness, dependency and impotence—a dozen who want their men to be more dominant, not less.[26]

There is an intergenerational angle. According to Gelles and Straus,[27] it is a myth that most battered and abused children grow up to become batterers and abusers themselves. They quote child development expert Edward Zigler of Yale University as saying "the majority of abused children do not become abusive parents" and "the time has come for the intergenerational myth to be placed aside."[28] But on the next page they cite researchers Rosemary Hunter and Nancy Kilstrom: "If they [abused children who grew up to be non-abusive parents] had been abused, it was by one parent, while the other parent served as a supportive life raft in a sea of trouble and pain."[29] In other words, the kids who survived abuse and became decent parents came from father-present families—*the two-parent family saved them*. So while Gelles and Straus think it's good that women should have "the economic resources they need to terminate a violent marriage,"[30] such termination transfers children from the patriarchal system which protects them to the matriarchal system where a disproportionate amount of child abuse occurs. In September, 1989 a social service officer in Milwaukee County,

---

25. Mary Daly, *Beyond God the Father* (Boston: Beacon Press, 1973), pp. 172ff.

26. Review of Simone de Beauvoir's *The Second Sex* in *Saturday Review*, 21 February, 1953.

27. Richard J. Gelles and Murray A. Straus, *Intimate Violence: The Causes and Consequences of Abuse in the American Family* (New York: Simon and Schuster, 1988), p. 121.

28. P. 121.

29. P. 122.

30. P. 113.

by name Terrence Cooley, wrote an inter-office communication titled "AFDC/Child Abuse Information," a copy of which found its way into the editorial office of *The Family in America*,[31] pointing out that of the 1,050 cases of child abuse and neglect in that county an astonishing 83 percent occurred in households receiving Aid to Families with Dependent Children (read: female-headed households).[32] "There has been," say Gelles and Straus,

> tremendous growth in paid employment of married women between 1975 and 1985. Our own research has found that paid employment of married women helps rectify the imbalance of power between spouses, and provides women with the economic resources they need to terminate a violent marriage.[33]

Also a non-violent marriage. Also a marriage in which the wife is not battered and oppressed but simply bored and fed up with the sexual regulation which the patriarchal system imposes upon her in exchange for her permitting a male to share her reproductive life and haul her out of the matriarchal system and place her under coverture in the patriarchal system.

Another way of saying the same thing is that it denies menn the resources and authority they need to hold a marriage together.

It "helps rectify the imbalance of power between the two spouses," say Gelles and Straus. They naively accept the whole Slaughtered Saints propaganda position, that women are poor violated victims in need of society's chivalry, an idea ancient in Mary Wollenstonecraft's day. In 1854 Barbara Leigh Smith Bodichon wrote a pamphlet, "Married Women and the Law," citing the familiar complaints about the patriarchy:

---

31. *The Family in America: New Research*, December, 1989; see Annex to Chapter I, page 284.

32. Things are worse than the 83 percent figure indicates, since among the remaining 17 percent of abuse cases there must be female-headed households *not* on AFDC.

33. Gelles and Straus, p. 113.

A man and wife are one person in law; the wife loses all her rights as a single woman, and her existence is entirely absorbed in that of her husband. He is civilly responsible for her acts; she lives under his protection or cover, and her condition is called coverture.

A woman's body belongs to her husband, she is in his custody, and he can enforce his right by a writ of *habeas corpus*.

The legal custody of children belongs to the father. During the life-time of a sane father, the mother has no rights over her children, except a limited power over infants, and the father may take them from her and dispose of them as he thinks fit.[34]

This tilting of the law in the favor of the male has been not just abolished but reversed, but it is still paraded in feminist literature (like the binding of Chinese women's feet) as proving how oppressed today's American women are. The 19th century husband was empowered to take his wife's children from her, *but he didn't*. Today's wife is empowered to take her husband's children from him *and she does* in millions of marriages, and the marriages in which her right is not exercised are de-stabilized by the knowledge that it could be exercised if the wife chooses. Gelles and Straus know this but they still talk as though the law tilted in favor of the husband rather than the wife. The "imbalance" which needs to be "rectified" is the reverse of what they suggest: what is needed is getting rid of the massive anti-male bias of the legal system which deprives husbands of virtually all rights and reduces ex-husbands to literal slavery.

Today's legal system has abandoned its responsibility to stabilize families and has become the principal enemy of the family. That such a thing could happen, and happen so rapidly and unobtrusively, suggests that the execrated pro-male 19th century legal system had the right idea. It sensed, if it did not explicitly understand, that women don't like marriage and

---

34. Quoted in Carolyn Heilbrun, *Writing a Women's Life* (New York: Ballantine Books, 1988), pp. 84f.

family life and would willingly do away with them if they could do so without forfeiting their benefits. "[I]f one imagined himself as newly arrived from Mars," writes feminist Carolyn Heilbrun,

> and were to read the descriptions of a woman's marriage in contemporary novels by women, one might well ask how on earth anyone could be expected to live out such a farce.[35]

She quotes a woman who opposed the ERA on the grounds that "I don't care to be a person":

> She understood, while misunderstanding the ERA, that to be a person and a wife are oddly incompatible.
> Why do contemporary men fail to see this?[36]

She scolds Christopher Lasch because he does not

> seem to recognize that the old, good life, which he, Yeats, Trilling, and all today's new conservatives feel such nostalgia for, rested on the willingness of women to remain exactly where today's women, in fiction at least, will not remain: at home. Waiting for husband-warrior to retreat to them from the wide world is no longer enough....[T]he woman who finds herself miserable at home when she is supposed to have everything she has always wanted, everything all women have always wanted—this woman, who would, decades ago, have been sent home by her analyst in search of a vaginal orgasm—is now seen as passing through a stage of development recognized in men but not hitherto associated with women: adolescence. A woman is not an adolescent at puberty in our society, because her search for identity does not take place then: rather it is a search for a husband in which she then engages. The search for self, Nora's search in Ibsen's *A Doll's House*, occurs deep into marriage and often with children left behind the slammed door....The real tension between...the fleeing

---

35. Carolyn Heilbrun, *Reinventing Womanhood* (New York: W. W. Norton, 1979), p. 175.
36. *Ibid.*

woman and those who struggle to preserve the family, is the tension between order and change, particularly evident in our society. It is most evident within marriage, where *the man desires order and the woman change.* If the women are unclear about what change should encompass, they know it begins with their departure.[37]

"Why do contemporary men fail to see this" *indeed*? Women don't like the regulation marriage imposes upon them. The feminist/sexual revolution is an attempt to get rid of this regulation without forfeiting the economic and status advantages its acceptance formerly conferred.

What Dr. Heilbrun says comes close to what the Seneca Falls feminists complained about, that women were moral minors with whom contracts—including marriage—were worth nothing because they could renege on them if they wished. Such irresponsibility justified the pro-male tilt of the law. 19th century men needed the pro-male tilt—and so do men today. "Why do contemporary men fail to see this?"

"Women will not remain at home," says Dr. Heilbrun. Not if they can make themselves economically independent (as they are doing) or if they can implement the feminist program of making divorce an economically viable alternative to marriage (for women) and, after inducing males to thrust their necks into the matrimonial guillotine, induce lawmakers to enact child support rules "that aim at equalizing the standards of living of the two parties after divorce."[38]

Dr. Heilbrun speaks of women's delayed "adolescence," their final growing up, postponed beyond its proper period by the necessity of having a husband while they are nubile and dependent and may wish to procreate a child or two. This delayed adolescence "begins with their departure" (read: divorce), when they demonstrate their maturity by repudiating the marriage contract upon which men and children must depend but which they and Dr. Heilbrun and the legal system correctly perceive as a mere piece of paper.

---

37. P. 179; emphasis added. "Departure" is feminese for expelling Dad.
38. See note 11.

"The man desires order and the woman desires change." The man desires a stable patriarchal family system; the woman desires a return to matriliny and de-regulation, a return to the sexual anarchy of the Stone Age and the ghetto and the Indian reservation. The only possible resolution of this is to make women grow up and choose either to accept sexual regulation as the quid pro quo for the benefits of patriarchy or to reject the benefits along with the regulation.

"The clearest memory of my wedding day," says Susan Crain Bakos,

> is what was going on in my head as I walked down the aisle in my white satin dress with the floor-length lace mantilla billowing around me: "No. No way is this going to be forever, for the rest of my life. *No.*"
>
> I said "I do" because that's what young women wearing white dresses have traditionally said in front of altars in churches. But in my mind, at least, the choices were still there.[39]

This shows her maturity: she is passing through the adolescence that males pass through at puberty. And the legal system agrees with her that her vows and her marriage contract are non-binding: her choices are still there. The difference is that the male's maturity makes his contracts dependable and Ms. Bakos's maturity makes hers undependable. The difference between these two kinds of maturity was the reason Victorian society decreed that "the legal custody of children belongs to the father"—and it is the reason our society ought to do the same.

"When I was no longer married," continues Ms. Bakos,

> I found it easy to share Kara's philosophy: Don't trust men; only sleep with them. The experience of multiple partners led us both to the same obvious conclusion: There would always be someone new, someone better, some other man to make love to us, so why not leave when a relationship grew boring or difficult or too complicated? It was what men deserved anyway.

39. Susan Crain Bakos, *This Wasn't Supposed to Happen: Single Women Over 30 Talk Frankly About Their Lives* (New York: Continuum, 1985), p. 20.

Why limit ourselves to one man when lots of men were available?

I got divorced so that I could join the generation of women, my generation, who kept their options open, put their own needs first, and considered sex a natural right. Together with the men of our generation, we weren't very good at "working things out," but we were certainly wonderful at "moving on." We knew how to break up. Our music about breaking up and moving on was upbeat and positive. The civilized divorce was surely our invention.[40]

She quotes "Kara":

"When men began talking about commitment, I got out. Making a commitment meant marriage; and for women, marriage means giving a man too much power in your life. I just knew I wasn't going to do it; and I was glad we lived in a time where a woman could have sex, all the sex she wanted, without getting married.

"I thought in vague terms of having a kid someday, of being a single mother. I didn't give up on having kids then, just marriage."

We chose sex, not marriage.[41]

Marriage means giving men responsibility and a meaningful reproductive role and these gals couldn't care less about male responsibility—aside from the responsibility of paying child support money. They want to schlepp back into promiscuity, recreational sex, matriliny and the free ride, like the squaws on Indian reservations and the welfare matriarchs of the ghettos.

The contempt for women's parasitism which Betty Friedan expressed in 1963 has now been replaced by a demand for compensation for something Ms. Friedan never hinted at, *men's* parasitism. Merely equalizing things, says Dr. Daly,

---

40. P. 22.
41. P. 23.

will not mean an immediate "give and take," as if those who have been deprived of their own life should "give on a fifty-fifty basis." Since what males have to give has in large measure been sapped from women, "the equalizing of concentrations" can hardly be imagined as if from equal but opposite social positions. On the level of social interaction, what has to take place is *creative justice.* It is not a simple transaction that is demanded, but a restitution. It is absurd for men to look upon the relinquishing of stolen privilege as benevolence. It is absurd also for men to protest indignantly when women speak of wresting back our own stolen power and being.[42]

A principal thrust of Slaughtered Saints feminism is the continuing accusation of male domestic violence directed against "women and children"—these two being lumped together to indicate that the perpetrators of the violence are (who else?) husbands and fathers. The fact appears to be, however, that Mom is responsible for more domestic violence than Dad.[43]

---

42. P. 173.

43. This is acknowledged even by investigators as timid as Gelles and Straus, who write that "About one woman in twenty-two (3.8 percent) is a victim of physically abusive violence each year" and that "A little more than forty husbands in one thousand (4.6 percent) were recorded as victims of severe violence" (Richard J. Gelles and Murray A. Straus, *Intimate Violence: The Causes and Consequences of Abuse in the American Family* (New York: Simon and Schuster, 1988), p. 104).

This says that there is 21 percent more violence directed against husbands. But what is compared is evidently lesser violence against wives ("physically abusive violence") and greater violence against husbands ("severe violence"); so one must suppose that if the same kind of violence were being compared the wives are more violent than the 21 percent figure suggests. (If this inference is incorrect, Gelles and Straus cannot blame anyone other than themselves.)

The "tendency" of these writers can be inferred from their calling 4.6 percent "a little more than forty in one thousand." "A little less than fifty in one thousand" would be closer to the mathematical truth--but it would deviate from the party line mandated by Slaughtered Saints feminism.

It needs to be understood that books on the subject of domestic violence are read chiefly by feminists and must pass review in the feminist press. A book which departs from the feminist party line will be dead in the water. Gelles and Straus mention their colleague Suzanne Steinmetz's article on "The Battered Husband Syndrome" and indicate that "she was immediately attacked by feminists, social scientists, and a few journalists... Other social scientists who witnessed the abuse heaped on our research group--especially on Suzanne Steinmetz--have given the topic of battered men a wide berth" (pp. 105f.). In other words, feminist clamor frightened them away from saying things that feminists don't want the public to know about, lest women should appear to be something other than blood-drained Slaughtered Saints and men to be something other than ravening beasts.

According to Los Angeles policeperson Gloria Vargas, as quoted by *Los Angeles Times* writer Carol McGraw, "Kids grow up seeing their father get away with beating up mom. So what happens? They grow up and beat up their wife or resort to other violence."[44] "Typically," says McGraw, "the *victims*, afraid of even more violence, would not turn their *husbands* or *relatives* in, and in many cases would even join their *spouse* in attacking the police who came to their rescue, Vargas said."[45]

The *suggestio falsi* is that "victims" are female and "relatives" and "spouse" male. But there are as many male victims as female ones and the perpetrators protected by their "spouse" from police interference are frequently female. Boys are twice as likely as girls to be victims of assault (by Mom). Men often remain married to violent women out of concern to protect their children, who, in the event of divorce, would be placed in Mom's sole custody.

A mild protest against this sort of thing is registered by British feminist Lynne Segal, who complains that contemporary feminism "celebrates women's superior virtue and spirituality and decries 'male' violence and technology. Such celebration of the 'female' and denunciation of the 'male,' however, arouses fear and suspicion in feminists who, like me, recall that we joined the women's movement to challenge the myths of women's special nature."[46] According to the dust wrapper of Segal's book, "She argues against the exponents of the new apocalyptic feminism, among whom are Mary Daly, Andrea Dworkin and Dale Spender, which says that men wield power over women through terror, greed and violence and that only women, because of their essentially greater humanity, can save the world from social, ecological and nuclear disaster." Today, writes Segal,

> "like any Victorian gentleman, Robin Morgan, Adrienne Rich, Susan Griffin, Judith Arcana, Mary Daly, Dale Spender and their many followers, take for granted and celebrate women's greater humanism, pacifism, nur-

---

44. *Los Angeles Times*, 2 November, 1988.

45. *Ibid.*; emphasis added.

46. Lynne Segal, *Is the Future Female? Troubled Thoughts on Contemporary Feminism* (New York: Peter Bedrick Books, 1987), p. 3

turance and spiritual development. Robin Morgan tells us that only women can guarantee the future of life on earth. Ronald Reagan and the New Right in the US and anti-feminist conservatives here in Britain tell us much the same thing. Women can save the world from the nightmares of nuclear weaponry, which represents the untamed force of "male drives and male sexuality," through the power of the feminine mentality and the force of maternal concerns.[47]

Segal's is a minority view. As Robert Briffault truly says, "A defiant and rebellious attitude is found in women only where they occupy a position of considerable vantage and influence; it is not found where their status is really one of oppression."[48] Today's feminists occupy a position of considerable vantage and influence and they know that that position is secure only as long as the public accepts the "myth of the monstrous male"—and the victimized female.

Slaughtered Saints feminists have much to say about the beastliness of males, but nothing to say about what Ms. Friedan most emphasized in 1963: "the problem that has no name," *acedia*, the ennui deriving from a lack of meaning in their existence. Acedia is a spiritual problem, but a materialist like Ms. Friedan could conceive of it only as a problem with an economic or occupational solution—an elitist career. She misconceived "the problem that has no name" as not a blessing but a curse. It was a signal that a spiritual dimension was lacking in the lives of the educated middle-class women she wrote about. "Blessed are those who feel their spiritual need," said Jesus, "for the Kingdom of Heaven belongs to them."[49]

The women suffering from the problem that has no name were in the fortunate condition of having had their *other* problems solved by the patriarchal system. The acedia from which they suffered was the problem at the very apex of the "hierarchy of needs." "Only recently," says Ms. Friedan,

---

47. *Ibid.*, pp. 3-4.
48. Robert Briffault, *The Mothers* (New York: Macmillan and Company, 1927), I, 327.
49. Matthew 5:2; Goodspeed's translation.

have we come to accept the fact that there is an evolutionary scale or hierarchy of needs in man (and thus in woman), ranging from the needs usually called instincts because they are shared with animals, to needs that come later in human development. These later needs, the needs for knowledge, for self-realization, are as instinctive, in a human sense, as the needs shared with other animals of food, sex, survival. The clear emergence of the later needs seems to rest upon prior satisfaction of the physiological needs. The man who is extremely and dangerously hungry has no other interest but food. Capacities not useful for the satisfying of hunger are pushed into the background. "But what happens to man's desires when there is plenty of food and his belly is chronically filled? At once, other (and higher) needs emerge and these, rather than the physiological hungers, dominate the organism."[50]

In a sense, this evolving hierarchy of needs moves further and further away from the physiological level which depends on the material environment, and tends toward a level relatively independent of the environment, more and more self-determined. But a man can be fixated on a lower need level; higher needs can be confused or channeled into he old avenues and may never emerge.[51]

Ms. Friedan complains that the need for "self-actualization" has been wrongly interpreted as a "sexual need," something she calls an "explanation by reduction." But the career-elitism which she proposes to her female readers as the solution for the problem that has no name is equally an explanation by reduction, equally an "evasion of growth," equally unsatisfying, as is shown by a flood of disillusioned feminist books like *A Lesser Life, Unnecessary Choices, This Wasn't Supposed to Happen, The Divorce Revolution, Mothers on Trial,* et cetera.

---

50. The quoted words are from Abraham Maslow's *Motivation and Personality,* p. 83.
51. *The Feminine Mystique,* pp. 314f.

After pouring her contempt on the parasitism of American housewives, she proposes to make them grow "to their full capacities," to mass-produce "self-actualizers," people like Shakespeare, da Vinci, Lincoln, Einstein, Freud, Tolstoy. This will require a "massive attempt" by educators, parents, ministers, magazine editors, manipulators, guidance counselors, and a "GI Bill for Women":

What is needed now is a national educational program similar to the GI bill, for women who *seriously* want to continue or resume their education—and who are willing to commit themselves to its use *in a profession*. The bill would provide *properly qualified* women with tuition fees, plus an additional subsidy to defray other expenses—books, travel, even, if necessary, some household help.[52]

A free ride for women who want to be "professionals" and demand large fees from the people whose taxes give them their free ride. This is how liberated housewives will stand on their own feet. How can the "seriousness" and "proper qualification" of these women[53] be evaluated? Clearly on the basis that they *declare* themselves to be serious and properly qualified and choose to enter *professionally* oriented programs. In other words, idle housewives whose taking of a free ride from their husbands is held up to scorn and whose chief motivation is boredom with suburban lotus-eating and monogamous marriage, are to crowd into colleges and begin a subsidized existence paid for by taxpayers mostly less affluent than themselves. The subsidization will include funds to hire household helpers, women not serious about becoming *professionals*, who need wages solely to support their families.[54] These members of the lower orders will live on their trickle-down benefits, far more modest than those given to Ms. Friedan's elitists—of all classes

---

52. *The Feminine Mystique*, pp. 364, 370; emphasis added.
53. Men don't qualify for the free ride since they don't suffer from the problem that has no name.
54. Cf. *The Feminine Mystique*, p. 215: "Anyone with a strong enough back (and a small enough brain) can do these chores."

in society the ones least deserving of, or in need of, public assistance. Their subsidization is said to be a matter of "desperate...emergency":

> Their desperate need for education and the desperate need of this nation for the untapped reserves of women's intelligence in all the *professions* justify these emergency measures.[65]

After spending most of her book talking about the immaturity of American housewives, Ms. Friedan then compares them to male GIs, "matured by war," suggesting that "Women who have matured during the housewife moratorium can be counted on for similar performance"[56]—presumably because of the influence of the feminine mystique, elsewhere said to cause their infantilism. If the "housewife moratorium" (read: feminine mystique) is a maturing influence, why should it not lead these women to stand on their own feet "without sexual privilege or excuse" rather than to demand the exchange of one parasitism (on husbands) for another (on taxpayers)? The GI Bill gave ex-servicemen some compensation for their years of service to society. Ms. Friedan wants the same compensation for women because "society asks so little of women" and therefore (by Ms. Friedan's logic) must pamper these Sleeping Beauties yet more, rather than merely allowing their husbands to pamper them, which denies them independence and dignity.

Sleeping Beauty feminism was poorly adapted to becoming a mass movement despite Ms. Friedan's program for making it one. It was aimed at the minority of elitists whose non-spiritual problems had been solved and who were summoned to confront the spiritual crisis signaled by "the problem that has no name." The failure to recognize this crisis as a spiritual one has led not

---

55. P. 370; emphasis added. We need more lady lawyers, lady doctors, lady psychologists, lady philosophers, lady academics and lady executives like we need a trephine. What we do need is more day-care workers, more clerk-typists, more waitresses, more nurses, more street-crossing guards and more cleaning women, and it is in such occupations that most liberated women find themselves after they cast off patriarchal oppression and what Mrs. Pankhurst called "the great scourge" of marriage.

56. P. 370.

to its solution but its burial, its replacement by problems at lower levels in the "hierarchy of needs," things like paying the rent and the utilities and coping with roleless men—problems which have made today's Slaughtered Saints feminism what the Sleeping Beauty feminism of a generation ago could never have been, a mass movement.

The best thing for the women's movement now would be (if it were possible) to restore the patriarchal family and hope that it could once again solve women's lower-level needs and bring them back to where is could be said, "Blessed are those who feel their spiritual need." Let the Scriptures be fulfilled. The patriarchy which brought them this far couldn't carry them all the way to moksha experience but it was the best friend women ever had.

Slaughtered Saints feminists now affect to interpret the free ride as itself an affliction, as what feminist Jessie Bernard calls "the woman's extra load of economic dependency."[57]

She thinks this burden "has to be lightened" because

> A union between a man and a woman in which, *when it breaks down*, one loses not only the mate but also the very means of subsistence is not a fair relationship.[58]

It is not a relationship at all *when it breaks down*; and it breaks down chiefly because (thanks to the feminist/sexual revolution's insistence on a woman's right to control her own reproduction) marriage has become a non-binding contract. Women do not suffer from an "extra load of economic dependency"; they want to hang on to the dependency or get it back again—without having to fulfill the marital obligations which justify it.

The patriarchal system benefits women by *marriage*. The feminist program of wrecking the patriarchy aims to make it provide the same benefits *outside marriage*, thereby destroying marriage, the family, the male role and the whole patriarchal

---

57. *The Future of Marrige* (New Haven: Yale University Press, 1982), p. 288.
58. *Ibid.*; empahsis added.

system—and restoring matriliny. The only way for men to restore the patriarchy is to insist that there shall be no free ride outside of marriage and the acceptance of sexual regulation—no alimony, no child support payments, no affirmative action and comparable worth programs, no quotas, no goals-and-time-tables. To be independent means not to be dependent.

The suffering of single mothers—largely self-inflicted—is now deemed sufficient justification for the free ride:

The welfare system...should be replaced with a system under which single parents would be earners, but would have government guarantees of child support payments out of the earnings of the other parent, health care, and high quality child care.[59]

Wages Due Lesbians [is] an independent group of lesbian women who organize within Wages for Housework, particularly in regard to custody. Wages for Housework is an international organization fighting for money for all women so that they can lead *independent* lives.[60]

Benefits for divorced, separated, and never-married mothers and their children could be made more similar to benefits to widows either by increasing benefit levels or by making benefits available to single mothers regardless of income.[61]

For women as a group, the future holds terrifying insecurity: We are increasingly dependent on our own resources, but in a society and an economy that never intended to admit us as independent persons, much less as breadwinners for others.[62]

---

59. Barbara Bergmann, *The Economic Emergence of Women* (New York: Basic Books, 1986), p. 5.

60. Gillian E. Hanscombe and Jackie Forster, *Rocking the Cradle: Lesbian Mothers: A challenge in Family Living* (Boston: Alyson Publications, 1982), p. 46; emphasis added.

61. Irwin Garfinkel and Sara S. McLanahan, *Single Mothers and Their Children: A New American Dilemma* (Washington, D.C., Urban Institute Press, 1986), p. 26.

62. Barbara Ehrenreich, *The Hearts of Men: American Dreams and the Fight from Commitment* (Garden City, NY, 1984), p. 175.

The fact that women are overwhelmingly the caretakers of children is a key determinant of their secondary economic status. Whether within the two-parent family unit or in a single-parent family, women, for the most part, provide the nurturing, the day-to-day care, the hands-on childrearing.[63]

The feminist demand to be made independent by being made dependent appears paradoxical until its underlying idea is understood, which is this: What women want is not independence but de-regulation. They yearn to return to the "kind of role they had on the grasslands of Africa millions of years ago." [64]

De-regulation is the key idea which explains the feminist/sexual revolution. They like to talk about independence because it sounds self-approbatively heroic—and the talk is sincere in the sense that when they write agitprop or get together at conventions and take one another seriously they believe their own flim-flam. But when any tangible, especially economic, benefit enters the picture they opt for dependence. The more dependence—the more alimony, the more child support, the more legislative/bureaucratic/judicial chivalry, the more affirmative action, the more comparable worth, the more quotas, the more goals-and-timetables, the more anti-male discrimination, the more freebies—the better. If it's free they want it. What they don't want is the regulation of their sexuality which gives males a secure role within stable families.

The currently fashionable program for attaining this de-regulation is the subject of the following chapter, the program of casting themselves into poverty and squalor and dragging "their" children with them—and exhibiting the resulting predicament as proving their need to be rescued.

---

63. Ruth Sidel, *Women and Children Last: The Plight of Poor Women in Affluent America* (New York: Viking, 1986), p. 190.
64. See the quotation from Helen Fisher, page 5, *supra.*

V

The Mutilated Beggar Argument

In Cairo there exists a cottage industry which mutilates children to be used as beggars. The more gruesome and pitiable the mutilations, the more the beggars will earn. The disfigured children are placed on mats on street corners with a begging bowl and they ask for alms for the love of Allah.

The almsgiver is doing a good thing and a bad thing. The good thing is paying for the child's next meal. The bad thing is ensuring that more children will be mutilated.

The Mutilated Beggar technique is employed extensively in the contemporary war over the family. Ex-wives drag their children into poverty and then point to their sufferings as proving the need for ex-husbands or the welfare system to bail them out. The father (or taxpayer) who bails out Mom and the kids is doing a good thing—providing rent and food money—and a bad thing—subsidizing the destruction of this family and encouraging the mass divorce which is wrecking millions of others—in effect, undermining the patriarchy and restoring matriliny.

Here's a nineteenth century example. Ella May Wiggins, a factory worker with nine fatherless children, wrote "The Mill Mother's Lament" to exhibit her suffering and that of her children:

We leave our homes in the morning,
We kiss our children good bye,
While we slave for the bosses
Our children scream and cry....

How it grieves the heart of a mother,
You everyone must know,
But we can't buy for our children
Our wages are too low.

It is for our little children,
That seem to us so dear,
But for us nor them, dear workers,
The bosses do not care.

But understand, all workers,
Our union they do fear;
Let's stand together, workers,
And have a union here.[1]

Wiggins's problem is the fatherlessness of her nine children. The best social arrangement would be for her to have a husband to love, honor and protect her and those kids. Maybe she had a husband and he died and there exists no realistic prospect of a replacement for him. In that case Wiggins is a proper object of charity.

Wiggins doesn't want charity. She wants a union which will compel "the bosses" to subsidize her with an income suitable for the support of herself and nine children. She and the kids need the money. The bosses are wealthier than she is. Ergo they should be forced to share. Is she worth a larger salary than other employees who do the same work? Probably not. Probably her nine children decrease her efficiency and increase her absenteeism. If she were paid not the wage she is worth but the wage she needs, other employees who are worth the same amount would have to be given less and would probably seek employment elsewhere, where they were paid what they were worth. The bosses would find themselves losing their best workers and having to operate their mill with needy and desperate workers like Wiggins. If they have competition to meet, they would find themselves disadvantaged, possibly driven out of business, with the consequence that Wiggins and other needy people like herself would be out of jobs. Everyone would suffer and the results would be worse than if there had been no union and no wage increase for Wiggins.

Suppose Wiggins's problem were dealt with at the highest level. Suppose that (as in communist countries) there were a law against unemployment. Nobody would ever be destitute. Wig-

---

1. Quoted in Elise Boulding, *The Underside of History: A View of Women Through Time* (Boulder, Colorado: Westview Press, 1976), p. 640.

gins might think this would be a desirable reordering of society. So would a lot of feminists. It would greatly weaken, perhaps eventually destroy, the patriarchal system, making husbands unessential as family providers, making female chastity superfluous, since it would no longer be essential to reassure fathers and husbands concerning the integrity of their families. Sexually responsible behavior would be unnecessary. A reordering of society which would make mothers of nine fatherless children economically independent would pretty well shatter social arrangements, including the family. Incentives for divorce, for male abandonment of families, for the creation of female-headed families would be multiplied. There would be far more cases like Wiggins's and far fewer resources for bailing them out. Children would be at greater risk of delinquency and the other ills mentioned in Chapter I.

The fact is that in the *general* case (even if not in Wiggins's case) mothers and children are better served by the patriarchal system than by any other. The reason was well explained a century ago by Herbert Spencer, who showed how two very different principles operate within and outside of the family—"the law that during immature life benefit received must be great in proportion as worth is small, while during mature life benefit and worth must vary together."[2] Wiggins would abolish the distinction and have "the bosses" run their competitive business as though it were a family in which the bosses functioned as parents—much as New York's Governor Cuomo believes government should be a "family" for its citizens. The resulting social structure would come to resemble the Stone Age matriclan described in Chapter II. The matriclan creates little wealth and expends that little in keeping everyone marginally afloat. In it, the intense motivation created by the nuclear family is lost. Wiggins's hope is that the wealth will continue to be generated somehow and that she can corner her share of it by employing the Mutilated Beggar Argument to lay a guilt-trip on "the bosses." The system works poorly to generate wealth.

It will be useful to give one or two additional illustrations of the Mutilated Beggar Principle.

---

2. *Principles of Sociology*, III:, part 8; reprinted in *Herbert Spencer on Social Evolution* (Chicago: University of Chicago Press, 1972), ed. J. D. Y. Peel, p. 245.

Feminist Marilyn French, while rejoicing over women's new-found liberation, complains of some of the economic problems accompanying it:

> Old codes of marriage, divorce, sexuality, and child rearing have broken down, but the consequences of this breakdown have been mixed.

Here are the good things resulting from the breakdown of the "old codes," meaning the patriarchal sexual constitution:

> People can escape from unhappy marriages, they can use their sexuality as they choose on the whole.

And here are the bad things:

> At the same time, men are displaying an irresponsibility about their children that is equivalent in self-hatred to terrorist murder—for are not our children expressions of ourselves? Women and children are the new poor, and a growing class.[3]

It is "good" that women can escape from their marriages and be promiscuous ("use their sexuality as they choose"); but this wrecking of the marriage contract, which deprives the man of legitimate children, takes away his motivation for supporting Mom and her kids—for "our" children means Mom's children, taken away from Dad. Strange reasoning, this, which ignores the obvious causal connection between the breakdown of the sexual constitution, women's escape from marriage and their using their sexuality as they choose ("good" things) and the male rolelessness resulting from this female de-regulation. Why should a man be condemned and compared to a terrorist murderer for no longer performing a role of which he has been deprived? Why is it not rather the irresponsibility of the woman or the divorce court judge which is to be condemned for exiling

---

3. Marilyn French, *Beyond Power: On Women, Men and Morals* (New York: Summit Books, 1985), p. 22.

the children's provider? This is like disbanding the fire and police departments and blaming them for not putting out fires and preventing robberies, like refusing to pay the rent and blaming the landlord for *expelling* his tenants, like placing children in the *father's* custody and blaming Mom for not coming to his home to do his laundry, mop his floors and prepare his meals.

Another example. America is giving Madagascar a subsidy in a "debt-for-nature" swap, to encourage them to stop massacring their forests.[4] Environmentalists are said to be enthusiastic "because it helps raise awareness in developing countries of environmental issues."[5] The awareness which will be raised is that ecological irresponsibility pays: Madagascar wouldn't have gotten the money if it had behaved responsibly, would it?

Another. The Irish Law Reform Commission has proposed that the concept of "illegitimacy" should be abolished, since it is unjust to deny rights to innocent illegitimate children in order to benefit legitimate ones.[6] It is the institution of marriage which protects "innocent" children from the disadvantages imposed upon them by the irresponsibility of unchaste parents; and if there are no "illegitimate" children, there can be no "legitimate" ones—since either term is meaningless except in reference to the other— and fathers will no longer provide their offspring with the benefits formerly conferred by two-parent families. What is intended to benefit the child-victims creates more of them and maximizes their miseries, since fatherless children really are disadvantaged as the evidence in the Annex to Chapter I shows..

Here's a different application of the Mutilated Beggar idea, attempting to employ it to gain for women the benefits men earn by work and achievement. Janice Mall, writing a column titled "About Women" in the *Los Angeles Times*, quotes a feminist to this effect:

---

4. *The Los Angeles Times,* 4 August, 1989.

5. *Ibid.*

6. Phyllis Chesler, *Mothers on Trial: The Battle for Children and Custody* (New York: McGraw-Hill Book Company, 1986), pp. 365, 580.

One woman, in describing her own feelings about being a minority in her field, provided an image that could help men understand the difficulties: "Imagine that your lawyer, your doctor, your priest, rabbi or minister, your senator and representative, your mayor, the president of your institution, most of its trustees, almost all of the deans and most of your colleagues were all women. How would you feel?"[7]

A man would feel *awful*—like one of the millions of black youths standing around street corners in the ghettos, or like drifters on Skid Row, or prisoners in jail who see themselves excluded from all high status occupations. The complaining lady implies that there should be affirmative action to place her and her sisters in 51 percent of high status positions—but not in 51 percent of the far more numerous low status positions. The price a *man* pays for being one of the high status winners is accepting the chance of being one of the losers—a chance which is no part of any feminist program for helping women. Women already have "equal opportunity" to compete for the high status positions; what they now want is an affirmative action program to *confer* 51 percent of the high status positions on women without them risking the fall into the low-status positions, where real competition would place many of them.

Today there are millions of women caught in the Custody Trap (to be discussed in the following chapter), deprived of the economic security formerly given them by the patriarchal system. These millions of losers are an embarrassment to the feminist movement which is chiefly responsible for their predicament, but which would like them to believe they are victimized by having been compelled to make the "choice" of which feminists write so much: women, they say, were *pressured* by the sexist patriarchy into being "just a housewife," which was the reason so few of them ever became senators or corporation executives—but also, not incidentally, why so few of them ever became jailbirds or Skid Row bums. The solution, Ms. Friedan told them, was for them to repudiate the "choice," to liberate themselves to become elitists like Mr. Friedan herself, a mag-

---

7. *Los Angeles Times*, 14 December, 1986.

num cum laude from Smith, who writes best-selling books. Trouble was most of the women thus liberated were not magnum cum laude or magnum cum talent or magnum cum chutzpah or magnum cum luck and they were unwanted on the talk shows. They ended up as waitresses or salesgirls or on welfare and discovered that their role in the feminist system was not to be Joan-of-Arc's like Ms. Friedan,[8] but to be humble Mutilated Beggars whose afflictions could be pointed to as proving the need for more feminism and larger subventions from ex-husbands and from the Backup System—so that they could "stand on their own feet."

Charlotte Bunch complains about divorced women not getting as much of their ex-husbands' paychecks as they did during marriage: "No-fault divorce laws sounds like equality, but since male and female incomes are not equal and many women have worked for husbands for years, these laws cut off some women's badly needed and justified right to alimony."[9]

The wives have been working for the husbands, as she says. But the husbands have also been working for the wives. The wife's withdrawal of her services by divorce ends the husband's reciprocal obligations; and if the husband's income is greater, that proves the desirability of having a husband, not the justice of reducing an ex-husband to bondage. If being in need (Mutilated Beggar argument) were enough to ensure the subsidization of ex-wives by ex-husbands, marriage would become superfluous except as a preliminary to divorce. If a wife is a parasite for taking a virtual free ride on the back of her husband, an ex-wife who gets her free ride on the back of an ex-husband, for whom she provides no reciprocal services whatever, is trebly parasitic.

---

8. Betty Friedan, *The Second Stage* (New York: Summit Books, 1981), pp. 86f.: "Joan of Arc said, facing the flames, 'All that I am I will not deny.' ...I have known for a long time that what drove me to tangle with the tortuous questions, to take on the uneasy, almost inconceivable mission of the women's movement, and what drives me now, at the zenith of that movement and in the face of its remarkable accomplishments, to wrestle anew with its assumed direction, is the simple driving need to *feel good* about being a woman, about myself as a woman, to be able to affirm who I really am--*All that I am will not deny.* Not only in my secret heart of hearts, but in the reality of evolving life, in the world."

9. *Passionate Politics: Feminist Theory in Action* (New York: St. Martin's Press, 1987), p. 115.

Female economic need is one of the chief props of marriage. Meeting this need by *divorce* arrangements means subsidizing ex- wives simply because they are female—*a reductio ad absurdum* of Betty Friedan's insistence that American wives should stop being parasites, stand on their own feet "and compete without sexual privilege or excuse."[10]

The female-headed families which seek to exploit the Mutilated Beggar argument are the source of most social pathology. Feminists aver that this pathology results from the poverty of these families, the cure for which is more of somebody else's money. But better subsidization of female-headed families would mean more female-headed families, more crime, more illegitimacy and the rest of the ills cited in Chapter I.

The alternative to the female-headed family is not a better-funded female-headed family but the patriarchal family, which produces not only more money but less crime, more stability and higher achieving offspring. The props needed to make the patriarchal family once again normative could be easily restored—the father's control over his paycheck and society's guarantee of father custody in the event of divorce. Father custody would mean few husbands would divorce their wives, knowing that without them they would be overburdened with a double role of breadwinning and child care. It would mean few wives would divorce their husbands, knowing that divorce would cost them their children and their standard of living. It would place economic and psychological motivations on the side of marriage instead of pitting them against marriage.

Father-custody was formerly the accepted arrangement. The first feminists, meeting at Seneca Falls in 1848, made it one of their chief complaints that in cases of divorce fathers automatically got custody of their children.[11] The family stability created by this presumption of father custody was a major reason for the progress and achievement of the Victorian era.

10. *The Feminine Mystique* (New York: W. W. Norton, 1963), p. 346.

11. Miriam Gurko, *The Ladies of Senaca Falls: The Birth of the Women's Rights Movement* (New York: Shocken Books, 1976), p. 61: "Elizabeth [Cady Stanton, nineteenth century feminist] heard about women caught in miserable unhappy marriages who had managed to arrange separations or even divorce, but were not permitted to see their own children or have anything to say about their upbringing. Under the state laws, a father had exclusive rights of guardianship, no matter what kind of man he was or what the cause of separation had been."

Would women accept it? Yes, as they did in the 19th century, because it would stabilize marriage. Mary Ann Mason, writing in her recent book *The Equality Trap* says, "Something has gone very wrong with the lives of women. Women are working much harder than they have worked in recent history, they are growing steadily poorer, and they are suffering the brutality of divorce at an unprecedented rate....I fear that the present trajectory of women's lives is aiming toward a bleak future. I see my daughter...and her generation living alone most of their adult lives in small efficiency apartments. There are few children in this dreary vision. Women have given up on having children, not because they have committed themselves to career, but because they have learned too well from my generation that women cannot depend upon marriage to last the duration of child-raising. They have learned that mothers get stuck with an exhausting burden of work at home and in the marketplace."[12]

But whether women would accept the patriarchal system or not, men must insist upon it—insist that the implementation of the marriage contract shall be on the basis of the wording of the contract itself. They must get back to fundamentals, must insist that they enter into the marriage contract primarily to procreate legitimate and inalienable children. They must reject the socially destructive idea, now accepted as a matter of course by women, lawmakers and judges, that the purpose of marriage is to provide women with ex-husbands.

---

12. Quoted in *MS.*, October, 1988.

VI

The Custody Trap

"For many women," says feminist Dr. Alice Rossi, "the personal outcome of experience in the parent role is not a higher level of maturation but the negative outcome of a depressed sense of self-worth, if not actual personality deterioration."[1] "The heart of woman's oppression," says Shulamith Firestone, "is her childbearing and childrearing roles."[2] The predicament of these mothers is trebly pitiable when they are single heads of families. Single mothers complain especially of poverty—theirs and that of the children they drag into the Custody Trap to keep them company and give them a "role." They aver that the patriarchal family is a prison for the mother; but the mother is far more restricted, impoverished and miserable in a female-headed family, with reduced income and no partner to share responsibilities with.

There exists a medium sized library of books with titles like *Women and Children Last, Poor Women, Poor Families,* and *Working Your Way to the Bottom: The Feminization of Poverty,* whose message is that society must do something to rescue single mothers. The overriding concern of this literature is the need for more money for Mom, so that her mother-love may have the wherewithal required for its proper functioning.

No question, the poverty is a problem. According to Betty Friedan, "Statistics indicate that a child in a family now in poverty, headed by a man, has a fifty-fifty chance of getting out of poverty by his or her maturity—but that a child in a poverty family headed by a woman has no chance."[3] Divorced women,

---

1. Alice Rossi, "Transition to Parenthood," in Peter Rose, ed., *Socialization and the Life Cycle* (New York: St. Martin, 1979), p. 137.
2. Cited in Samuel Blumenfeld, *The Retreat from Motherhood* (New Rochelle: Arlington House, 1975), p. 112.
3. *It Changed My Life: Writings on the Women's Movement* (New York: Random House, 1976), p. 326.

according to MS. magazine, have the lowest household incomes of any group of women.[4] "Worldwide," according to Kathleen Newland, "between one-quarter and one-third of all families are supported by women; and worldwide, these families are leading candidates for poverty and hardship."[5]

But poverty is not the only problem, or the worst. 80 percent of children in psychiatric clinics come from female-headed homes.[6] Single women family heads have the highest rate of disease compared to all other women, far higher than the never married.[7] They report "less satisfaction with their lives than Americans in any other marital status, including widows and women who had never married."[8]

Writing of the problems of female heads of families, Barbara Gelpi, Nancy Hartsock, Clare Novak and Myra Strober say, "Associated with such extreme hardship is the high incidence both of health problems and of troubles with older children among these families."[9] The same point is made by Deborah K. Zinn and Rosemary Sarri:

> Women also encountered a variety of serious problems with their older children. More than one-third were called to school in 1982 for special conferences, and 21 percent eported that their children had been suspended at least once. A small number of children had been expelled, referred to the juvenile court, committed to institutions, and/or victimized by crime. The numbers, although small, exceeded those one would expect to observe in an average family.[10]

---

4. *Ms.*, May, 1978.

5. Kathleen Newland, *Women, Men and the Division of Labor*, p. 153; cited in Hilda Scott, *Working Your Way to the Bottom: The Feminization of Poverty* (Boston: Pandora Press, 1984), p. 22.

6. *London Observer*, 14 September, 1980.

7. *Los Angeles Times*, 5 November, 1981.

8. David Chambers, *Making Fathers Pay* (Chicago: University of Chicago Press, 1979), p. 42.

9. *SIGNS*, Winter, 1984, p. 206.

10. *SIGNS*, Winter, 1984, pp. 366f.

Girls in female-headed homes have more problems in sex role and personality development and in handling aggression.[11] Father-deprived sons frequently exhibit aggressive behavior, lack of social responsibility, a variety of intellectual defects, high delinquency potential, tendencies toward homosexuality, difficulties in interpersonal relations and low need for achievement.[12] More than one third of the children from female- headed homes drop out of school.[13]

Divorce researchers Judith Wallerstein and Joan Kelly were struck with the pervasive sadness they encountered among 6-to-8- year-olds in female-headed families—a sadness not seldom transformed into rage at the mothers.[14] E. Mavis Hetherington found that mothers in father-absent homes have more psychiatric symptoms than mothers in intact homes.[15] According to Patricia Paskowicz, one-third of children of divorce living with their fathers seem pleased with their situation, compared with only one-tenth of those living with their mothers.[16]

Women heads of families are less marriageable. "I am a nice-looking, 28-year-old divorced woman," one of them writes to Dear Abby. "I have no trouble getting dates, but my problem is that every man I date runs to the nearest exit when I tell him I have three kids....The last four men I dated seemed interested in me—until I told them I had three children. After that I ever heard from them again."[17]

---

11. Henry Biller, *Paternal Deprivation: Family, School, Sexuality and Society* (Lexington, MA: D. C. Heath, 1974), p. 109; Henry Biller, *Father, Child and Sex Role: Paternal Determinants of Personality Development* (Lexington, MA D. C. Heath, 1971), p. 111.

12. According to Fr. Juan B. Cortes, of Georgetown University, cited in *Catholic University Bulletin*, 23 February, 1973.

For fuller documentation, see Annex to Chapter I, pp. 240ff.

13. Starke Hathaway and Elio Monachesi, *Adolescent Personality and Development* (Minneapolis: University of Minnesota Press, 1963), p. 81.

For fuller documentation, see Annex to Chapter I, pp. 251ff.

14. Cited in Ciji Ware, *Sharing Custody Following Divorce: An Enlightened Custody Guide for Mothers, Fathers and Kids* (New York: Viking, 1982), p. 80

15. "The Effects of Father Absence on Child Development," in *Young Children*, March, 1971, p. 239.

For fuller documentation, see Annex to Chapter I, pp. 262ff.

16. *Los Angeles Times*, 16 December, 1984.

17. *Los Angeles Times*, 1 July, 1982.

A child living in a female-headed home is ten times more likely to be beaten or murdered.[18] According to *USA Today*, while working married women have the best health of any group of women, single mothers, working or unemployed, have the poorest.[19] According to Irma Moilanen and Paula Rantakallio, fatherless children are much more likely to develop psychiatric problems—boys three times as likely, girls four times. [20] According to Sara McLanahan and Larry Bumpass, Women who were raised in female-headed families are 53 percent likelier to have teenage marriages, 111 percent likelier to have teenage births, 164 percent likelier to have premarital births, 92 percent likelier to experience marital disruptions.[21]

The catalogue of miseries associated with female-headed families could be extended without limit. (See the Annex to Chapter I.)

Mother-custody has been the choice of divorce courts for a century. It is, as the foregoing paragraphs show, a tried-and-failed arrangement. It does not benefit women. It drags them into poverty and depression. It does not benefit children. It drags them into the same poverty and into a greater likelihood of educational failure and delinquency. It devastates men by depriving them of their children and their role. Dr. Lenore Weitzman's assertion that divorce bestows upon men a standard of living 42 percent higher than they enjoyed while married is a puerile falsehood which is not made less absurd by repetition.[22]

Betty Friedan believes that society asks "little" of women. The little refers most importantly to the obligation of wives to bear legitimate children. A wife's reneging on this obligation ought to forfeit her right to subsidization and social approval. The primary reason for marriage, formerly made explicit in the priest's instructions to the groom and bride in the marriage

---

18. *The Legal Beagle*, July, 1984.
19. *USA Today*, 11 April, 1984.
20. "The Single Parent Family and the Child's Mental Health." *Social Science Medicine* 27 [1988], 181-6; cited in *The Family in America: New Research*, October, 1988.
    For further documentation, see Annex to Chapter I, pp. 262ff.
21. "Intergenerational Consequences of Family Disruption." *American Journal of Sociology* 4 [July, 1988], 130-52; cited in *Family in America: New Research*, October, 1988.
22. See Chapter VIII.

ceremony in the Book of Common Prayer, is the procreation of children. Men undertake the responsibilities of marriage and fatherhood primarily for the purpose of procreating these children, who are properly called "legitimate" by reason of having a father and because society, in order that it may not be burdened with the social costs described in the foregoing paragraphs, recognizes the importance of their having a father. The social crisis indicated by the title of the present book and the social pathology indicated in Chapter I have resulted from the failure of the legal system to safeguard the Legitimacy Principle.

The high correlation between crime and fatherless families is indisputable. According to the *Los Angeles Times*,

> The nation's prison population jumped by a record 46,004 inmates in the first six months of 1989, for a total of 673,565 men and women behind bars,[23] the Bureau of Justice Statistics said. The increase broke the record not only for half-year increases but also was higher than any annual increase recorded during the 64 years the government has counted prisoners, the bureau said. The 7.3% surge in prison population during the first half of 1989 was brought about by increases of 7% in the number of men imprisoned and 13% in the number of women, the bureau said. Since 1980, the number of state and federal prisoners serving sentences of more than one year—known as sentenced prisoners—more then doubled from 315,974.[24]

Not much can be done now about the damaged lives of the mostly fatherless children who grow up to become these incarcerated prisoners, or the less damaged lives of the larger numbers who avoid incarceration. These less-damaged people survive the high-crime ages, 14-to-24, and enter middle age as underachieving, confused, unhappy adults, permanent semi-

---

23. Estimates differ considerably. *U.S. News and World Report*, 4 November, 1988 estimated that one million people would be behind bars by 1989. According to the *Los Angeles Times* of 1 October, 1989, "more than one million citizens are behind prison and jail bars" and another 2.6 million are on probation or parole. The *Times* article here quoted evidently excludes the *jail* population.

24. *Los Angeles Times*, 11 September, 1989.

casualties with weakened families of their own.[25] What needs
to be done is to stop the flow of messed-up kids through the
pipeline running from the divorce courts and into female-headed
families, through pathological childhoods into disruptive adolescence and demoralized adulthood—the process now in full swing
and programmed to continue into the next Garbage Generation
in the 21st century.

The failure of the judges and policymakers responsible for
most of these female-headed families to understand their responsibility for them and for the disruption, crime, demoralization and illegitimacy they produce derives from the disastrous
but natural mistake of supposing that because the female-
headed family form is biologically based, whereas the father-
headed family form is merely a social creation, society ought to
support the biologically based form by choosing Mom for custodian of the children in case of divorce. They cannot grasp the idea
that the reproductive pattern found among lower animals is
unsuitable for humans.

The fact is that the family, like the civilization it makes
possible, is an artificial creation. Civilization is artificial. And
fragile.[26]

Patriarchal civilization came into existence when men became equal sharers in human reproduction. The biological
marginality of the male required that this sharing should be
buttressed by artificial social supports, the most important
being society's recognition of fathers as heads of families. The
present destruction of the father-headed family is felt to be
justified by the sacredness of motherhood, which causes judges
and lawmakers to acquiesce when women demand that their
marriages be terminated and that they be made heads of families.[27] Female headship of families is disastrous. Mom, whose

---

25. Two examples: (1) People born around 1950 have a 2,000 percent greater
likelihood of experiencing depression by age thirty than people bron before 1910
(Los Angeles Times, 9 October, 1988). (2) The suicide rate of white males age 15-
24 rose almost 50 percent between 1970 and 1983 (U. S. Bureau of the Census,
Statistical Abstract of the United States, 1987, 107th ed., p. 79; cited in *The Family
in America*, October, 1988.)

26. The desirability of giving fathers rather than mothers custody of the children
of divorce is discussed in Chapter X.

27. As indicated in Chapter II, note 10, page 13, most divorce actions are initiated
by wives.

role is a biological fact, doesn't need society's props; Dad, whose role is a social creation, does. Society must use the strength of the mother-infant tie not as a lever for wrecking the two-parent family, but as a prop for preserving it—by guaranteeing to the *father* the headship of his family and the custody of his children. Then mothers, knowing that divorce will separate them from their children and from Dad's paycheck, will reconcile themselves to accepting the patriarchal, two-parent family arrangement. Marriage will be stabilized. There will be no feminization of poverty, no general acceptance of the female-headed family and its social pathology.

By society's guarantee of father custody the roles of both spouses are re-affirmed, children are brought up in two-parent families, and society can hope for the kind of stability, creativity and productivity found in societies with stable families, societies such as that of the Victorian age and contemporary Japan.

When Margaret Mead speaks of the female role as a biological fact she refers to the *mammalian* female role. The female role in patriarchal, civilized society is every bit as artificial as the male role. "What is now called the nature of women," wrote John Stuart Mill in 1869, is an eminently artificial thing."[28] He meant the nature of patriarchally socialized women. What is called the nature of man is, in patriarchal society, equally artificial. Mill himself was an artificial thing—if he hadn't been, his books wouldn't be worth reading. Civilization is an artificial thing, something men and women chafe under, as Freud explained in *Civilization and Its Discontents*, because civilization is built on repression and frustration—and the toleration of frustration, a toleration motivated by the sexual law-and-order of family living which ties sexuality to long-term goals, to the past and the future, to ancestors and descendants, to home and children.

There is no way to motivate males to accept the coercion-imposed frustration feminists and the divorce courts want to inflict on them by compelling them to subsidize ex-families, and that is the reason why, in the words of Louis Roussel,

---

28. J. S. Mill, *The Subjection of Women* (Cambridge, MA: M. I. T. Press, 1970; original publication, 1869), p. 22.

What we have seen between 1965 and the present, among the billion or so people who inhabit the industrialized nations, is...a general upheaval in the whole set of demographic indicators.

In barely twenty years, the birth rate and the marriage rate have tumbled, while divorces and illegitimate births have increased rapidly. All these changes have been substantial, with increases or decreases of more than fifty percent. They have also been sudden, since the process of change has only lasted about fifteen years. And they have been general, because all industrialized countries have been affected beginning around 1965.[29]

This is why, in other words, we have a Garbage Generation growing up in female-headed households. The feminist-sexual revolution is an attempt to get back to the pre-patriarchal pattern of the Stone Age, to mobilize and unleash the discontents resulting from civilization's demand that women accept sexual law-and-order. (Civilization makes even more onerous demands upon men, as men's 7 or 8 year shorter life-span shows. For all of which, women and men both live longer under patriarchy than under matriliny.)

What's in it for women? Stable marriage and its economic and status advantages. The task of the patriarchy is (1) to convince women that these advantages are the quid pro quo they get for participation in the patriarchal system (acceptance of sexual law-and-order, sharing their reproductive lives with men) and are not otherwise obtainable; (2) to convince lawmakers and judges that they must support the patriarchal family rather than trying to create a divorce-alternative to it.

This divorce-alternative, this disastrous idea now held by the legal system (and of course by feminists) that divorce ought to provide ex-wives with the same benefits that marriage provides to wives, is the chief underminer of patriarchy. "The idea of compensatory payment," says Mary Ann Glendon in discussing the French synonym for alimony,

29. Louis Roussel, "Demographie: Deux Decennes de Mutations," paper presented at the Fifth World Conference of the International Society on Family Law, July 8-14, 1985, Brussels, Belgium; cited in Mary Ann Glendon, *The Transformation of Family Law*, (Chicago: The University of Chicago Press, 1989), p. 144.

is to remedy "so far as possible" the disparity which the termination of marriage may create in the respective living conditions of the spouses....It depends on the establishment of the fact of a disparity between the situations of the ex-spouses, and its aim is to enable both of them to live under approximately equivalent material conditions.[30]

The idea of the "compensatory payment" is to transfer money from the possession of the male who earns it to the possession of a female who does not earn it and who has no claim to it other than her status as a Mutilated Beggar. "Compensatory" for *what*? For the withdrawal of the services which during marriage justified her enjoyment of a 73 percent higher standard of living?[31]   Why doesn't her withdrawal of services justify the husband in withdrawing *his* services? Why *should* they both live "under approximately equivalent material conditions"? Why should there *not* be a "disparity" in their incomes, since the ex-husband earns his income and the ex-wife does nothing which entitles her to share his earnings? *Vive la disparite*! This "disparity" is the principal reason she married him.[32] Patriarchal civilization is built on this disparity. The male devotes the greater part of his energies to creating this disparity, believing that it will make him attractive to females and that by offering it to one of them he can induce her to share her reproductive life with him and thereby enable him to create a family and procreate legitimate and inalienable children who will benefit from this disparity by having a higher standard of living and by receiving the patriarchal socialization which will civilize them— make them stable and law-abiding and educationally successful.

---

30. Glendon, p. 210.
31. The 73 percent figure is Dr. Lenore Weitzman's estimate discussed in Chapter VIII.
32. Vance Packard, *The Sexual Wilderness: The contemporary Upheaval in Male-Female Relationships* (New York: David McKay Company, 1968), p. 268: "Overwhelmingly the women saw the man's role as being that of 'breadwinner.' This was mentioned by nearly nine out of ten wives, and two-thirds of all the wives put it in first place."
See the fuller quotation, Chapter VIII, note 24.

It is thus that patriarchal society puts sex to work to motivate males to create wealth and social stability—the wealth and stability which feminists and the legal system are undermining in order to liberate women and return society to matriliny. The disparity which feminists and the courts want to get rid of is virtually synonymous with the wealth of society which they want to latch onto. They imagine that eliminating the disparity means raising the standard of living of women rather than lowering the standard of living of everybody. There exists no such disparity in ghettos and on Indian reservations because the males in ghettos and on Indian reservations have no bargaining power and no motivation to acquire it by work and self-discipline. They lack the frustration-tolerance which sexual law-and-order and dedication to family living make endurable. They are willing to accept the one-night stands and the stud-status which their women are willing to offer them. And so, alas, are increasing numbers of males in the larger society. And policy-makers, lawmakers and judges are willing to re-order society to make it conform to this matrilineal pattern which makes men studs instead of fathers. And this is why there is a Garbage Generation.

Dr. Glendon tells us that French law

> authorized compensation (sometimes very substantial) for such harms allegedly resulting from the divorce as the loss of esteem suffered by a divorced person, loneliness, or the loss of social position by one who has become accustomed to a high standard of living.[33]

The divorced person referred to is the female. She is deprived of her high standard of living. But the ex-husband is equally deprived of his ex-wife's reciprocal services, presumed to be of equal value to the high standard of living he bestowed on her— or else why was she entitled to the high standard of living? If each is deprived, and if the deprivations are of equal value, why is the woman entitled to compensation and the man not?

---

33. Glendon, p. 215.

In West Germany things are much the same: support of the ex-wife "is to be determined with reference to the marital standard of living."[34] In other words: (1) the ex-husband is penalized by the ex-wife's withdrawal of her services; (2) the ex-wife is rewarded (at the ex-husband's expense) for withdrawing them. Compensation for services rendered is replaced by compensation for services withdrawn. If the woman is to be liberated, the man must be doubly penalized. This is the upshot of the feminist movement which a generation ago told the American housewife to stop taking a free ride on her husband's back, to give up her parasitism, to be independent, to stand on her own feet and face life's challenges on her own without "special privileges because of her sex...without sexual privilege or excuse."[35]

The woman is said to be entitled to compensation because she suffers from divorce. She *should* suffer from divorce. The man suffers more, because judges discriminate massively against him in order to ease the suffering of the woman. "In terms of mental and physical disease and life expectancy," says George Gilder, "divorce damages the man far more than the woman."[36] To say that divorce hurts women is to say that marriage benefits women. Marriage should and must benefit women. This is what gives men bargaining power and therefore motivation. This is why they are willing to toil to create their families' (and society's) wealth, why their energies and talents can be directed into useful channels rather than disrupting society as they do where families are headed by women. The feminist/legal program to supply women with comparable benefits from divorce is destroying the whole patriarchal system, which works by encouraging men to earn money so that they have something to offer women in exchange for their accepting sexual of law-and-order. Men must have something which will induce women to live in patriarchal, two-parent families— that something being the disparity between men's and women's earnings. Patriarchy makes this disparity the great bulwark of family stability. The feminist/legal program wants to convert this disparity into a means whereby the patriarchal two-parent family may be destroyed.

---

34. Glendon, p. 220.
35. Betty Friedan, *The Feminine Mystique*, pp. 374, 346.
36. George Gilder, *Men and Marriage*, p. 66. See the fuller quote in Chapter VII, p. 153.

VII

The Gilder Fallacy

"The crucial process of civilization," says George Gilder, "is the subordination of male sexual impulses and biology to the long-term horizons of female sexuality. The overall sexual behavior of women in the modern world differs relatively little from the sexual life of women in primitive societies. It is male behavior that must be changed to create a civilized order."

Untrue. There is a striking difference in the behavior of males in civilized and in primitive societies—the difference between motivated, productive, stable males in the former and disruptive or idle or macho or narcissistic drones, or at best hunters and warriors, in the latter. However the most essential difference between the two societies is one less conspicuous but more pivotal: In the civilized society the females accept the regulation of their sexuality on the basis of the Sexual Constitution—monogamous marriage, the Legitimacy Principle, the double standard and female loyalty and chastity; in the primitive society the females reject sexual regulation and embrace the Promiscuity Principle, a woman's right to control her own sexuality. The female behavior is more basic, since it determines whether the males can be motivated to accept a stable and productive lifestyle. The key issue is not, as Gilder imagines, whether men can be induced to accept the Sexual Constitution which he imagines women try to impose, but whether women themselves can be induced to accept it. What causes women in civilized society to accept it is the knowledge that the economic and status rewards bestowed by patriarchal civilization can be obtained in no other way.

---

1. George Gilder, *Men and Marriage* (Gretna, LA: Pelican Publishing Company, 1986), p. 5.

Sexual regulation may take unsubtle forms—enforced wearing of veils and chadors, the confinement of women to gynecia, mutilation of female sexual organs, wearing of chastity belts and so forth. In more sophisticated societies the control is internalized and leads to feminist complaints such as the following from Peggy Morgan:

> We're really out of control of our sexuality when we see our desires as dirty and troublesome....This leaves us open to being controlled from the outside—letting others (especially men) convince us that we want what they want us to want.[2]

Here, from John Dollard's *Caste and Class in a Southern Town,* is an example of such manipulative regulation "from the outside"—males persuading females that they are really regulating themselves:

> One of the rituals of the university dances is that of a fraternity of young blades entitled the Key-Ice. During the intermission the lights are turned out and these men march in carrying flaming brands. At the end of the procession four acolytes attend a long cake of ice. Wheeled in on a cart it glimmers in the torches' flare. Then the leader, mounted on a table in the center of the big gymnasium, lifts a glass cup of water and begins a toast that runs: "To Woman, lovely woman of the Southland, as pure and as chaste as this sparkling water, as cold as this gleaming ice, we lift this cup, and we pledge our hearts and our lives to the protection of her virtue and chastity."[3]

For "protection" Peggy Morgan would (correctly) read *enforcing.*

There can be no civilization without the regulation of female sexuality. As Dr. Gerda Lerner says in discussing the creation of the system of patriarchal civilization, "The [ancient] state had

---

2. Peggy Morgan, cited in *off our backs,* May, 1988.
3. John Dollard, *Caste and Class in a Southern Town,* 3d ed. (Garden City, N.Y.: Doubleday, 1957), p. 138.

an essential interest in the maintenance of the patriarchal family....Women's sexual subordination was institutionalized in the earliest law codes and enforced by the full power of the state. Women's cooperation in the system was secured by various means: force, economic dependency on the male head of the family, class privileges bestowed upon conforming and dependent women of the upper classes, and the artificially created division of women into respectable and non-respectable women."[4] Dr. Lerner's wording acknowledges the fact, unrecognized by Gilder, that the Sexual Constitution is a *male* idea imposed upon females. "Social and ethnological facts," says Robert Briffault,

> afford no evidence that the influence of woman has ever been exercised in the direction of extending sexual restrictions and tabus, and of imposing chastity on men....Feminine morality consists in unquestioning assent to established estimates and usages....Feminine conservatism defends polygamy and sexual freedom as staunchly as it does monogamy and morality.[5]

What is true of the Sexual Constitution is true of civilization itself:

> Those achievements which constitute what, in the best sense, we term civilization [says Briffault] have taken place in societies organized on patriarchal principles; they are for the most part the work of men. Women have had little direct share in them.[6]

Precisely the opposite of Gilder's view that "civilization evolved through the subordination of male sexual patterns—the short-term cycles of tension and release—to the long-term female patterns."[7] "In creating civilization," says Gilder,

---

4. Gerda Lerner, *The Creation of Patriarchy* (New York: Oxford University Press, 1986), p. 9.
5. Robert Briffault, *The Mothers* (New York: Macmillan, 1927), III, 507.
6. Briffault, III, 507.
7. Gilder, p. 31.

women transform male lust into love; channel male wanderlust into jobs, homes, and families; link men to specific children; rear children into citizens; change hunters into fathers, divert male will to power into a drive to create. Women conceive the future that men tend to fell; they feed the children that men ignore.[8]

Why, if so, didn't civilization precede patriarchy and the regulation of *female* sexuality? This regulation was the precondition enabling males to create stable families from which they could not be expelled. The earlier matriarchal pattern is this: "The women are not obliged to live with their husbands any longer than suits their pleasure or conscience...."[9] In such a society women, including married women, are sexually autonomous and the men can do nothing about it. That's the way women prefer things. When Ann Landers asked her female readers whether they would, if they had the chance over again, make the decision to become mothers, 70 percent said no.[10] Alexandre Dumas, in *Les Femmes Qui Tuent*, writes that a distinguished Roman Catholic priest had told him that eighty out of one hundred women who married told him afterwards that they regretted it.[11] These women were not trying to impose the Sexual Constitution upon men; they were trying to escape from its control over their own lives. "In the most primitive human societies," says Briffault,

> there is nothing equivalent to the domination which, in advanced societies, is exercised by individuals, by classes, by one sex over the other. The notion of such a domination is entirely foreign to primitive humanity; the conception of authority is not understood. The ultimate basis of the respective status of the sexes in advanced patriarchal societies is the fact that women, not being

---

8. P. 5

9. J. G. E. Heckewelder, *History, Manners and Customs of the Indian Nations*, p. 154; cited in Briffault, I, 437.

10. Cited in Shirley Radl, *Mother's Day Is Over* (New York: Charterhouse, 1973), p. xiv.

11. Cited in Havelock Ellis, *Views and Reviews*, 2d series (Boston: Houghton Mifflin, 1932), p. 6.

economically productive, are economically dependent, whereas the men exercise economic power both as producers and as owners of private property....The development of durable private property, of wealth, the desire of the constitutionally predatory male to possess it and to transmit it to his descendants, are, in fact, the most common causes of the change from matriarchal to patriarchal institutions.[12]

In primitive societies the loose bonds of matrimony permit much sexual freedom and women outside of these loose bonds enjoy total promiscuity. Briffault again:

In all uncultured societies, where advanced retrospective claims have not become developed, and the females are not regularly betrothed or actually married before they have reached the age of puberty, girls and women who are not married are under no restrictions as to their sexual relations, and are held to be entirely free to dispose of themselves as they please in that respect.

To that rule there does not exist any known exception.[13]

No exceptions. Women are promiscuous unless male-created social arrangements compel or induce them to be otherwise. The truth about the creation of civilization is the opposite of what Gilder imagines it to be. Despite his belief that "greater sexual control and discretion—more informed and deliberate sexual powers—are displayed by women in all societies known to anthropology,"[14] American women are today more adulterous than their husbands.[15] 77 percent of the female readers of *Glamour* magazine approve of women having children out of wedlock.[16]

---

12. Briffault, I, 433f.
13. Briffault, II, 2.
14. Gilder, p. 12.
15. *Private Lives*, May, 1987, citing a survey by *New Woman.*
16. *Glamour*, November, 1985.

"Civilized society," says Gilder, "is not more natural than more degenerate social states. It represents a heroic transcendence of the most powerful drives of men."[17] Civilized society is far *less* natural than primitive society. That's why the Stone Age lasted a million years and civilization has lasted only a few thousand. Civilization represents a heroic transcendence of the most powerful drives of *women*—the imposition upon them of male regulation.

"The female responsibility for civilization," Gilder says,

> cannot be granted or assigned to men. Unlike a woman, a man has no civilized role or agenda inscribed in his body. Although his relationship to specific children can give him a sense of futurity resembling the woman's, it always must come through her body and her choices. The child can never be his unless a woman allows him to claim it with her or unless he so controls her and so restricts her sexual activity that he can be sure that he is the father.[18]

Not *unlike*, but *like* a woman, a man has no civilized role or agenda inscribed in his body. A woman's reproductive mechanism, like a woman's arms and legs, may be used for civilized or for uncivilized purposes, and the same is true of the man's reproductive mechanism and his arms and legs. Civilization depends on what is in peoples' *minds*, and the "choices" made in women's minds during the million years of the Stone Age were the same as they are among sexually unregulated women of today who demand the "sacred right to control their own reproduction" without male interference. A sense of futurity "always must come through her body and her choices," says Gilder. But it *didn't* come until "The Creation of Patriarchy" imposed male control and largely confined female sexuality within patriarchal families.

"Depending chiefly on the degree that the wanton male sex drive succumbs to maternal goals and rhythms," says Gilder,

---

17. Gilder, p. 76.
18. *Men and Marriage*, p. 13.

any society is capable of a variety of sexual states. Civilized and productive societies reflect the long-term disciplines of female nature, upheld by religious and marital codes.[19]

Upheld by *male-created* religious and marital codes. Hear how feminist Adrienne Rich feels about these codes:

These are some of the methods by which male power is manifested and maintained. Looking at the schema, what surely impresses itself is the fact that we are confronting not a simple maintenance of inequality and property possession, but a pervasive cluster of forces, ranging from physical brutality to control of consciousness, which suggests that an enormous potential counterforce is having to be restrained.[20]

Feminist Marilyn French contrasts the different way things are done in the matriarchy and in the patriarchy:

But "feminine" cultures do not work like "masculine" cultures. "Masculine" cultures aim at success (power, control), are concerned with rules and techniques and instrumentality. "Feminine" cultures are concerned with affection, bonding, cooperation, with being and being-together.[21]

Gilder's "civilized and productive societies" are French's "masculine" societies, which, apart from the wealth they generate, feminists would fain do away with, since they correctly perceive the current sexual encounter as a "struggle for our reproductive rights—for our sexuality, our children and the *money we need.*"[22]

---

19. P. 76.

20. Adrienne Rich, "Compulsory Heterosexuality and Lesbian Existence," in *Feminist Frontiers: Rethinking Sex, Gender, and Society*, ed. Laurel Richardson and Verta Taylor (Reading, MA: Addison-Wesley Publishing Company, 1983), p. 222.

21. *Beyond Power: On Women, Men and Morals* (New York: Summit Books, 1985), p. 387.

22. Adrienne Rich, *Of Woman Born: Motherhood as Experience and Institution*, tenth anniversary ed. (New York: W. W. Norton, 1986), foreward, p. xxi; emphasis added.

The women best able to resist this patriarchal interference, educated career women, commonly reject the role which Gilder supposes all women to cherish. "Highly educated women," says Marie Richmond-Abbott,

> are more likely to remain childless than are women with less education...Thus, women who are highly educated and more likely to have careers are less likely to want children because of perceived conflict with their work roles.[23]

It is such women who ask "Where are the men for women like us, men who can deal with women like us...?" "Are they threatened by our new power—or just afraid that we won't need them?"[24] What these autonomous women want is not, as Gilder supposes, to impose their long-term sexual horizons upon males, but to share the male freedom from maternity and regulation. "They envied their husbands who did not have to make similar compromises," says Richmond-Abbott.

An article in the December 4, 1988 *Los Angeles Times Magazine*, dealing with the lifestyle of six Los Angeles women who "had it all," "the personal stories of six women who have found success," indicated that the six women had altogether a total of two children, both offspring of one woman married to a house-husband and employing a full-time live-in housekeeper.

A 1985 survey showed that executive females—of all women those most at liberty to be their true selves and exhibit "long-term disciplines of female nature" (if they have them)—were three-fourths divorced or single, and that only 20 percent of them were in their first marriages (versus 64 percent of male executives who were in their first marriages.)[25] Ms. Friedan interprets such female independence as showing that money is a "love-spoiler."[26] She is thinking of *men's* money as inhibiting women's promiscuity. From the man's point of view, it is the

---

23. Marie Richmond-Abbott, *Masculine and Feminine: Sex Roles Over the Life Cycle* (Reading, MA: Addison-Wesley Publishing Company, 1983), p. 262.
24. Betty Friedan, *The Second Stage* (New York: Summit Books, 1981), p. 122.
25. *Los Angeles Times*, 24 February, 1985.
26. *It Changed My Life*, p. 224.

woman's money which is the love-spoiler, or at least the marriage and maternity spoiler. It is the man's aim to integrate love, marriage and maternity into family life, using the male paycheck as the binder; but these economically and sexually emancipated women are able to use their own paychecks to avoid such commitment to marriage and maternity. The birthrate of such women is minuscule, their divorce rate is far higher than that of economically dependent wives, as is their adultery rate, otherwise known as "a woman's right to control her own body." The answer to the question "Where are the men for women like us?" is that there aren't many, because most men want families— because it is men, not women, or not *autonomous* women, who have the long-term sexual horizons.

If men are not deflected from such women by their statistics for divorce and adultery, they might be deflected by those on coronary heart disease. According to the Framingham Heart Study, men married to women with thirteen or more years of education were 2.6 times more likely to have coronaries. If these women are in addition liberated to work outside the home the men are 7.6 times more likely to have coronaries.[27]

Men ought to avoid such women as they avoid the plague, the Internal Revenue Service, nuclear waste and low-density lipoproteins. Understandably, feminists and house-males hold a different view. Hear one of them, Professor Herb Goldberg:

> Finally, the best insurance against losing everything to a wife in a divorce or custody battle is the choice of a woman partner who delights in her own separate identity, has a history of relating to men by taking equal responsibility, does not see women as victims of men, and has created a fulfilling autonomous life for herself prior to meeting you.[28]

Worse advice for a man who wants a family would be hard to find. "Women," says Marie Richmond-Abbott, and she means elitist career-women,

---

27. *Los Angeles Times*, 2 August, 1983.
28. Herb Goldberg, *The New Male-Female Relationship* (New York: William Morrow and Company, 1983), p. 173.

have been delaying marriage, getting higher education, and entering nontraditional jobs. They have come to marriage with their own incomes and ideas of equality. They want fewer children and demand more power in their families. Women are participating more in the occupational world and in politics. While it will be difficult for poor women to follow this pattern, middle-class women who have established it are unlikely to give it up.[29]

As will be explained in Chapter IX, these women have climbed the "marriage gradient": their education and economic independence (both major goals of feminism) put them where there are few men to "marry up" to. They are less likely to marry, less likely to procreate, more likely to divorce, more likely to be unfaithful, more likely to settle for "alternative life styles." Their redeeming virtue, as indicated, is their low birthrate. "If sex role change is to occur at the individual level," says Ms. Richmond-Abbott (and you can believe she is working in her academic grove to facilitate such change),

men and women would have to socialize their children in a different manner. They would have to be aware of their own expectations and of their behavior toward their children, and they would have to monitor the environment in which their children grow and play so that it is nonsexist.[30]

She offers the familiar suggestions about non-sexist toys and non-sexist socialization, so that boys will be encouraged to be nurses, elementary school teachers and airline attendants, girls to be astronauts, soldiers and policepersons. Males will vacate the family-provider role to enable females to take it over, while the liberated women vacate their traditional role as housewives and mothers, turning these functions over to the lower orders and the pigmented races.[31]

29. Richmond-Abbott, p. 406.
30. P. 407.
31. "Women have outgrown the housewife role...a task for which society hires the lowliest, least-trained, most trod-upon individuals and groups." (Betty Friedan, *The Feminine Mystique*, pp. 308, 215).

Speaking of what he perceives as the sexual superiority and greater sense of responsibility of females Gilder has this:

> Her very body, her whole being, tells her that she will have to make long-term commitments to children, that her life is not something that runs from moment to moment, from one momentary pleasure or intrigue to another, but that she is engaged in a larger purpose that extends into the future.[32]

Why doesn't the female body convey this useful information to the one and one-half million women who abort their unwanted pregnancies every year?

Here is an episode from Kate Chopin's feminist classic *The Awakening* describing her heroine and her lover and illustrating female resentment over male regulation:

> "Why have you been fighting against it?" she asked. Her face glowed with soft lights.
> "Why? Because you were not free; you were Leonce Pontellier's wife....Something put into my head that you cared for me; and I lost my senses. I forgot everything but a wild dream of your some way becoming my wife."
> "Your wife!"
> "Religion, loyalty, everything would give way if only you cared....Oh! I was demented, dreaming of wild, impossible things, recalling men who had set their wives free, we have heard of such things."
> "You have been a very, very foolish boy, wasting your time dreaming of impossible things when you speak of Mr. Pontellier setting me free! I am no longer one of Mr. Pontellier's possessions to dispose of or not.[33] I give myself where I choose. If he were to say, 'Here, Robert, take her and be happy; she is yours,' I should laugh at you both."

....

32. *Conservative Digest*, November, 1986, p. 39.
33. Chopin is careful to make her heroine economically independent by giving her an inheritance from a *female* relative.

"I love you," she whispered, "only you; no one but you. It was you who awoke me last summer out of a life-long, stupid dream. Oh! you have made me so unhappy with your indifference. Oh! I have suffered, suffered! Now you are here we shall love each other, my Robert. We shall be everything to each other. Nothing else in the world is of any consequence."[34]

Nothing else—not for the next half hour or for the whole weekend or until her husband returns from his business trip. It is the boyfriend and the husband who think in terms of long-term sexual horizons and marriage, the heroine who thinks in terms of the present, who is willing to end it all rather than submit to being confined by the patriarchal sexual constitution to long-term commitments to her husband and her children. When, at the end of the book, the heroine drowns herself in order to escape this trap,

She felt like some new-born creature, opening its eyes in a familiar world that it had never known....She thought of Leonce and the children. They were a part of her life. But they need not have thought that they could possess her, body and soul. How Mademoiselle Reisz would have laughed, perhaps sneered, if she knew! "And you call yourself an artist! What pretensions, Madame! The artist must possess the courageous soul that dares and defies!"[35]

Kinsey was radically mistaken in thinking that women control the moral codes: If they support these codes, they do so because of compulsion or perceived advantage or simple conservatism, not because their bodies tell them they have to make long-term commitments.

The "intuition of mysterious new realms of sexual and social experience," says Gilder, "evoked by the body and spirit of woman, is the source of male love and ultimately of marriage."[36]

---

34. Kate Chopin, *The Awakening* (New York: Bantam, 1981), pp. 142f.
35. P. 152.
36. *Men and Marriage*, pp. 13f.

Very edifying. But it fails to explain that where women run things, as in the ghettos, little attention is paid to marriage or to long-term cycles of sexuality, and instead there are so many one-night stands, so many children having children. Where men run things, as in Oriental families, the long-term cycles extend backward to ancestor worship and forward to education, careers, the family's good name, and care for the hereditaments and the *patri*mony. The women Gilder writes about have long-term sexual horizons because men have socialized them to have them. Feminist anthropologist Evelyn Reed has people like Gilder in mind when she writes of

> the modern puritanical outlook on female sexuality, and...the reluctance of men in patriarchal society to acknowledge the independence and freedom of primitive women in sexual intercourse. That this independence existed cannot be doubted if one reads the reports of settlers and missionaries; they were quite offended by it.[37]

She cites the observations made by Father Jacob Baegert on the Indians of southern California two hundred years ago:

> They met without any formalities, and their vocabulary did not even contain the words "to marry"....The good padre complained that the women were independent and "not much inclined to obey their lords," and that after the wedding ceremony at the mission "the new married couple start off in different directions...as if they were not more to each other today than they were yesterday...." Worst of all, they failed to suffer from shame, fear, jealousy, or guilt about their sexual freedom:
>
>> They lived, in fact, before the establishment of the missions in their country, in utter licentiousness, and adultery was daily committed by every one without shame and without any fear, the

37. Evelyn Reed, *Woman's Evolution: From Matriarchal Clan to Patriarchal Family* (New York: Pathfinder Press, 1975), p. 264.

feeling of jealousy being unknown to them. Neighbouring tribes visited each other very often only for the purpose of spending some days in open debauchery, and during such times a general prostitution prevailed.[38]

That's the way it was with savages in California two hundred years ago, and that's the way it is coming to be in California today. When Marabel Morgan, the born-again Christian antifeminist spoke to an audience of women about the importance of pleasing men in bed, and confessed she sometimes found it difficult because her husband's sex drive resembled that of a 747 and hers that of a tiny Piper cub,

Morgan's breezy delivery gave no clue that she saw anything at all odd about this admission, but many of the women in the audience responded as though she had said something truly bizarre. As one commented, "The women I know are the 747s—and they're all griping because the men they married aren't even Piper Cubs. They're gliders."[39]

These are the women who ask, "Where are the men for women like us, men who can deal with women like us?"[40] There aren't many. "Women like us" turn men off, as Marabel Morgan tried to explain to them. Their contempt for Mrs. Morgan suggests that they enjoy turning men off. They might have made out quite well with the Digger Indian males of two hundred years ago but they should be—and are—shunned by males with long-term horizons.

Fear of intimacy, according to sexperts, "is an endemic feature of relationships in the 80s. Sex is perhaps the ultimate act of intimacy, and people can feel profoundly vulnerable in the letting go of defenses that it entails. In getting 'close' they may be afraid of getting hurt."[41]

---

38. *Ibid.*
39. Mary Donovan in the *Los Angeles Times*, 14 December, 1986.
40. Betty Friedan, *The Second Stage*, p. 121.
41. *Newsweek*, 26 October, 1987.

The Morgan quote comes from a review of *Remaking Love: The Feminization of Sex,* by Barbara Ehrenreich, Elizabeth Hess and Gloria Jacobs. These ladies, according to the *Newsweek* reviewer, think that

> The real sexual revolution...has occurred in the atti-
> tudes and behavior of women, and this revolution has
> taken place at the behest of women, not of men....[T]he
> backlash against sexual permissiveness we're witness-
> ing today needs to be viewed as a backlash against
> women's quest for autonomy.[42]

Autonomy—otherwise known as the Promiscuity Principle, otherwise known as the First Law of Matriarchy. What is being rejected is the patriarchal socialization which led Gilder to suppose they possessed long-term sexual horizons and wanted men to be sexually responsible *just like themselves*. The fact is that males, precisely because it is they who have the long-term sexual horizons, find such promiscuous women unattractive. Feminist anthropologist Evelyn Reed understands these things better than Gilder. Paraphrasing Engels, she writes:

> It was the drastic social changes brought about by the
> patriarchal class institutions of the family, private prop-
> erty, and the state which produced the historic downfall
> of the female sex. In the new society men became the
> principal producers, while the women were relegated to
> home and family servitude. Dispossessed from their
> former place in society at large, they were robbed not
> only of their economic independence but also of their
> former sexual freedom. The new institution of monoga-
> mous marriage arose to serve the needs of men of
> property.[43]

This freedom, which Gilder supposed to be the *male* pattern, is the pattern of unsocialized, unpatriarchalized females, who view the requirement of chastity and loyalty as their "historic

---

42. *Ibid.*
43. Evelyn Reed, *Problems of Women's Liberation: A Marxist Approach* (New York: Pathfinder Press, 1971), p. 24.

downfall." Men insist on marriage and female chastity because this is the only way they can have legitimate children, the motivators of the wealth-creation Ms. Reed speaks of. Patriarchy and wealth are the good twins; matriarchy and violence the bad twins. It is the wealth created by the patriarchal system which reconciles females to renouncing the feminist Promiscuity Principle and accepting patriarchy's Legitimacy Principle.

More from Reed:

> It was only when their own communal society was overthrown that these former governesses of society were defeated and sent, dispersed and fragmentized, into individual households and the stifling life of kitchen and nursery chores.
>
> All this knowledge that we can gain from a study of prehistory will not only help women to understand their present dilemma but also provide guidelines on how to proceed in the struggle for women's emancipation, which is again coming to the fore.[44]

They smell victory. As S. L. Andreski says of the decline of fatherhood, "one of the most important changes taking place in our society,"

> If the trend...continues without a reversal we shall have witnessed a turning-point in the evolution of mankind: perhaps a return to matrilineal descent, which may have been common before it was replaced by patriarchy at the dawn of the more complex civilizations.[45]

No perhaps about it. Patriarchy was the precondition for the more complex civilization.

"It is sometimes imagined," says Gilder,

> that the gynocentrism of many poor black families is a strength—the secret of black survival through the harrowing centuries of slavery and racism. In a sense, of

---

44. *Ibid.,* p. 26.
45. *Times Literary Supplement,* 10 June, 1977.

course, this is true. In any disintegrating society, the family is reduced to the lowest terms of mother and child. The black family has long rested on the broad shoulders and heart of the black woman.

Yet this secret of black survival is also a secret of ghetto stagnation. It is quite simply impossible to sustain a civilized society if the men are constantly disrupting it.[46]

Most of the male disrupters had mothers who undermined patriarchal sexual stability by divorce, marital disloyalty, or promiscuity. It is the female who initiates the cycle which culminates in the visible male disruption. Gilder blames the male; the law imprisons the male; and as crime continues to increase undeterred by punishment, society imagines it must compensate for the withdrawal of males from the system by increased subsidization of females—subsidization which causes them to imagine themselves independent of males and free to follow the Promiscuity Principle. Improperly socialized women like things this way because they *lack* the long-term horizons Gilder ascribes to them.

It is, complains feminist Ellen Goodman, "by and large men who define 'normal,' even while committing 90 percent of the *violent* crimes, and waging nearly all the wars."[47] The violent crimes, she says—those requiring lots of testosterone and heavy musculature, crimes which are therefore male specialties. There are, however, crimes which both men and women commit; and if it is desired to know whether men or women are more virtuous it will be proper to consult the statistics for such crimes—check violations, forgery, perjury, child abuse. Ask a supermarket manager whether men or women commit more check violations, ask a social worker whether fathers or mothers commit more child abuse, ask a lawyer whether men or women commit more perjury, and you will learn something about the double standard of morality of which feminists complain.

---

46. *Sexual Suicide* (New York: Quadrangle/The New York Times Book Co., 1973), pp. 117f.

47. *Los Angeles Times*, 23 May, 1986.

Male antisociality is typically violent; female antisociality is typically sexual. The relationship between the two is indicated by Ramsey Clark's statistic that three-quarters of criminals come from "broken" (read: female-headed) homes. The way to stop generating these violent male criminals is to clean out their breeding places—to stop creating female-headed homes.

It is now feminist doctrine that the creation of the female-headed family need not be preceded by the formalities of marriage and divorce, that all extra-patriarchal females are entitled to a free ride for violating th Legitimacy Principle. Feminist Professor Barbara Bergmann wants child support payments from absent fathers to be "the same for children born out of wedlock as for children of divorced or separated parents."[48] The woman has all the rights, the man all the obligations. The female-headed family is to be the norm, as in the ghetto, with the resulting male disruptiveness serving as propaganda-grist for further female rejection of the patriarchy.

Here is another assertion of the Promiscuity Principle, from America's wise woman, Abby Van Buren: "There is only one reason to make love, and that's because you feel like it."[49] Also: "to marry because you want to be a mother is a poor reason for marriage."[50] This means getting rid of the patriarchal Sexual Constitution and returning to the Promiscuity Principle of the Digger Indians.

The existing policy is that such socially sanctioned unchastity gives Mom title to her children and to her ex-husband's or ex-boyfriend's paycheck. The biological tenuousness of paternity suffices to establish the social centrality of Mom's role and to make her economic subsidization imperative.

This repudiation of patriarchy implies the repudiation of Betty Friedan's Sleeping Beauty feminism, which averred that "women have outgrown the housewife role"[51] and should seek self-actualization in the real world of male achievement. But most women who hope to liberate themselves by creating father-

---

48. *The Economic Emergence of Women* (New York: Basic Books, 1986), p. 309.
49. *Los Angeles Times*, 11 August, 1985.
50. *Los Angeles Times*, 1 June, 1987.
51. *The Feminine Mystique*, p. 308.

less families will find themselves, like the women of the ghettos, not free to pursue high status careers but locked in more securely than ever to the hated maternal functions from which feminism promised to liberate them.[52]

Here is the crux of the Gilder fallacy. "Men," he says, "have no ties to the long-term human community so deep or tenacious as the mother's to her child."[53] Check. "Only the woman has a dependable and easily identifiable connection to the child—a tie on which society can rely."[54] Check. But the facts cited show that this tie does not create a tie to the *husband*, not one which stabilizes the two-parent family. The way to stabilize the two-parent family (which society needs because it produces better behaved and higher achieving children) and to prevent the creation of the female-headed family (which produces most of the criminal class) is for *society to maintain the tie between the child and the father* by guaranteeing to him that his wife cannot take his child from him. It is for the purpose of providing this guarantee that patriarchal society exists.

As will be more fully explained in Chapter X, the only way for society to provide this guarantee is to reverse the existing custody disposition in divorce cases and return to the 19th century practice of awarding custody of children to fathers rather than mothers.

"The human race," thinks Gilder, "met the challenge of transition from hunting to agriculture and from agriculture to industry in part by shifting the male pursuit from game to women."[55] Men had always pursued women. What was needed to motivate men to accept the "long-term horizons" Gilder writes about was the assurance that the pursuit of women would lead to the "creation of patriarchy," a political system based not on a

---

52. Again and again Ms. Friedan tells her readers to hire a cleaning *woman* so they can go to law school, medical school or graduate school. One is reminded of the feminist John Stuart Mill's complaint that women should be expected to do "the work of servants," or of the feminist Elizabeth Cady Stanton's complaint that women had to spend so much of their time conversing "with children and servants." It doesn't occur to these elitists that few women have servants.

53. *Men and Marriage*, p. 168.

54. P. 7.

55. George Gilder, *Men and Marriage*, p. 37.

matriline but on the *family*, of which the man knew himself to be the permanent head, not liable to be exiled at the pleasure of the mother. Only such a stable reproductive arrangement could motivate a man to accept long-term family responsibilities, to commit himself to a lifetime of work and the creation of wealth, wealth which his wife would have to know to be unobtainable outside of patriarchal family arrangements. This is the motivational basis of civilization.

"In this process," continues Gilder, "society became strongly dependent on the institutions by which the hunter is domesticated—chiefly now the institution of marriage. In general, across the range of modern life, marriage became indispensable to socializing the mass of males."

Gilder fails to see that it became no less indispensable to socializing females, a fact well understood by feminists such as Adrienne Rich, Gerda Lerner and Betty Friedan, who emphasize women's reluctance to submit to traditional marriage and their wish to gain its economic advantages for themselves without submitting to patriarchal constraints.

Gilder is on the mark when he says

> The desire of *men* to claim their children thus emerged as the crucial impulse of civilized life. It is chiefly in the nuclear household that the man's connection to his children becomes central. He is the key provider. His fatherhood is direct and unimpeachable, and he identifies, loves, and provides for his offspring. His role as provider then becomes almost as crucial for the maintenance of the family as the mother's role. He thus can feel equal to the mother within the family and he can join it without damage to his sense of himself as a man.[56]

But not only is Gilder unable to see the reluctance of many women to accept this nuclear family arrangement, so necessary to men, he is unable to see how it is being destroyed by a 50 percent divorce rate. "His fatherhood [in the nuclear household] is direct and unimpeachable," he says. Not for the 50 percent

---

56. *Men and Marriage*, p. 37; emphasis added.

exiled by divorce. "Marriage became essential to socializing the mass of males," he goes on. Half of them are no longer the beneficiaries of this socialization, and the other half realize that the "essential" prop formerly provided by society's support of the conjugal family is no longer dependable. The desire of men to *retain* their children is as much "the crucial impulse of civilized life" as their desire to procreate them in the first place; and since neither aim now has society's guarantee, the entire system of male motivation based on the conjugal family is in process of destruction by women's unwillingness to submit to its constraints and by society's acceptance of this unwillingness as a woman's right.

Gilder acknowledges "that economic growth and capitalism depend in crucial degree on familial and sexual organization"[57] and that "the role of the male is the Achilles' heel of civilized society,"[58] but he imagines that what is required is simply for men to *consent* to conjugal family arrangements which women in large numbers are refusing to consent to. "By the late 1970s," say Barbara Ehrenreich, Elizabeth Hess, and Gloria Jacobs,

> a majority of women—of all ages—had accepted with pleasure progressive attitudes toward sex....Many of Cosmo's readers were as sexually satisfied as Redbook's (the median reported was nine lovers per woman) and a little more brazen to boot: "I have lovers because sex feels good," said one, and claimed another, "I have lovers because what else is there in life that's so much fun as turning on a new man, interesting him, conquering him?" Among Playboy's readers in 1983, young married wives were "fooling around" more than their husbands....[T]he true heart of the sexual revolution was a change in women's behavior, not men's.[59]

It may be that *patriarchally socialized* women can motivate fathers, but unsocialized women are the enemies of the patriarchal arrangement, and women, socialized or not, do little, as Briffault truly says, directly to create civilization itself.[60] Gilder

57. *Men and Marriage*, p. 35.
58. P. 45.
59. *Ms*, July, 1986; emphasis added.
60. See the quotation from Briffault, p. 123.

emphasizes the essentialness of the conjugal family to civilization; but he cannot see that it is the male who is most motivated
to create and preserve it. He understands that all societies
(including savage societies) are built upon the tie between
mother and offspring. But whereas both biology and experience
inform the female that this tie is dependable in any sort of society
with any sexual arrangements, and that accordingly women
need not have the long-term sexual horizons Gilder claims for
them, biology and experience both inform the male that the
father-child tie is precarious and requires him not only to take
long-term views but also to create social structures which will
guarantee the legitimacy and inalienability of his children.
Gilder refuses to see that this guarantee has now been lost, that
society is returning to matrilineality, and returning likewise to
the patterns of short-term, compulsive sexuality which Gilder
associates with males but which are grounded in matrilineality
and found consistently in such matrilineal societies as those of
the Tongans and the Todas and the Takelomas and the Mandans
and the Montagnais and the Canelas and the Caraijas and the
Nandi and the Masai and the Baila and the Akamba and the
Morus and the Dume Pygmies and the Kadza and the !Kung and
the Gidjangali—and the ghettos.

Gilder quaintly assumes that most marital breakdown results from "powerful men" abandoning the wives of their youth
and lusting after their young secretaries.[61] A moment's reflection would convince him that there aren't that many "powerful
men," and that high status men have a lower divorce rate than
most other males. Besides which, he ought to know that most
divorces are initiated by, and granted to, women.[62]

---

61. Gilder, "Family and Nation: Moynihan's Welfare Turnaround," in *Catholicism
and Crisis*, June, 1986; reprinted in *Human Events*, 26 July, 1986.

62. Lenore Weitzman, *The Divorce Revolution: The Unexpected Social and Economic
Consequences for Women and Children in America* (New York: The Free Press, 1985), p.
460: "These researchers [Robert Schoen, Harry N. Greenblatt, and Robert B. Mielke]
report that 78 percent of all divorce petitions in California were filed by wives..." P. 147
[quoting attorney Riane Eisler]: "By social convention, the vast majority of divorces were
filed by women." P. 174: "In California, in 1968, under the adversary system, over three-
quarters of the plaintiffs—those who initiated the legal divorce proceedings—were wives
filing charges against 'guilty' husbands." According to David Chambers, *Making Fathers
Pay* (Chicago: University of Chicago Press, 1979), p. 29, "the wife is the moving party in

"Unless marriage is permanent and sacred," he says, "it becomes an increasingly vulnerable and embattled institution that collapses before every temptation and crisis."[63] The way to make it permanent is not by urging men to submit to women's "long-term sexual horizons" but by ensuring that marriage offers women long-term economic and status advantages unavailable outside marriage.

---

divorce actions seven times out of eight." According to the *Legal Beagle*, February, 1986, 72 percent of divorce filings are made by wives. According to Yuanxi Ma, Chinese feminist, about 60 percent of China's divorces are initiated by women (*off our backs*, April, 1988). According to Joan Kelly, author of *Surviving the Breakup*, "Divorce is sought about three to one by women" (cited in *Joint Custody Newsletter*, January, 1988). According to Christopher Lasch, *NYRB*, 17 February, 1966, three-quarters of divorces are granted to women. According to Elsie Clews Parsons's *The Family: An Ethnographical and Historical Outline* (New York: G. P. Putnam's Sons, 1906), p. 331, "A large majority of divorces are obtained by women." According to a three-day survey by the County Clerk's Office in Orange County, California, two of every three divorce petitions listed the wife as the plaintiff (*Fathers' Forum*, August, 1987). According to court records in Marion, Howard, Hancock, Grant and Ruch counties in Indiana in 1985, of 2,033 dissolutions granted, 1,599 (76.6%) were filed by wives, 474 (23.3%) were filed by husbands (National Congress for Men *Network*, Vol. 1, #3).

Where women enjoy greater independence, divorce rates are higher. Marilyn French says (*Beyond Power: On Women, Men and Morals* (New York: Summit Books, 1985), p. 59: "As in all matrilineal cultures, marriages were easily dissolved." According to Phyllis Chesler (*Mothers on Trial: The Battle for Children and Custody* (New York: McGraw-Hill Book Company, 1986), p. 569: "Divorce is especially rare among those tribes where custody is retained by fathers." According to Lucy Mair, author of *Marriage*, there is more divorce in matrilineal than in patrilineal societies (cited in Elise Boulding, *The Underside of History: A View of Women Through Time* (Boulder, Colorado: Westview Press, 1976), p. 145. According to Nicholas Davidson (*Gender Issues*, May, 1988), "In America today, 70 percent of divorces are initiated by women."

Things have always been thus. Writing nearly two centuries ago, Louis Gabriel Ambroise, Vicomte de Bonald wrote (*Du Divorce*, Paris, 1818 [original ed., 1801]), p. 144, "Divorce is provoked by wives more often than by husbands; and, according to Madame Necker, "the confederacy of women who call for divorce is extremely numerous." p. 182: "It must not be forgotten that most divorces are provoked by women; which proves that they are weaker or more impassioned, not that they are more unhappy." According to the 4th century writer Servius, the Great Goddess Demeter "execrated marriage," and presided not (as tradition would have us believe) over marriage but over *divorce*. "The same character,", says, Briffault, "appertains to all the Great Goddesses of the Eastern Mediterranean world" (*The Mothers* (New York: Macmillan and Company, 1927), III, 171).

According to Shere Hite (*Women and Love: A Cultural Revolution in Progress* (New York: Alfred A. Knopf, 1987)), p. 459, "ninety-one percent of women who have divorced say *they* made the decision to divorce, not their husbands."

For further documentation, see Chapter II, note 10 (page 13).

63. *Human Events*, 26 July, 1986.

The following passage suggests that Gilder never heard of Tawney, that he supposes capitalism is a Roman Catholic creation, that the present sexual crisis is not a post-World War II problem but originated in the eighteenth century, and that a generation ago girls were as promiscuous as they are today:

> Around the world, social decline and sexual chaos is the universal harvest of reliance on secular, rationalist moral codes. In *two centuries* of effort, secular humanists have yet to come up with a way of transmitting ethics to children or persuading girls to say No. Without a religious foundation, embracing all the essentials of Catholic teaching, neither marriage nor civilization, neither capitalism nor democracy can long survive in the modern world.[64]

The present sexual anarchy has not resulted from "two centuries of secular humanism"; it has developed mostly within the last generation (not, to be sure, without predisposing causes), and it has occurred largely in consequence of government welfare programs, the pressures of feminism, the 50 percent divorce rate and society's error in supposing that its props are required for the strongest link in the family, the mother's role, rather than for the weakest link, the father's role.

There can be no greater contrast than that between what Gilder imagines women to think and what women actually do think once they have rejected the patriarchal socialization men have imposed on them for the last several millennia. Prior to the imposition of this patriarchal socialization, the relations between the sexes were governed by the first law of matriarchy: "Women control our own bodies."

---

64. *Ibid.* The improvement in sexual morality during the Victorian Era, when Gilder imagines it to have been deteriorating, was formerly well known. According to Joseph McCabe's *Rationalist Encyclopedia* (London: Watts and Co., 1950), p. 306,

In England and Wales the ration of illegitimate to total births declined from 67 per 1,000 in 1841 to 54 per 1,000 in 1871-80, and there was not at that time any wide knowledge of contraceptives.

Cf. In the same reference work the article "Illegitimacy in Catholic Countries" and Alfred Kinsey's *Sexual Behavior in the Human Female* (Philadelphia: W. B. Saunders Company, 1953), p. 443.

"Some distinguishing features of a woman-centered social system," says Paula Gunn Allen, "include free and easy sexuality and wide latitude in personal style."[65]

The 7th century Bedouin poetess Maysun was a woman who knew both the civilized life of a caliph's wife and the free, wild and matricentric life of the nomad. In the following verses she lamented how her condition as a wife bound her to the contract of marriage. She had no yearning (such as Gilder supposes women to have) to impose this contract or to impose civilization and family stability on a lawless male. It was a male who imposed it on her and she didn't like it:

> Breeze-flowing tents I prefer
> to ponderous halls
> And desert dress
> to diaphanous veils.
> A crust I'd eat in the awning's shade,
> not rolls,
> And watched by a dog that barks
> not a cat that smiles,
> I'd sleep to the wind's time,
> not to the tambourine.
> A youth's impetuous sword,
> *not a husband's wiles,*
> Uncouth slim tribesmen I love,
> not corpulent men.[66]

"Women," says Adrienne Rich,

> have married because it was necessary, in order to survive economically, in order to have children who would not suffer economic deprivation or social ostracism, in order to remain respectable, in order to do what was expected of women because coming out of "abnormal" childhoods they wanted to feel "normal," and because heterosexual romance has been represented as

---

65. Paula Gunn Allen, *The Sacred Hoop: Recovering the Feminine in American Indian Traditions* (Boston: Beacon Pess, 1986), p. 2.

66. Quoted in Elise Boulding, *The Underside of History* (Boulder, Colorado: Westview Press, 1976), p. 303; emphasis added.

the great female adventure, duty, and fulfillment. We may faithfully or ambivalently have obeyed the institution, but *our feelings—and our sensuality—have not been tamed or contained within it.*[67]

Protests of this sort are lost on Gilder, who imagines the patriarchally socialized female is the real thing:

> The difference between the sexes gives the woman the superior position in most sexual encounters. The man may push and posture, but the woman must decide. He is driven; she must set the terms and conditions, goals and destination of the journey. Her faculty of greater natural restraint and selectivity makes the woman the sexual judge and executive, finally appraising the offerings of men, favoring one and rejecting another, and telling them what they must do to be saved or chosen. Managing the sexual nature of a healthy society, women impose the disciplines, make the choices, and summon the male effort that support it.
>
> Modern society relies on predictable, regular, long-term activities, corresponding to the sexual faculties of women. The male pattern is the enemy of social stability.[68]

Modern society relies on predictable, regular, long-term activities, corresponding to the sexual demands of the hated Double Standard, imposed by men over the resistance of women, as the pattern found in *non*-modern, *non*-patriarchal societies shows. In such societies, as Robert Briffault truly says, and as the condition of the ghettos and the Indian reservations sufficiently proves, "there is no original disposition in women to chastity":

---

67. Adrienne Rich, "Compulsory Heterosexuality and Lesbian Existence," in *Feminist Frontiers: Rethinking Sex, Gender, and Society,* ed. Laurel Richardson and Verta Taylor (Reading, MA: Addison-Wesley Publishing Company, 1983), p. 230; emphasis added.
68. *Men and Marriage,* p. 12.

[W]hile we everywhere find chastity imposed by men upon women, it would be difficult to find any instances of a corresponding imposition of chastity by women upon men apart from the primitive tabus which have reference to menstruation, pregnancy and suckling.[69]

The selectivity of which Gilder writes is that of civilized—patriarchally socialized—women with economic and status motives for behaving themselves as men wish them to behave. But even within civilized society, continues Briffault, "Whenever individual women enjoy...a position of power, far from imposing or observing chastity, they avail themselves of their independence to exercise sexual liberty."[70] Then they talk little about the sanctity of motherhood and sound instead like this:

I have what I call the "gang boyfriend motif." I have one boyfriend I've had for eleven years. He's been married twice in that time, and I know and his wife knows we're both better off not having him full-time. He's my main man. Then I have other boyfriends, usually out of town, who I see fairly regularly. I also have one other boyfriend in town, who I really like a lot. They all add up to one big boyfriend, and all my needs get taken care of.[71]

What Gilder supposes to be female nature is what Betty Friedan describes as a "mask" designed to deceive the Gilders of the world:

I protest—on behalf of women and men and my ever-deepening respect for the power and the glory and the mystery of human sex. I protest that passionate sexual human love cannot be experienced if it is divorced from what we really are ourselves. Those obsolete masculine and feminine mystiques—the masks we've been wearing which didn't let us be or know each other. The Biblical word for sexual love is *knowing*.

---

69. Robert Briffault, *The Mothers*, abridged ed., p. 387.
70. *Ibid.*, p. 387.
71. Barbara Ehrenreich, Elizabeth Hess and Gloria Jacobs, *Re-Making Love: The Feminization of Sex* (New York: Anchor Press, 1986), p. 190.

Locked in those iron masks, we finally choke with impotent rage and become immune to each other's touch.[72]

Referring to the growing economic independence of women, she says, "We are in a state of transition now"—transition to a society where women can show how they really feel, which is this:

The bitterness, the rage underneath the ruffles, which we used to take out on ourselves and our kids and finally on the men in bed, is out in the open now, scaring us in its corching intensity, goading men to exasperation and despair. And now the men are letting it hang out, too: how they really feel about female parasites, the dead weights, alimony, the sexual nothingness, the lonely lovelessness of the manipulated breadwinner.[73]

"Female parasites" *motivated by economics and a desire for status within the patriarchal system* to assume the masks which deceive the Gilders, but which Betty Friedan and her feminist sisters see through. Here is one of Ms. Friedan's friends:

I've messed up my kids, devoting my life to them that way. I've been giving my husband a very hard time these last few years. All my hostility is coming out. And now he is a successful lawyer, he has made enough money, he wants to have a good time. He wants me with him, sailing, skiing, entertaining, and I'm in school, making up for lost time. I'm alive again. I don't know what's going to happen to my marriage. My husband is a handsome, successful man. A lot of women are after him. If I have to choose between my own life and my marriage, I have to save my life and take the consequences.[74]

It's a safe bet these consequences will be calculated with an eye on economics and on what her lawyer tells her she can expect in alimony and child support money from the divorce court.

---

72. *It Changed My Life*, p. 232.
73. *Ibid.*
74. *Ibid.*, p. 234.

What Ms. Friedan says about female autonomy is the same as what Monica Sjoo and Barbara Mor say, with the difference that Ms. Friedan tells women they should be ashamed of themselves for not sharing in patriarchal achievement, while Sjoo and Mor tell women the arena of patriarchal achievement should be destroyed:

> When women control our bodies, our daily lives, our environment, and our goals, we don't inflict on ourselves the terrible split between motherhood and self-realization that patriarchy and the nuclear family inflict on us. The split is a structural one, indigenous to male-dominated environments.[75]

The way to get rid of this terrible split is by women's achieving "total sexual and reproductive autonomy" [see page 18 above], autonomy which confers upon women the right of not being subsidized by, and therefore dependent upon, males. Total autonomy means abolishing the contract of marriage and men's responsibilities to women.

The "male pattern" which Gilder thinks the enemy of social stability is not the male pattern in patriarchy but the male pattern in matrilineal societies such as the ghetto, the pattern where males acquiesce in female promiscuity ("autonomy"), because they have too little bargaining power to do anything about it.

Why should the phrase "the male pattern" be used to designate male acquiescence in female promiscuity? Why should it not rather be used to designate the pattern of regulated sexuality *imposed* by wiser patriarchal males who understand the relationship between unregulated female sexuality and the disruptive masculine displays which *Gilder* perceives as "the male pattern"?

"*He* must make a durable commitment," says Gilder. Why say he must when, with a 50 percent divorce rate, he cannot?

> Even then [says Gilder] he is dependent on the woman to love and nurture his child. Even in the context of the family, he is sexually inferior. If he leaves, the family may survive without him. If she leaves, it goes with her.

75. Monica Sjoo and Barbara Mor, *The Great Cosmic Mother: Rediscovering the Religion of the Earth* (San Francisco: Harper and Row, 1987), p. 200.

He is replaceable; she is not. He can have a child only
if she acknowledges his paternity; her child is inexorably
hers.[76]

Dependent on the woman to love and nurture his child? Not
if she can (like Winston Churchill's mother) afford a nanny, or
can (as feminists are trying to do) screw the government for free
child care. If she leaves the family goes with her? Not in
Victorian society, where women like Lady Caroline Norton
complained of the loss of their children following divorce and
where J. S. Mill complained that "they are by law *his* children."
(When the suggestion was made to Mill that mothers, rather
than fathers, should be given the custody of the children of
divorce, he thought the idea had merit, but he refused to
advocate it publicly because he said it was an idea for which the
public's mind was insufficiently prepared to make such advocacy
useful.)

Not according to the *Corpus Juris*, which says, "at common
law and under some statutes, the primary right to the custody
and care of minor children is generally in the father."[77] Not in
sixteenth century Germany, where "illegitimate children, who
abounded, were usually taken into the father's home after
marriage."[78] Not in Freud's Austria, where the great psychologist stipulated in his will that if he died before his children were
grown, they should be taken from their mother and placed in a
foster home. Not in Iran, where father-custody is automatic
following divorce.[79] Not in Renaissance Venice, where, "even in
cases of adultery, the wife's lover had to pay for her expenses if
she became pregnant, then had to rear the child, and the wife
was returned to her husband after the birth."[80] Not in Ibsen's
Doll's House, where Nora acknowledges that her husband Thor-

76. *Men and Marriage*, p. 13.

77. Cited in R. F. Doyle, *The Rape of the Male* (St. Paul: Poor Richard's Press, 1976), p. 87.

78. Will Durant, *The Reformation* (New York: Simon and Schuster, 1957), p. 303.

79. Farazaneh Taidi, Iranian actress, describes her divorce: "However, I think because I did not love my husband--my marriage, as far as I was concerned, was a marriage of convenience--it did not work. I had to get a divorce. Divorce came during the late Shah's regime and despite his Family Protection Courts, divorce meant that I had to separate from my 3 1/2 year old son. Custody of children automatically goes to husbands in Iran. Separation from my child was most hurtful to me." (*off our backs*, November, 1987)

80. Review by Diane Broughton of Guido Ruggiero's *The Boundaries of Eros: Sex Crime and Sexuality in Renaissance Venice, Los Angeles Times*, 10 March, 1985.

wald is better able to rear the children than she is. Not in America in 1848, when the Seneca Falls feminists complained that women automatically lost their children in the event of divorce, and when judges made assertions such as this from the bench:

> It is a well-settled doctrine of the common law, that the father is entitled to the custody of his minor children, as against the mother and everybody else; that he is bound for their maintenance and nurture, and has the corresponding right to their obedience and their services.[81]

Gilder imagines that the way things have been in the 20th century American matriarchy is the way they have always been and always must be. "He is readily replaceable; she is not"? He is replaceable if his paycheck can be taken from him or if the government will subsidize female promiscuity, illegitimacy and matriarchy via AFDC. Without these subsidizations, it would be found that a mother-surrogate is far more easily obtainable (in the form of a paternal grandmother, a stepmother, a nanny or a housekeeper) than a breadwinner.[82]

---

81. State v. Richardson, 40 NH272 (NH 1860), p. 273; cited in Andre P. Derdeyn, M. D., "Child Custody Contests in Historical Perspective." Paper presented at the 129th annual meeting of the American Psychiatric Association, Miami Beach, Florida, May 10-14, 1976: *American Journal of Psychiatry*, 133: 12 Dec. 1976.

82. Terry Arendell quotes a divorced mother as follows:

Most men simply have no concept of what we're up against, even when they're single parents and have custody. Men still have this whole troop of women—mothers, aunts, sisters, friends—to wish them luck and give them household help and child care. And they've got enough money so they can afford to pay for such things if the women around them don't come through.

Another:

It really disgusts me to watch single men who have custody of their children get so much attention. Friends invite them over to dinner. My friends who are couples don't invite me and my children over; they just expect that I can manage. Men have double the income and can afford to pay for all the services they need, but they get treated as if they'r wonderful to be doing all this and must be really overloaded. I've never had that kind of support from anyone.

Arendell's comment:

These women felt especially deserted and segregated when they heard frequent cultural messages to the effect that children raised by divorced mothers are likely candidates for delinquency, homosexuality, or abnormal social behavior. Already overburdened with financial and emotional responsibility for their children, they found societal indifference hard enough to tolerate; blanket criticisms based on negative stereotypes outraged them. (Terry Arendell, *Mothers and Divorce: Legal, Economic and Social Dilemmas* (Berkeley: University of California Press, 1986). p. 100.)

"Only a specific woman can bear a specific child" says Gilder,

> and her tie to it is personal and unbreakable. When she
> raises the child she imparts in privacy her own individ-
> ual values. She can create children who transcend
> consensus and prefigure the future, children of private
> singularity rather than "child-development policy." She
> is the vessel of the ultimate values of the nation. The
> community is largely what she is and what she demands
> in men.[83]

Her tie to "her" child is "unbreakable." It is in the American
matriarchy, as it is among the Tekelmas, the Mandans, the
Canelas and other savages—whereas the father's tie in these
savage societies is easily breakable, which is why these savages,
like ourselves, have underachieving children. "She imparts her
own individual values"? Either she fails to, or her values are
defective, for what she imparts is the socialization which produces 75 percent of the criminal class.

Gilder gets so swept away by his own rhapsodizing about
mothers and maternity that the logic of what he dealing with
eludes him. He tells of the central position of women in both
home and civilization, of mother-love, of long-term ties of the
mother to her child and their depth and tenacity, of the need for
her to transmit her values to her offspring and of how the success
or failure of civilization depends on this transmission, of her
deep moral, aesthetic, religious, nurturant, social, sexual concerns, which involve the ultimate goals of human life, of how she
is the repository of the ultimate values of the nation and of how
the community is largely shaped by her, of the existence of a
uniquely feminine moral sense rooted in webs of relationships
and responsibility, in intimacy and caring, a moral sense superior to the masculine one of rules, hierarchy, aggression, lust and
abstraction. He assures us that the mother's tie to her child is
the ultimate basis of all morality, based on the preciousness of
life, beginning in the womb and breast, morally paramount,
unimpeachable, and so on and on. What, then, of the fact which
will not go away—the one about three-quarters of criminals

---

83. *Men and Marriage*, pp. 168-9.

coming from female-headed homes where they reaped the benefits of this superior virtue, this uniquely feminine moral sense so much nobler than that of the male? These criminals had the benefits of all of Mom's goodness without any dilution by masculine influence.

Gilder's answer: "If children lack the close attention of mothers *and the disciplines and guidance of fathers* they tend to become wastrels who burden and threaten society rather than do its work."[84] This is supposed to show the importance of Mom's influence. It's like arguing that milk will cure scurvy. The cure for scurvy is not milk but vitamin C; and the analogue of Gilder's argument is to insist that patients deprived of milk *and vitamin C* suffer from scurvy, and therefore they need more milk. The criminal class doesn't suffer from mother-deprivation. It suffers from father-deprivation. Mom has stinted *nothing*—she has given her *all* to the criminal class. Criminals have many problems, but mother-deprivation is not one of them.

"In terms of mental and physical disease and life expectancy," says Gilder, "divorce damages the man far more than the woman":

> Divorced men of every age group between thirty-five and sixty-four have a mortality rate three and a third times as high as divorced women....Divorced men are three and a half times as likely as divorced women to commit suicide, and four times more likely to die in an accidental fire or explosion. Murder claims three divorced men for every divorced woman, as does cirrhosis of the liver. And, in the realm of more conventional mortality, divorced men are six times as likely as divorced women to die of heart disease.[85]

Gilder writes as though men and women passed through the same experience. This is like comparing a female driver and a male pedestrian who experience the same "accident," and inferring from the resulting injuries that females are tougher than

---

84. P. 168; emphasis added.
85. *Men and Marriage,* p. 66.

males. Both parties experience "divorce," but the man experiences in addition the massive anti-male discrimination of the divorce court, where he loses his children, his home, his property, his future income—his *role*. If wives were deprived of all these things, if ex-wives were rounded up and jailed on Mother's Day for not subsidizing their ex-husbands, as ex-husbands are commonly rounded up on Father's Day by clambering District Attorneys and thrown in jail for not subsidizing their ex-wives, we would hear something about *men's* greater ability to survive the trauma of divorce.

Here, from David Chambers's *Making Fathers Pay*,[86] is the way the male is handled in divorce cases. Can one imagine a judge ordering an ex-wife to clean her ex-husbands's home and then scolding her for failure to do so in some such manner as this?

The Court:	All right, Mr. Connors, bring up Mr. Neal. (Mr. Neal approaches the bench.)
The Court:	Mr. Neal, do you know why you're here?
Defendant:	Yes.
The Court:	I can't hear you.
Defendant:	Yes.
The Court:	Why are you here?
Defendant:	Back alimony.
The Court:	It's not alimony; I never ordered alimony.
Defendant:	No.
The Court:	You were never ordered by Judge Johnston to pay alimony.
Defendant:	No, support.
The Court:	That's right. You were ordered to pay support for your children, not alimony for your wife. And that was back in '63, and he only made you pay ten dollars per week per child. You have five, is that right?
Defendant:	Yes.
The Court:	Do you know how much you're in arrears?

---

86. David Chambers, *Making Fathers Pay: The Enforcement of Child Support* (Chicago: University of Chicago Press, 1979), pp. 3ff.

Defendant: Yes.

The Court: How much?

Defendant: It's over ten thousand.

The Court: Well, why are you that far behind? Why haven't you paid something on it?

Defendant: Well, I had other bills and trying to make a living myself; I just couldn't seem to pay nothing.

The Court: Well, what do you mean "other bills"? You knew you had these children.

Defendant: Yes.

The Court: These children didn't ask to be brought into the world, Mr. Neal. How did you expect those children to get food in their little stomachs and clothes on their back, shoes on their feet, boots in the winter time? Where were you working all this time?

Defendant: I had different jobs.

The Court: Well, why haven't you held a steady job? What's your trouble? I'd like to know.

Defendant: Nothing.

The Court: Well, then, why haven't you held onto a steady job if nothing's wrong with you?

Defendant: Just trying to find something that pays more money.

The Court: But you can't do it—

Defendant: No.

The Court: —going from one insignificant job to another. Were you born here in Flint?

Defendant: Yes.

The Court: You knew that you could make a hundred and fifty, hundred and sixty dollars in the factory here. Why didn't you apply to the factory?

Defendant: I did. They won't take me back because I got a hernia and I couldn't pass the test again.

The Court: You got married [a second time] in '65. Did you marry a Flint woman?

Defendant: Yes.

The Court: Is she working?

Defendant: No. She can't work; she's a diabetic now.

The Court: You knew you had these five children be fore you married her. These are the ones that come first. I don't care about your second wife. But these children are too small and I'm not going to let them go around in garbage cans looking for food or something, or to put shoes on their feet. If you're strong enough to marry a second time and go to bed, you're strong enough to get a job that will pay and feed these children. You have no business assuming that responsibility when you had five little tots to take care of. They didn't ask to be brought into this world, Mr. Neal. You've defied this court. You think that laws were made for everybody but you. Well, I'm going to teach you a lesson. Do you have anything to say why I shouldn't cite you for contempt of Court?

Defendant: (No audible response.)

The Court: Do you have anything to say, I asked you?

Defendant: No.

The Court: You have nothing to say in mitigation of what you've done to these children?

Defendant: I know I did wrong.

The Court: Yes. If you would have sent at least ten dollars a week for the five of them, at least we would have seen that you were making an effort. You didn't even send a nickel.

Defendant: I did send money off and on, but right to them; I didn't send it to the court.

The Court: Oh, really, and you expect the court to believe that?

Defendant: No.

The Court: You're darn tooting I don't believe it. This court finds nothing wrong with you. Hernia or no hernia, you had no business leaving the Fisher body when you were building up seniority, fringe benefits, everything. You take a leave of absence and go to Florida with a new wife. You may have gotten that hernia at Fisher's for all you know. Anyhow, the court finds you in contempt of court for violating this support— violating the judgment of divorce, wherein support was made for five small children at ten dollars per week [per child]. And that isn't even enough. The court finds nothing wrong with you, hernia or no hernia. There are many men who work with hernias; they are physically and mentally able. If you are capable of remarrying, you are capable then of supporting your children. You are to be confined to the county jail for one year unless you come up with half, at least five thousand dollars, and a wage assignment of at least the current fifty dollars, plus twenty-five dollars on the back. Let him make two or three telephone calls and see if he can get somebody to take him out.[87]

Mr. Neal was sentenced to a year in prison, but got two months off for good behavior.

If Mr. Neal had been more articulate he might have replied to the Court's invitation to speak in his own behalf as follows:

You say that you are imprisoning me for contempt of court. You are lying. You are imprisoning me for debt, in violation of the law which you have sworn to uphold. You are denying me my right to be tried by a jury of my

---

87. Chambers, pp. 3-6.

peers, divorced males, in violation of Article III, section 2 of the Bill of Rights, which you have sworn to uphold.

You tell me that I have no business marrying a second wife. If you know anything about the statistics of sociology, or if you have read George Gilder's *Men and Marriage*, you would know that married men earn nearly twice as much as single men. If you are concerned, as you affect to be, that I earn as much as possible, you would encourage me to remarry.

You tell me that you care nothing for the welfare of my second wife, and I believe you; but if I failed to support *her*, you would be tantruming at me for the welfare costs she would require of the State of Michigan, and telling me that you cared nothing for my first wife, and that since she is *not* my wife I am not responsible for her, which is true.

You say I have no business assuming responsibility for a second wife. I say to you, you have no business assuming responsibility for my children, and that in taking that responsibility upon yourself and placing them in a fatherless home in the custody of a woman incapable of providing for them, you are responsible for their poverty. By placing them in a female-headed home you are placing them where their likelihood of becoming delinquents is several times greater than if they were in a father-headed home. You destroyed my family, and you are trying to shift your responsibility for destroying it onto me by blaming me for the law's incompetence to protect my children and for the fact that I am unable to support two households with an income sufficient only for one.

You say that my children didn't ask to be brought into the world. I say to you that they didn't ask to be taken from a two-parent family where they were decently provided for *by me* and placed *by you* in a one-parent family where they are impoverished and at greater risk of delinquency and educational failure.

You ask me why I haven't held a steady job. You want to know what my trouble is. My trouble is that you have

destroyed my family—destroyed the system of motivation which formerly made me a productive, stable and
useful member of society—and are now about to make
me a jailbird who can contribute nothing to society. My
trouble is the same trouble as that of tens of millions of
other American males—that you and the other members
of your profession are, by destroying half of America's
families, destroying the basis of patriarchal civilization.
My trouble is that you and your fellow judges imagine
that by raging and tantruming at males like myself you
can compensate for the damage you are inflicting upon
society by your own weakness of character, your own
lawlessness in refusing to keep your oath of office and
administer justice impartially, and your lack of cognitive skill.

You say you aren't going to let my children rummage
in garbage cans. It is because you placed them in a
female-headed home that they are rummaging in garbage cans. They never rummaged in garbage cans when
they were in my custody.

You may imagine that your demonstration of indig-
nation is benefiting the State of Michigan. It will cost the
State between $20,000 and $25,000 to imprison me for a
year. During that time my ex-wife and my children will
be entirely on public welfare. During that time I will
earn nothing and will therefore be withdrawing another
$25,000 worth of productivity from the Michigan econ-
omy. My future employability will be impaired once I
have a jail record. I will be paying no taxes for the next
year and reduced taxes in the future—perhaps none at
all, since I may find myself driven into the underground
economy, or compelled to leave the state in order to
escape your bullying.

Your concern is not, as you pretend, for the best
interests of my children. You never lost thirty seconds
of sleep over my children or any of the other children you
placed in fatherless households where they are far more
likely to be impoverished and delinquent. Your concern
is to practice cheap judicial chivalry at my expense and

to preserve a mindless legal rule-of-thumb which will save you the necessity of performing the duty for which you receive your salary, the duty of administering impartial justice and of thinking about what you routinely do when you destroy families and place children in their mothers' custody.

In the *Mahabharata*, the ancient epic of India, the character Pandy says, "Women were not formerly immured in houses and dependent upon husbands and relatives. They used to go about freely, enjoying themselves as best they pleased....They did not then adhere to their husbands faithfully; and yet, O beauteous one, they were not regarded as sinful, for that was the sanctioned usage of the times....The present practice of women being confined to one husband for life hath been established but lately."[88]

In the early 19th century, a traveller named De Roquefeuil visited the Marquesas Islands and reported that nearly every woman there had at least two husbands.[89]

In the 24th century B. C., when civilization was a recent human achievement, an edict of King Urukagina of Lagash declared that, "Women of former times each married two men, but women of today have been made to give up this crime."[90] *Made* to give it up—clearly the idea of monandry originated with males and was imposed on females.

Contrary to what Gilder imagines, there must be something congenial to female nature in the state of promiscuity which existed in India in the age of the Pandavas, in the Marquesas Islands in the 19th century, in Lagash before the time of King Urukagina. What else is to be inferred from the fact that the most strident and frequently repeated demand of feminists is for "a woman's right to control her own body"—to abolish the Legitimacy Principle and re-establish the Promiscuity Principle?

88. Quoted in Robert Briffault, *The Mothers*, abridged ed. (New York: Grosset and Dunlap, 1959), p. 76.

89. Edward Westermarck, *Three Essays on Sex and Marriage* (London: Macmillan and Company, 1934), p. 296.

90. Cited by Gerda Lerner, *The Creation of Patriarchy* (New York: Oxford University Press, 1986), p. 63.

"The right of women to full sexual equality with men," says Ms. Friedan, "and to the dignity and privacy of their own person must be secured by federal statute recognizing the right of every woman to control her own reproductive life."[91]

That means a federal law legitimizing fornication for unmarried women and adultery for married women, a federal law denying to men any rights under the marriage contract.[92]

"Only economic independence can free a *woman* to marry for love," says Ms. Friedan.[93] Men's money may be a "love-spoiler,"[94] but women's own money is romance itself—and isn't necessarily connected with marriage at all. She explains:

> "Marriage as an institution is doomed" is the feeling of many women in the movement for whom the essence of women's liberation sometimes seems to be *liberation from marriage.*
>
> ....
>
> "There's no real economic base for marriage any more," says a learned friend of mine. "When women needed a man for economic support, and men needed women economically to run a home, when they needed to have children to secure their old age, marriage was real then and sex outside of marriage was not sanctioned. There's no real basis for that now. That's why marriages now are breaking up as soon as the children get old enough or even before."[95]

She illustrates from the experience of a liberated friend:

> She is currently involved with two married men in two different cities. Over the last week she has seen both, spent two intense days with one, several with the other, but does not quite know when she'll see either one again. This has been going on for several years. Neither has

---

91. *It Changed My Life,* p. 102.

92. Although, as we learn elsewhere in Ms. Friedan's writings, she has no intention of terminating men's *obligations* under that contract, even after the termination of the contract itself. (*The Second Stage,* p. 19.)

93. *The Feminine Mystique,* p. 371; emphasis added.

94. *It Changed My Life,* p. 224.

95. *It Changed My Life,* p. 238.

any interest in leaving his wife, nor would she really want to marry either one of them. Other than the fact that neither is available on weekends, Sundays or holidays, or for long vacations or dinner every night—her relationship with both is quite perfect. Marvelously intense conversation, sex, emotion, dinners, letters—more intense surely than if they were together every day. She is not at all jealous of their wives.

"What could be better?" asks her married friend. "You can enjoy all that, the closeness, the emotion, the sex, the fun and games—and you don't ever have to do the laundry, so to speak, or stop doing your thing to make his dinner. You live your own life. You only have yourself to think about. How I envy you!"[96]

Just like Romeo and Juliet. No money worries. No love-spoiling (male) money to interfere with the fun and games by bribing and buying up women as though they were property. The woman has her own money (or her husband's) and can use it to enjoy her sacred right to promiscuity, a right which ought to be guaranteed by federal law. This is the reality behind what Gilder perceives as women's long-term sexual horizons, horizons which, however, become long-term chiefly when contaminated by economic considerations.

The females in primitive societies and in the women's liberation movement covet a promiscuity which would deny to males a secure family role. By contrast, patriarchally socialized females in civilized societies accept the Sexual Constitution (or did until recently), and their chastity and loyalty to their husbands enable these husbands to be heads of families, a headship motivating the stable and productive male behavior which Gilder takes to be the primary difference between civilization and savagery. Both male and female behavior differ, but the difference in female behavior, consequent upon its regulation by the patriarchal sexual constitution, is the more fundamental.

---

96. P. 239.

Writing of the "creation of patriarchy" in the second millen-
. nium B. C., Dr. Gerda Lerner says:

> The class position of women became consolidated and
> actualized through their sexual relationships....[Different
> groups of women] shared the unfreedom of being sexu-
> ally and reproductively controlled by men....Class for
> men was and is based on their relationship to the means
> of production: those who owned the means of production
> could dominate those who did not.[97]

It has to be that way for patriarchy to work. Male status is
based on work and the creation of wealth, motivated by the
male's role as head of the family. For this system to exist it is
necessary that society should do what Dr. Lerner complains of
its doing—consolidate the "class position" (status) of women
through their sexual relationships:

> It is through the man that women have access to or are
> denied access to the means of production and to re-
> sources. It is through their sexual behavior that they
> gain access to class. "Respectable women" gain access to
> class through their fathers and husbands, but breaking
> the sexual rules can at once declass them.[98]

The threat of being de-classed is essential to the system, which
would be destroyed by the acceptance of the Promiscuity Principle. Accordingly, the acceptance of the Promiscuity Principle
is the major thrust of feminism: "Our liberation process consists
in large part in gaining control over our own bodies, which are
our own selves, our own lives."[99] According to Helen Diner, "A
free disposition over one's own person is an original right in a
matriarchal society"[100]—and women want the right restored.
Lesbian feminist Susan Cavin insists that "patriarchy must
control female sexuality, or else patriarchy cannot exist....The

97. *The Creation of Patriarchy,* p. 215.
98. P. 215.
99. Amy Hoffman, *Gay Community News,* December, 1982.
100. *Mothers and Amazons: The First Feminine History of Culture* (Garden City,
N.Y.: Anchor Books, 1973), p. 31.

creation and maintenance of patriarchy or any other form of male-ruled society is based on the control of female sexuality."[101]

To recapitulate. Patriarchal civilization is made possible by the regulation of female sexuality on the basis of the Sexual Constitution. Given freedom, females do not use their influence to impose this Sexual Constitution on males but to escape from it, to wreck the hated patriarchal system, as they have done in the ghettos. Surely it is significant that in the vast feminist literature dealing with the economic miseries of single mothers and their children, there is *nowhere* any suggestion to return to the Sexual Constitution and the patriarchal family—the only realistic means by which the economic problems of most single mothers can be solved. The entire thrust of this literature is to demand alternate methods of improving the standard of living of female-headed families without going back to the family and the Sexual Constitution which Gilder imagines them to be yearning for.

---

101. *Lesbian Origins* (San Francisco: Ism Press, 1985), p. 8.

VIII

The Weitzman Fallacy

Dr. Lenore Weitzman's book *The Divorce Revolution*[1] argues that ex-husbands owe ex-wives far more alimony and child support money than divorce courts now compel them to pay. She deems it unjust that the ex-husband should walk away from his marriage with his earning ability intact while the ex-wife has little earning ability to walk away with. This male earning ability, the principal inducement the man had to offer the woman for marriage, is referred to as an "asset of the marriage," and therefore (by feminist logic) belongs equally to the *un*married (divorced) woman and the *un*married (divorced) man, while the children, the chief asset of the marriage from the man's point of view, are presumed to be the property of the woman by biological right.

The statistics Dr. Weitzman offers in support of her contention—the divorced man's standard of living is said to rise by 42 percent, the divorced woman's standard of living to fall by 73 percent—have become an established part of the folklore of feminism. The original feminist position, given in Betty Friedan's *The Feminine Mystique*, had been that women ought to be independent, to stand on their own feet and face life's challenges on their own "without sexual privilege or excuse."[2] Ms. Friedan withdrew this view when the cold winds of economics began blowing and her feminist followers began blaming her for the loss of their husbands' paychecks:

> We did not realize the trap we were falling into [wrote
> Ms. Friedan in her 1976 book *It Changed My Life*]. We
> fell into a trap when we said, "No alimony!" because

1. Lenore Weitzman, *The Divorce Revolution: The Unexpected Social and Economic Consequences for Women and Children in America* (New York: The Free Press, 1985).
2. Betty Friedan, *The Feminine Mystique* (New York: W. W. Norton, 1963), p. 346.

housewives who divorced were in terrible straits. We
fell into another trap by accepting no-fault divorce
without provision for mandatory settlements.[3]

Being independent was great as long as it meant not having
reciprocal responsibilities; losing the free ride was less great. It
was accordingly necessary to devise a new justification for the
ex-wife's retaining of the ex-husband's money, this being that
most of the "assets of the marriage" consist of the husband's
earning ability. The argument is thus stated by feminist Terry
Arendell:

Most of these [divorced] women viewed their husband's
earnings and earning ability as rightfully being a community property issue.[4]

Ms. Arendell regards it as proper that ex-husbands should
subsidize ex-wives but wholly unfair that ex-wives, if they re-
marry, "would lose all financial help from their former husbands" while "their ex-husbands...could re-marry at will and
still lose nothing of what they had taken out of their marriages."
No matter that they had also taken their earning ability into
their marriages. No matter that the first marriage no longer
exists, having been dissolved by divorce. No matter that the
second marriage does exist and that the man's earning ability is
benefiting his second family, to which he is bound by legal and
affectional ties. No matter that the ex-husband cannot suffer
any deprivation by his re-marriage because the ex-wife never
gave him anything of which he might be deprived.

The husband's economic-provider services were common
property during the marriage *because the wife's reciprocal services were also common property*. But by divorce the wife has
withdrawn her services. She doesn't go to her ex-husband's
home to do his laundry, mop his floors, and prepare his meals.
What Ms. Arendell's argument comes to is this: she agrees with

---

3. *It Changed My Life: Writings on the Women's Movement* (New York: Random
House, 1976), p. 325.
4. *Mothers and Divorce: Legal, Economic, and Social Dilemmas* (Berkeley: University of California Press, 1986), p. 34.

Ms. Friedan that "society asks so little of women"[5] that (apart from bearing his children) the wife's contribution to the husband bears no comparison to the husband's contribution to the wife. In withdrawing her services at the same time that she withdraws her really substantive contribution to the marriage, the children, she is withdrawing something so trifling that Ms. Arendell can truly say the ex-husband is walking away with most of the assets of the marriage.

Hence, according to feminist reasoning, the women who make themselves independent by divorce are entitled to perpetuate their dependence by alimony and child support awards.

Dr. Weitzman's statistics concerning the ex-husband's improved and the ex-wife's deteriorated standard of living are spurious. But suppose they were valid. What then?

First, it follows that there are excellent economic reasons for placing children of divorce in the custody of fathers rather than mothers.

Second, it follows that during the marriage the husband performed extremely valuable services for the wife, so valuable that when they are withdrawn her standard of living falls by 73 percent.

(The wife's "unpaid" services to the husband during marriage are frequently referred to in feminist literature as something justifying compensation. How can a woman's standard of living be lowered by 73 percent by divorce if all she is losing is the non-payment of *nothing*?)

Third, it follows that the husband performed these services at great sacrifice to himself, so great that even with his continued subsidization of her by alimony and child support payments, and despite the ex-wife's withdrawal of her "unpaid services" worth $25,000 a year (Gloria Steinem's estimate), his own standard of living, once he is partially emancipated from her, skyrockets by 42 percent.

Fourth, it follows that during the marriage the husband had nothing to show for having raised his wife's standard of living by 73 percent at a cost of a 42 percent lowering of his own—nothing except the loss of his children and his motivation (not to mention

---

5. *The Feminine Mystique* (New York: W. W. Norton, 1963), p. 338.

the probable loss of his home, etc.). But this loss of children and motivation is an *economic* fact of the first importance. From the economic standpoint, the ex-husband's greatest asset is not his skill, not his degrees and credentials, not his customer goodwill, not his reputation, but his motivation, which in the typical case (since most divorce actions are initiated by wives)[6] the wife herself destroys—and then demands to be compensated for.

Fifth, it follows that Dr. Weitzman is glaringly inconsistent in maintaining on the one hand that the wife's contribution to the marriage is the reason for the husband's (and ex-husband's) economic success, and on the other that he owes her a post-marital free ride *despite the fact that she has been a ball-and-chain on him,* lowering his standard of living by 42 percent. One is reminded of Betty Friedan's assertion that "There are, of course, many reasons for divorce, but chief among them seems to be the growing aversion and hostility that men have for the feminine millstones hanging around their necks."[7]

Sixth, it follows that Dr. Weitzman disproves her own contention that the wife's contributions to the marriage account for the husband's financial success, and that his *future* earnings— "assets of the marriage" for which *withdrawn* services cannot be responsible—ought for this reason to be shared by the ex-wife. These contributions are said to consist largely of "moral support." Why is not this moral support as much community property as the male earning ability it is said to generate? Why is not its withdrawal by divorce a justification for the withdrawal of the earning which is said to result from it?

Seventh, it follows from Dr. Weitzman's estimate of the value of the wife's contributions to the marriage that the husband sustains a crippling loss from her withdrawal of these contributions. If they are the reason for the husband's economic achievement, then their denial entitles him not only to withdraw his earnings, but to be compensated.

Eighth, it follows that if the 42 percent statistic is valid, the ex-husband is entitled to compensation from the ex- wife for her *lowering* of his pre-divorce standard of living by that amount.

---

6. See Chapter II, note 10, page 13, and Chapter VII, note 62 page 142 for the evidence.
7. *The Feminine Mystique,* p. 273.

(Such a claim would correspond to the demand made by ex-wives to be compensated for the careers they forfeited by marriage.)

Dr. Weitzman wants it both ways: the woman marries the man and demands post-marital recompense because marrying him was a favor; she divorces him and demands post-marital recompense because divorcing him was a favor. She asks us to believe that the motivations provided by the wife make the man an underachiever (by 42 percent) while they are acting upon him during marriage, but then function proleptically to make him an overachiever once they are withdrawn by divorce.

In writing of the predicament of divorced women, Dr. Weitzman complains of the "assumption that it is fair to divide *family* income so that the *wife* and children share one-third, while the *husband* keeps the other two-thirds for himself."[8] There is no "family"; the woman is not a "wife"; the man is not a "husband." A family is created by marriage and destroyed by divorce. The economic predicament of the woman has virtually nothing to do with "no fault" divorce as Dr. Weitzman's book tries to prove. It is due to divorce itself. The greater misery of ex-wives today is not owing to change in divorce procedures (there has been none), but to the greater number of divorces.

During marriage the wife did get from the husband what Dr. Weitzman wishes the ex-wife (read: non-wife) to have from the ex- husband (read: non-husband). The only unfairness is that to the children whom the ex-wife drags into poverty with her to be used as mutilated beggars. It is schizophrenic to insist on the continuing existence of the "family" as a means of justifying the destruction of that family itself. It is like feeding a cow its own milk—taking away its substance in order to nourish it. What such schizophrenia testifies to is Dr. Weitzman's own recognition that the family—the real, nuclear, patriarchal family—is the true source of the wealth she is grasping for, while at the same time she works to destroy it.

She complains of the predicament of "an older housewife who has spent twenty or thirty years in the family home" and then loses it when her marriage ends. This woman has spent twenty or thirty years living in a home she could probably not have

---

8. *The Divorce Revolution, p. 396; emphasis added.*

provided for herself, enjoying a standard of living 73 percent higher than she could have earned, bestowed upon her by a husband who forfeited 42 percent of his own standard of living for her sake during marriage. Which partner is entitled to compensation?

It is a commonplace in feminist literature that women should be freed from what Zillah Eisenstein calls the "patriarchal image of woman as dependent on man." "In this view," she says, "she is still primarily a mother and therefore needs a man to support her."[9] Dr. Weitzman's demand for the subsidization of ex-wives by ex-husbands constitutes a reactionary reversion to this obsolete patriarchalism, which keeps women from "learning to stand alone."[10]

It was the thrust of Betty Friedan's *Feminine Mystique* that it is contemptible and infantile of women to be economically dependent upon husbands, that the childish "mystique" they affected for the purpose of perpetuating this dependence and jollying men into supporting them was stifling, undignified, inhibitive of women's growth, and that they should discard their economic dependence and stand on their own feet. "Why," asked Ms. Friedan, "isn't it time to break the pattern by urging all these Sleeping Beauties to grow up and live their own lives?"[11] The thrust of Dr. Weitzman's *Divorce Revolution* is the precise opposite: that women must remain economically dependent on men, even when they divorce them and withdraw the trifling services upon which Ms. Friedan poured her ridicule and contempt. They must rely upon the Motherhood Card and the Mutilated Beggar argument which permit them to drag their children into the Custody Trap where they wallow in self-generated economic misery and self-pity.

Dr. Weitzman proposes that this parasitism should never end. Even after the children are grown, says Dr. Weitzman, "Long- married older *wives* must also be assured of an equal share of all of their *husband's* career assets."[12] But "wives" *are* assured of their husbands' career assets, an assurance they

---

9. *The Radical Future of Liberal Feminism* (New York: Longman, 1981), p. 212.
10. Betty Friedan's words, *The Feminine Mystique*, p. 134.
11. *The Feminine Mystique*, p. 304.
12. *The Divorce Revolution*, p. 380; emphasis added.

enjoy because of marriage, the stability of which Dr. Weitzman is seeking to undermine by her attempt to make divorce into an alternative institution capable of giving women the same benefits marriage gives them. She cannot see where her own evidence leads. She urges women not to trust their husbands' loyalty (now eroded by the feminist/sexual revolution) but instead to trust feminist agitation, lawyers, bureaucrats and lawmakers. Trust in lawyers, bureaucrats and lawmakers is misplaced. Betty Friedan told women to trust *themselves* and to acquire the skills which would make them economically independent. Now Ms. Friedan, like Dr. Weitzman, is reduced to speaking of such an undeliverable promise as a "trap" leading women into economic disaster.

These women "deserve some special recognition and compensation for their contributions, not harsher treatment," says Dr. Weitzman.[13] They *receive* special recognition and compensation in the form of a 73 percent higher standard of living; and it was one of the main contentions of *The Feminine Mystique* that this compensation was excessive and unmerited and that wives should be ashamed of themselves for taking it. Hear Betty Friedan:

> In our culture, the development of women has been blocked at the physiological level with, in many cases, no need recognized higher than the need for love or sexual satisfaction. Even the need for self-respect, for self-esteem and for the esteem of others—"the desire for strength, for achievement, for adequacy, for mastery and competence, for confidence in the face of the world, and for independence, and freedom"—is not clearly recognized for women. But certainly the thwarting of the need for self-esteem, which produces feelings of inferiority, of weakness, and of helplessness in man, can have the same effect on woman. Self-esteem in woman, as well as in man, can only be based on real capacity, competence, and achievement; on deserved respect from others rather than unwarranted adulation. Despite the

---

13. *The Divorce Revolution*, p. 382.

glorification of "Occupation: housewife," if that occupation does not demand, or permit, realization of woman's full abilities, it cannot provide adequate self-esteem, much less pave the way to a higher evel of self-realization.[14]

"The most glaring proof," said Ms. Friedan, "that, no matter how elaborate, 'Occupation: housewife' is not an adequate substitute for truly challenging work, important enough to society to be paid for in its coin, arose from the comedy of 'togetherness.' The women acting in this little morality play were told that they had the starring roles, that their parts were just as important, perhaps even more important than the parts their husbands played in the world outside the home."[15] "Most of the energy expended in housework," she says, "is superfluous."[16] It is this "underused, nameless-yearning, energy-to-get-rid-of state of being housewives"[17] that is now said to be the justification for prolonging dependence after divorce. "The problem seemed to be not that too much was asked of them, but too little."[18] "The husbands of the women I interviewed," says Ms. Friedan, "were often engaged in work that demanded ability, responsibility and decision. I noticed that when these men were saddled with a domestic chore, they polished it off in much less time than it seemed to take their wives."[19]

Dr. Weitzman gives an example of how divorce arrangements perpetuate women's dependence (though Dr. Weitzman wants more, not less, of this dependence):

> Consider the following situation as an example of the typical legal (and social) issues that may arise with remarriage. A remarried man is legally obligated to support his two children from a former marriage and the young child he has fathered with his new wife. At the same time, his wife's two children from her former

14. *The Feminine Mystique*, p. 315.
15. P. 248.
16. P. 238.
17. P. 207.
18. P. 252.
19. P. 241.

marriage are currently living with him, and by virtue of their presence in the household (at his dinner table, etc.) he finds himself supporting them as well. While he is not legally obligated to support his wife's children if he has not legally adopted them—and let us suppose that neither he nor the children's natural father wants that adoption to take place—in practical terms, he inevitably contributes to their support because they are members of his new household. The situation is further complicated by the fact that his new wife's ex-husband has also remarried and started a new family, and has not been paying her court-ordered child support. Our man feels the law should either relieve him of his financial obligation to support his own two children by his ex-wife (who are now living in another man's household) or force his present wife's ex-husband to pay his support obligations. He is disconcerted to learn that there are no legal guidelines to allocate and apportion support responsibilities among several families.[20]

Which is to say, because he is a male the legal system cannot be bothered about his rights. This man is paying the price for the liberation of *three* women: (1) the current wife, who deserves his support because of his marriage-vow to her and hers to him, in compliance with which she performs reciprocal services; (2) his former wife, who deserves nothing, since his marriage vow to her has been annulled by the divorce court and since she has withdrawn her services from him; and (3) the new wife of the old husband of his present wife, who gets a free ride because she is able to spend her husband's entire paycheck.

This man is perpetuating the ills feminism was created to end, by keeping these three women from growing up and standing on their own feet "without sexual privilege or excuse," with "self- respect, courage, strength," with "spirit, courage, independence determination...strength of character," "assuming true equality with men," "learning to stand alone," "launch[ing] forth, as men do, amid real, independent stormy life" doing "the work

20. Weitzman, p. 161.

[they] are capable of, [which] is the mark of maturity," accepting the hard but necessary truth that "freedom is a frightening thing...frightening to grow up finally and be free of passive dependence."[21]

Here is another of Dr. Weitzman's cases:

On the other hand, consider how the present system may provide a windfall for a second spouse while unjustly depriving the first. At age 58, a corporate vice president falls in love with his secretary and decides to divorce his wife of 34 years. (The two children of this marriage already have families of their own.) Aside from a substantial home the major assets of this marriage are in the husband's career, in generous company benefits (including full medical, hospital and life insurance and an excellent retirement program) and executive perks (a luxurious car, a large expense account, investment options and extensive travel at company expense). His secretary, who is 28 at the time of the marriage, has two young children whom the executive agrees to adopt. If, let us say, the executive has a heart attack the following year and dies suddenly, in most states, a third to a half of his estate would go to his new wife, with the remainder divided among the four children (two from his last marriage and his new wife's two children). His first wife will receive nothing—neither survivors' insurance nor a survivor's pension nor a share of the estate—and both she and his natural children are likely to feel that they have been treated unjustly. A legal rule that would allow some weighted apportionment between the two wives would seem more just.[22]

Such a rule would defeat the whole purpose of feminism and reinstate the "patriarchal image of woman as dependent on man"— the idea that a woman "needs a man to support her." It would deny to women the privilege of standing on their own feet "without sexual privilege or excuse," "with self-respect, courage,

---

21. *The Feminine Mystique*, pp. 346, 92, 38, 127, 134, 387.
22. Weitzman, pp. 161f.

strength," et cetera. It would turn the clock of feminist progress back a quarter of a century and revert to the ills of the old system—with the principal difference that patriarchal marriage, which formerly gave wives security, has now become so destabilized that the security no longer exists. The original feminist complaint was that "society asks so little of women."[23] The new demand is that an ex-wife should retain her free ride even after divorce has emancipated her from the performance of that "little."

Dr. Weitzman sees no social value in the executive adopting his second wife's two children. In discussions of divorce, it is common to hear much about "the best interests of the children"; but such concern for children gets expressed only when the children are attached to Mom—when it is the rights or advantages of a man, not those of a woman, which a court or a lawmaker wants a pretext to ignore. Why shouldn't the man who earns the money and the perks be permitted to be magnanimous with them for the purpose of benefiting his second wife's children? For what better purpose could his money be spent? Dr. Weitzman would like to imply that the money and perks are not really earned by the man but accrue to him by virtue of his ex-wife's previous ministrations or are created out of nothing by lawmakers, lawyers and divorce court judges, whose generosity is generosity with the money of someone else, always male.

In this case, the best interests of the children are very well served by this wealthy gentleman—and also by the good sense of the young secretary who invests *her* assets—including her youth and attractiveness—in a new marriage, thereby becoming "assets of a *marriage*" in the fullest sense of the word, assets promoting the welfare of her husband, her children and herself. If the first wife has lost similar assets, this is principally the consequence of the weakening of the institution of marriage, a weakening, let it be remembered, which it has been one of the chief objects of feminists to bring about. Much is written in feminist literature about the predicament of divorced women, but nowhere in that literature is there expressed a wish to help women avoid this predicament in the only way most of them can be helped—by

---

23. *The Feminine Mystique*, p. 338.

strengthening the contract of marriage. Dr. Weitzman would like to transfer some of the man's assets to the first wife; but her proposal (strengthening divorce as an alternative to marriage) would have the effect of further weakening all marriages and creating more cases like that of the first wife for whom she is concerned. (She loads the case by making the executive wealthy. Her principle, once established, would be applied to wealthy and non-wealthy alike, with the consequence that few divorced men could afford to re-marry—or would be worth re-marrying.)

Dr. Weitzman describes the scenario as a "windfall" for the second wife, the word suggesting that her marriage to a wealthy man is the result of chance, while the loss of this wealth to the first wife is "unjust." Chance had no place in the decision of either the second wife or the man. The plea that the first wife is unjustly treated has a justification only on the supposition that she had a *right* to expect marriage to be a stable institution. Neither Dr. Weitzman nor any other feminist desires the stabilization of marriage. What they do desire is for the benefits of marriage to be replaced by comparable benefits from divorce— in the present case by giving the first wife, who has withdrawn her services from the marriage, an unearned windfall at the expense of the ex-husband and his second wife, who perform valuable services for each other and who are therefore the ones entitled to enjoy the assets of the only *marriage* which exists, their own.

Dr. Weitzman's proposals for transferring the earnings and pensions and bank accounts and insurance programs and real estate and annuities and stocks and bonds of ex-husbands to ex-wives would lead men to take all sorts of socially undesirable self-defensive measures—squirreling money into coffee cans, renting rather than buying a home, opening a secret bank account in the Cayman Islands, reducing or liquefying attachable assets, minimizing take-home pay—so that the wife would have fewer incentives for divorce. The possession of assets such as these formerly promoted marital and social stability. Dr. Weitzman, by offering them, or a moiety of them, as rewards to divorcing wives, is making them into de-stabilizers of marriage—in effect de-motivating men from creating the wealth she covets. A husband who creates such wealth and acquires such assets under the threat Dr. Weitzman is holding over his head is simply buying insecurity for himself.

Dr. Weitzman makes much of the fact that a middle-aged divorced woman is economically disadvantaged. Her greatest economic disadvantage by far is the burden of child custody, which should indeed be taken from her and placed upon the father, for everyone's benefit, especially the children's. With this burden removed she might still claim to be disadvantaged in the sense that she has less work experience and fewer vocational skills and will accordingly probably earn less than the ex-husband. But her needs are less than his, especially if he has custody of the children. She is not going to have a second family, as he may have—and as wise social policy might well encourage him to have. She has only herself to provide for. Affluence will not make her more attractive to most prospective second husbands: a man contemplating marriage with a woman cares very little how much money she has. A woman contemplating marriage with a man is primarily concerned with his ability to provide for her.[24] In particular, a middle-aged ex-husband will need an attractive bank account and stock portfolio if he hopes to be taken seriously by a prospective second wife, for without these she would prefer a younger man. He may need to finance the rearing and college education of children yet unborn—and society might well encourage him to do so, for there are few more socially useful ways for him to spend his money. A second family would enhance his motivations, his wealth-creation, and his social stability in a way that subsidizing an ex-wife would never

---

24. Vance Packard, *The Sexual Wilderness: The Contemporary Upheaval in Male-Female Relationships* (New York: David McKay Company, 1968), p. 268: "Overwhelmingly the women saw the man's role as being that of 'breadwinner.' This was mentioned by nearly nine out of ten wives, and two-thirds of all the wives put it in first place. The second most-mentioned role of the man of the house was 'father,' which again suggested responsibilities rather than any interpersonal relationships with the 'mother.' In third place in terms of mentions was the man's role as 'husband.' Altogether, somewhat less than half of all the wives thought to mention the husband at all. And only one in eight thought the man's role as husband deserved to be ranked as first in importance. The wives, then, saw, the husband primarily as a supplier of income for the home..."

Practically the entire text of Dr. Weitzman's book could be cited as proving the same thing--that women aren't nearly as much interested in men and marriage as in men's paychecks, and that the paycheck of an ex-husband is every bit as good as the paycheck of a husband.

do. Dr. Weitzman, by creating "rules that require (rather than allow) judges to redistribute the husband's post-divorce income with the goal of equalizing the standards of living in the two households,"[25] would penalize the man and his second wife and their children and society itself by making the man into an under-motivated, rather than a highly motivated, worker in order to provide a free ride for the woman whom Betty Friedan, in *The Feminine Mystique*, sought to salvage from a life of meaningless parasitism.

Dr. Weitzman perceives the family in terms of what Vance Packard calls "the Peripheral-Husband Marriage":

> [H]e is a bystander. He is economically useful but stands outside the basic family unit as perceived by his wife. This basic unit consists of herself, *her* children, and *her* home."[26]

The problem of the feminist movement, as Dr. Weitzman articulates it, is to use the Motherhood Card and the Mutilated Beggar argument to get that peripheral male out of the home without losing his paycheck. The problem of patriarchal society and of the men's rights movement is to ensure that this separation of a man from his paycheck and his family does not occur.

Dr. Weitzman's concern is with the economics of divorce and how it disadvantages women and children. It does indeed. A minority of the elitist women addressed by Betty Friedan's *Feminine Mystique* have achieved the cherished goal of economic independence from men, though few of these women have children. For large numbers of women the skyrocketing divorce rate has meant independence at the price of poverty or near-poverty. Dr. Weitzman's book is a storehouse of data proving to the hilt that children would be economically better off in the custody of fathers rather than mothers.

But important as the economic argument for father custody is, it is less important than the greater likelihood of delinquency imposed on the children by mother custody, a fact alluded to earlier. A recent study of 25,000 incarcerated juveniles made by

---

25. P. 380.
26. *The Sexual Wilderness*, p. 267.

the Bureau of Justice Statistics indicates that 72 percent of them came from broken homes (read: mostly female-headed homes). 74 percent of the nation's children live with two parents, 26 percent with one parent (read: Mom). In other words, 74 percent, coming from intact homes, produce only 28 percent of the juvenile crime; 26 percent, coming from mostly female-headed homes, produce a staggering 72 percent of the crime. The ratios of delinquency probability in the two groups can thus be stated numerically by dividing the size of the group by the proportion of the delinquency it generates. 72 divided by 26 for the female headed group gives 2.76; 28 divided by 74 for the intact group gives .378. The ratio of the delinquency generated by the two groups is thus 2.76 divided by .378, or 7.3. If the findings of this study are to be trusted *a child growing up in a single-parent home (usually female-headed) is seven times as likely to be delinquent.*[27]

The delinquency may be greater than the statistic suggests. According to the *Los Angeles Times*, "Researchers found that many of the young adult offenders had criminal histories that were just as extensive as those of adults in state prisons."[28] In other words, when the careers of these youngsters have become as long as the careers of older criminals, they will have committed far more crimes.[29]

---

27. Statistics from *Los Angeles Times*, 19 September, 1988. See Annex to Chapter I, p. 216.
28. *Ibid.*
29. The expression "single-parent home" lumps fatherless homes together with motherless homes and suggests they are equally likely to generate delinquency. This is untrue. If you ask the boys' vice principal of your local high school, the man concerned with discipline problems, who the troublemakers are, he will tell you they are boys from fatherless homes. (The girls' vice principal will tell you about the problems--especially the sexual ones--of the girls from fatherless homes.) Those from motherless homes are not a problem. Readers desirous of seeing documentation for this will find it in the third and fourth chapters of my *Back to Patriarchy*.

IX

Hypergamy

For years IBM has run a magazine ad showing two pairs of colored infant booties, pink and blue, with the question "GUESS WHICH ONE WILL GROW UP TO BE THE ENGINEER." Underneath there is this:

As things stand now, it doesn't take much of a guess.
Because by and large, *he* is encouraged to excel in math and science. *She* isn't.
Whatever the reason for this discrepancy, the cost to society is enormous because it affects women's career choices and limits the contributions they might make.
Only 4% of all engineers are women.
Only 13.6% of all math and science Ph.D.'s are women. An encouraging, but still low, 26% of all computer professionals are women.
In the past ten years, IBM has supported more than 90 programs designed to strengthen women's skills in these and other areas. This support includes small grants for pre-college programs in engineering, major grants for science programs at leading women's colleges, and grants for doctoral fellowships in physics, computer science, mathematics, chemistry, engineering, and materials science. We intend to continue supporting programs like these.
Because we all have a lot to gain with men and women on equal footing.

IBM

What IBM thinks of as the promotion of equality is better understood as the undermining of hypergamy, one of the pillars of the patriarchal system. Hypergamy, or the "marriage gradient," means that women "marry up," men "marry down." A cinder girl may hope to marry Prince Charming, but a chimney sweep cannot hope to marry Princess Charming. A male doctor might well marry a female nurse, but a female doctor would hardly consider marrying a male nurse. The female nurse may be underpaid, but in the marriage market her prospects are better than those of the female doctor because there are more desirable males she can hope to "marry up" to.

The social implications of the IBM program may be suggested by asking some other questions concerning the possessors of the blue and pink booties:

GUESS WHICH ONE IS TWENTY-FOUR TIMES MORE LIKELY TO END UP IN JAIL.

GUESS WHICH ONE IS MORE LIKELY TO END UP ON SKID ROW.

GUESS WHICH ONE IS MORE LIKELY TO COMMIT SUICIDE.

GUESS WHICH ONE IS MORE LIKELY TO EXPERIENCE A CRIPPLING ACCIDENT, TO BECOME AN ALCOHOLIC, A DRUG-ADDICT.

IBM's question implies that society's arrangements tilt in favor of males. The fact is that society's arrangements produce more male winners *and more male losers.* One principal reason for the success of the male winners is the knowledge that they might be losers: they must earn their success and are motivated to earn it partly by the greater risk of failure. IBM proposes to intervene in society's arrangements to *confer* benefits on females which will increase the number of female winners without increasing the number of female losers. What will increase is the number of male losers, since the male engineers will be competing not only with each other but with females enjoying a conferred advantage denied to males. Another question:

> WHICH ONE WILL BE PRIVILEGED TO ATTAIN
> STATUS BY MARRIAGE AND WHICH ONE WILL
> HAVE TO EARN IT FOR HIMSELF/HERSELF BY
> WORK AND SELF-DISCIPLINE?

With IBM interfering with "market forces" this question might have to be re-worded: "attain status by marriage *or by IBM's largess.*" As IBM offers women more status, marriage has less to offer them—men have less to offer them. Men's marriageability is decreased because they have relatively less to offer women; women's marriageability is decreased because they have fewer men to "marry up" to. As IBM transfers status from those more dependent on work and self-discipline to those less dependent on work and self-discipline, men will become less motivated, since the rewards for work and self-discipline are reduced. The effect, though at a higher level of income, will be what is observable in the ghetto, where women enjoying the handouts of the welfare bureaucracy, become economically and status-wise independent of men, with the consequence that large numbers of men become de-motivated and less marriageable.

Two more questions:

> WHICH ONE IS MORE LIKELY TO DIVORCE
> HIS/HER SPOUSE?

> WHICH ONE WILL HAVE HIS/HER LIKELIHOOD
> OF DIVORCE INCREASED BY A FACTOR OF FIVE
> IF HE/SHE IS EDUCATED AND ECONOMICALLY
> INDEPENDENT?

The consequences of IBM's favors to females can be found on page 42 of Nickles and Ashcraft's *The Coming Matriarchy*:

> [Those women] who work prefer smaller families, and
> fewer children means more time to devote to personal
> and nondomestic interests. Our survey revealed that
> the working woman not only prefers a smaller family

but, in fact, fewer have children. Only 61 percent of the working women we surveyed had children, compared with 85 percent of the nonworking women....Our survey also showed that working women have less successful marriages....[A] woman who works was *five times* as likely to have a disrupted marriage as one who did not work....[W]orking wives are more than twice as likely as housewives to have had affairs by the time they reach their late thirties....Researchers have found that the longer a wife is employed, the more both partners think about divorce—an increase of one percentage point for each year of her employment. Things get worse as she earns more money. Vassar economist Shirley Johnson calculated that every $1,000 increase in a wife's earnings increases her chance for divorce by 2 percent....These working women, who earn $20,000-plus, are the most likely of all women to be separated or divorced.[1]

According to research by three Yale sociologists, "women wed to less-educated or younger men had marital dissolution rates at least 50% greater than those marrying similarly educated or older men. Better-educated husbands brought no increased risk to the marriage....[2]

Writing of high-achieving executive women, Edith Gilson says:

When we turn to our women's private lives, we see more reasons for distress. Surely, some of their careerfrustrations could be offset by the emotional support of husbands and children...but for a startling number of the women, marriage and children are comforts they live without. According to this study, the odds that an executive woman will never marry are four times greater than for the average American woman. Only 5 percent of most women age thirty and up have never wed (the 1985 Census), whereas 21 percent of our executive women have never been brides.

1. Elizabeth Nickles and Laura Ashcraft, *The Common Matriarchy: How Women Will Gain the Balance of Power* (New York: Seaview Books, 1981), pp. 42f.; cf. pp. 105f.; emphasis in original.
2. *Wall Street Journal,* 5 September, 1989.

Even if our women do marry, the probability of their divorcing is twice as great as the norm. Thirty percent are currently divorced, and another 10 percent are on second or third marriages. Forty percent of all our women have therefore been divorced—compared with just 20 percent of most women in their same age range.

The differences between our women and their male peers are even more striking. Less than half (48 percent) of our women are currently married—compared with a whopping 96 percent of executive men....What's more, just 11 percent of the men have been divorced, compared with nearly four times as many of our women.

Many of the women I interviewed felt that men couldn't handle being married to women as or more successful then they. "Here we've gone and sweat blood to become independent, to become women the men can have intelligent conversations with—and they don't want us!" lamented Laura, the pretty magazine editor.[3]

A man's friends would never congratulate him for "marrying up." They would make jokes about his eligibility for membership in the Dennis Thatcher Society, an organization "honoring" the husband of the British Prime Minister. On the other hand, one of the most damning things a woman's friends can say of her (behind her back, naturally) is "Margaret married beneath herself."

Let's project IBM's program into the future. Let's suppose the wearers of the blue and pink booties grow up and both become engineers. Then:

WHICH ENGINEER IS MORE LIKELY TO BE CHILDLESS?

IF BOTH MARRY, WHICH IS LIKELY TO HAVE MORE CHILDREN WHO WILL BENEFIT FROM HIS/HER SUPERIOR EDUCATION?

3. Edith Gilson with Susan Kane, *Unnecessary Choices: The Hidden Life of the Executive Woman* (New York: William Morrow, 1987), p. 62.

Virginia Woolf thought as IBM thinks: families would make great sacrifices to educate their sons, few sacrifices to educate their daughters. She failed to understand the reason: education enables sons to have families, to provide for wives and children who would benefit from the sons' education economically and by the transmission of the knowledge and the values embodied in the education. Educating daughters does not enable them to provide for husbands, and greatly decreases likelihood of their having stable marriages. The birthrate of educated women is far lower than the birthrate of educated men. (Ms. Woolf herself was childless, as are most feminists.) What Bernard Lentz says of professional men and women of the period 1890-1940 is true of other eras:

> Even for the "superperformers" [the most successful professional women]...marriage still led to diminished success, resentment, and a distracting tension in their personal lives. In contrast, men at this time found marriage had numerous advantages in their climb up the professional hierarchy....[4]

Ergo, society has a greater interest in encouraging and furthering the education of males. Educating a boy enables him to have and to support a family, to give children an advantage in life, to transmit family values and strengthen the patriarchy, to create social stability. Educating a girl enables her to escape marriage, or if she marries, to escape childbearing or to have a smaller family. Education, which increases her independence, will enable her more easily to expel her husband and inflict upon her offspring (whose custody is virtually guaranteed her) the disadvantages accompanying fatherlessness. Feminists see these options as desirable, but why should IBM or the rest of us see them as desirable?

---

4. Review in *Academe*, Nov/Dec, 1987 of Penina Migdal Glazer and Miriam Slater's *Unequal Colleagues: The Entrance of Women into the Professions, 1890-1940* (New Brunswick, N.J.: Rutgers University Press, 1987).

Hypergamy worked the same way four thousand years ago. Feminist Dr. Elise Boulding writes of "Urbanization, the Rise of the State and the New Conditions for Women" in the second millennium B. C.:

> What I have been describing is certainly not "equality" for women. Military action became increasingly important throughout the second millennium, and each new arms levy, each new conscription of soldiers, and each new round of booty brought home from a successful war, would enhance the power differential between women and men of the elite. The women's access to the new resources was far more limited than that of men. Power was shared, but not shared equally.[5]

Not shared equally—meaning that the women didn't share equally with the *victorious* males, the males who took the risks and endured the ardors of military life and *earned* the booty. How much of the booty was earned by the women? None, and that is why they were lesser sharers. For every victorious male there was a defeated male who lost the booty and perhaps his freedom or his life. Dr. Boulding makes no comparison between women and these male losers—just as feminists see themselves discriminated against by the absence of women in the Senate and the upper echelons of corporate power and the engineering profession, but choose not to notice that there is a similar absence of women in prison and on Skid Row. IBM's question, carried back four millennia, would be: "Which one is more likely to earn booty?" Another relevant question would be: "Which one is more likely to have booty conferred upon him/her?" IBM's implied argument is: Since men are more likely to earn benefits, women deserve to have more benefits conferred upon them.

Feminist-economist Dr. Barbara Bergmann offers a little paradigm-story about Pink People and Blue People earning their living by picking berries on an island. Like women and men in our own society the Pinks and Blues have sex-segregated occupations. Dr. Bergmann thus illustrates "the crucial point":

---

5. Elise Boulding, *The Underside of History: A View of Women Through Time* (Boulder, Colorado: Westview Press, 1976), p. 211.

If a group is segregated and furthermore is crowded into a relatively narrow segment of labor-market turf, its members will as a result be less productive, and their economic rewards will be lower.[6]

(It is a sufficient refutation of this to point out that Senators are a segregated group occupying a narrow segment of the labor-market turf, but they do not suffer from low economic rewards.)
She continues:

The line of argument will be made clearer if we resort to a simplified example. Consider an island inhabited by the two tribes of people, the Pinks and the Blues, both of whom make their living gathering berries....If all gatherers were allowed to range over the whole island, individual gatherers' yields would vary with their talent, energy, and luck. Given our assumption that the two tribes have equal average talents, the average yield per gatherer would be the same in both tribes.

However, suppose the island's territory was partitioned between the tribes, so that gatherers were allowed to pick berries only in the territory assigned to their tribe. Were each tribe assigned a share of the territory about proportional to its size, and of equal average quality per acre, then again the yield per gatherer in the two tribes should be about the same. However, suppose the Blue tribe were to be assigned exclusive possession or a disproportionately large share of territory. In that case, the work of members of the Blue tribe would on average bring in a greater yield than the work of members of the Pink tribe. If the land the Blue tribe got was higher in quality than the Pink's, the Pink tribe's disadvantage would be greater still.

Dr. Bergmann's Blues like to imagine they don't discriminate against the Pinks:

---

6. *The Economic Emergence of Women* (New York: Basic Books, 1986), p. 128.

The way things are arranged on our mythical island, no
one says to a Pink worker, "Because you are a Pink, we
will see to it that you get less than a Blue." The
mechanism that arranges for Pinks to get less is a set of
rules about who may work where. As long as everyone
follows the rules and all hands keep to their place, the
Pinks will average less production per person than the
Blues and will take home less "pay" for their efforts.

The restriction of the Pinks to a relatively small
territory reduces the efficiency of labor on the island as
a whole. The total number of berries picked on the island
would rise were the territorial restrictions on the Pinks
to be relaxed. If some Pinks were allowed into the Blues'
territory, it would relieve the overcrowding in the Pinks'
part of the island.

The assumption is that there is a labor shortage—one in high
status occupations—never an unemployment problem.

If a boatload of social scientists were to visit the island
portrayed in our example, they might hear from theore-
ticians belonging to the Blue tribe that its success was a
sign of innately superior talent and greater attention to
business. They might also hear that all Pinks voluntar-
ily restricted themselves to their own territory. If,
however, these social scientists observed the segregation of the two tribes, the relative devices used to keep
Pinks from infiltrating Blue territory, they might very
well conclude that the inequality of rewards was connected to the exclusion of Pinks from the Blues' territory.

What they would notice, if the Blues and Pinks resembled
men and women, is the greater aggression and motivation of the
Blues—and that the island society had organized itself to utilize
this greater aggression and motivation. Dr. Bergmann alludes
to African societies which fail to do this:

There are certain societies in Africa where women do all
of the heavy agricultural work, all of the business deal-
ings, and all of the work of family care. The men are at

leisure full time. In such a society, presumably no tasks are unsuitable for women. The designation of some jobs as unsuitable for women in any particular society is a matter of social convention rather than a reflection of women's inherent disabilities or inborn dislikes for certain kinds of work. People's ideas about suitability can and do change when the economy changes.[7]

The problem is the waste of *men's* talents. Would Dr. Bergmann care to live in such a society? The jobs are equally available to men and women, but the men will not take them and therefore the society fails to thrive. There is no reason for men to work and create wealth to make themselves attractive to women because women work for themselves and because sex is unregulated and available to men without their having to work.[8] The goals of feminism have been achieved—and society remains at the level of the Stone Age.

If men cannot outperform women they will not perform at all, and society will be lucky if male energies are merely wasted in narcissistic display rather than in disruptive violence and machismo. A man with nothing to offer a woman save a paycheck the size of her own is impossibly disadvantaged. He will know, and his wife will know that he knows, that the words "I don't need you, Mister" are always at her disposal and, thanks to the anti-male bias of the divorce court, she has an authority in the family greater than his own.

Patriarchal capitalism prospers because it creates an arena of work wherein males are allowed to succeed and create wealth and where they are *motivated* to do so and rewarded for doing so by the satisfactions of family living.

---

7. Bergman, p. 37.

8. The amotivation of males in such societies is thus described by Rousseau: "Being confined to the purely physical aspect of love, and fortunate in being ignorant of those preferences which irritate the passions and increase the difficulties in the way of their satisfaction, savage men must needs feel less frequently and less powerfully than we do the ardours of temperament; and consequently disputes amongst them are less frequent and less cruel. Imagination, which plays havoc amongst ourselves, has no power over the mind of the savage; each awaits peacefully the impulse of nature, yields to it without exercising choice, with more pleasure than fury, and, the need being satisfied, all desire is extinguished." (J. J. Rousseau, "Discours sur l'origine de l'inegalite parmi les hommes," *Oeuvres completes*, vol. i, p. 548; quoted in Robert Briffault, *The Mothers* (New York: Macmillan, 1927), II, p. 141.

The key idea of the alternative matriarchal/feminist system is thus stated by Faye Wattleton, President of Planned Parenthood:

> Together we can work to achieve the most important goal of Planned Parenthood—*to give all people the right and the ability to decide for themselves whether and when to bear children.*[9]

All people signifies all female people. Wattleton demands the right of all female people to deny to all male people any reproductive decision-making:

> I believe that no *woman*, black or white, rich or poor, can ever truly be free without the right to control her own reproductive life. [Emphasis added]

Ms. Wattleton's pitch for "reproductive rights" and Dr. Bergmann's pitch for taking better jobs away from men to confer them on women come to the same thing: men are excluded from meaningful participation in reproduction. Men become superfluous members of families. The basis of civilized society is that men shall share equally in reproductive decision-making, and shall earn the right to do so by working. The program of feminism is to deny men this right by undermining the sexual constitution, the Legitimacy Principle, marriage and the family. When they talk about women's reproductive rights and about making women economically independent of men, this is what they mean.

.   .

---

9. From a letter circulated by Planned Parenthood, November, 1986.

X

Our Paychecks, Our Selves:
Why Fathers Must Demand Custody

Short of total annihilation, there can be no more fundamental change in a society than the one taking place in ours, a change which has no name and whose nature is unrecognized because its separate facets—crime, delinquency, drugs, sexual anarchy, educational underachievement, family breakdown, feminism— are perceived as separate problems, or as not problems at all, but progress. The essence of the change is the abandonment of the system of social organization based on male kinship and the reversion to the older system of social organization based on female kinship. The statistics which measure this change inch upward only one or two percentage points a year, but viewed historically it is happening with electrifying speed.

What makes it possible is the sexual de-regulation of women, with (in the words of feminist Helen Colton) "no man, be it husband or physician, telling [a woman] what she may or may not do with her own body."[1] The idea strikes at the basis of the patriarchal system, which requires that males shall share equally in reproductive responsibility. Patriarchy achieves this sharing by imposing the system of *agnation*, kinship through males, in place of kinship through females such as is found in the ghettos, the islands of the Caribbean and surviving Stone Age societies.

What men must do to salvage the male kinship system is to safeguard the male paycheck—to prevent anyone, ex-wife, house male judge or house male lawmaker, from telling him what he may or may not do with that paycheck, and that if he enters into a contract of marriage to share that paycheck with a wife in exchange for her sharing of her reproductive life with him, this contract shall not be abrogated for the purpose of depriving him of his children and his paycheck.

---

1. Helen Colton, *Sex After the Sexual Revolution* (New York: Association Press, 1972), p. 235.

Early Roman society was divided into the *plebeians*, meaning "the people" (the base of the word survives in *plebiscite*, a vote of the people), and the *patricians*, the "father-people" (from *patri*, father), a term which can have come into existence only in a society where mother-kinship was normative and idea of kinship based on fatherhood was an innovation. The success of the innovation made Roman government, law and civilization possible. The patricians were wealthier, more stable; and in time the plebeians saw the advantages of father-kinship, which became the norm for all of Roman society. Learning how to govern their families on patriarchal principles made the Romans capable of governing the world.

The social structure based on mother-kinship is found in relatively pure form in Haiti—the most impoverished, most squalid, most matriarchal nation in the Western Hemisphere.[2] Haitian women enjoy the sexual liberation Ms. Colton covets for American women: the typical Haitian woman has children by three different fathers, none of whom, needless to say, has a family in any meaningful sense of the word,[3] none of whom, needless to say, can be motivated to work very hard.

Poverty is the hallmark of societies (or areas within societies) based on female kinship. When the complaint is made that the rich get richer and the poor get poorer, what is meant is that patriarchal families get richer and female-headed families get poorer. Feminist agitprop calls this "the feminization of poverty" and tries to combat it with the Mutilated Beggar argument, or with affirmative action and comparable worth programs and quotas favoring women.

---

2. Also the most ecologically devastated. Ecofeminists like to portray ecological spoliation as resulting from the ruthlessness of capitalist patriarchy. Aerial photographs show Haiti, once heavily forested, to be surrounded by oceans made brown by erosion of the soil from that happy matriarchy.

3. *Los Angeles Times*, 1 June, 1989. "Sexual promiscuity," says the *Times*, "has been almost a way of life in Haiti." It is estimated that there will be over a million AIDS cases there by the year 2005.

"Port-au-Prince," writes Joan Chittister, "is a cesspool. The poor are everywhere; the streets are gullies and the buildings are in various stages of collapse...The people are free only to starve...Cardboard shacks lined mud paths barely more than a car-width wide. Children, literally thousands of them, played in the mud and dirt...Starving dogs move slowly among the children...Crowds gathered quickly, all young men and boys, pushing and asking for money, candy, pens, eyeglasses. Anything at all." ("The Anguish of Haiti," in *The Witness*, January, 1990.)

As indicated in Chapter I, the wrecking of the patriarchal system is obscured by two facts: the generation-long time-lag between cause and effect and the sex-switch between generations. Let's illustrate. In 1980 crime increased by a startling 17 percent. Los Angeles Police Chief Daryl Gates was flabbergasted; nothing in the economy, he said, could explain it. What did explain it was the huge increase in divorce and illegitimacy in the mid-1960s. Back then nobody paid much attention. The children from the newly created female-headed families didn't walk out of the divorce courtroom and start committing crimes. But by the early 1980s the fatherless kids were entering the crime-prone years, 14-24, and the skies were darkening with clouds of chickens coming home to roost.

Nothing has been done to lessen crime since then because nothing has been done to prevent the family breakdown and illegitimacy which underlie it: men are excluded from responsible participation in reproduction more effectively than ever. The number of incarcerated prisoners is today almost double what it was in 1980. The prisoners are nearly all male, a fact dwelt upon lingeringly in feminist literature, which likes to contrast the dangerous violence of the male with the harmless gentleness of the female. Feminist literature passes silently over the fact that three-quarters of the male prisoners grew up in female-headed households.

The necessity of regulating female sexuality in order to create the stable families which ensure male participation in reproduction was the discovery made by our wise ancestors who created the patriarchal system several thousand years ago—following the million year prehistorical coma of the Stone Age, during which society was matrilineal—built on female kinship (and female promiscuity), the arrangement to which we are now reverting.

Dr. Gerda Lerner has been quoted in Chapter II, describing the means employed to impose the patriarchal system in the times of Hammurabi (18th century B.C.). Under Hammurabi's law code, "the wife enjoyed considerable and specified rights in marriage" but was sexually her husband's "property."[4] She was

---

4. Gerda Lerner, *The Creation of Patriarchy* (New York: Oxford University Press, 1986), p. 114.

sexually regulated by the Babylonian state, which understood, as our society does not, the necessity for such regulation.

Hammurabi's legislation *benefited women.* The woman's willingness—or in the absence of her willingness, her obligation—to submit to sexual regulation gave her the bargaining power to claim the "considerable and specified rights in marriage" Dr. Lerner alludes to. It enabled her to offer a man something he very much wanted—a stable family and legitimate children—something he could not obtain from a sexually unregulated female.

Betty Friedan's 1963 book *The Feminine Mystique* told American housewives that the "considerable rights" they obtained through marriage were an overpayment for the trifling services they performed: "Society asks so little of women....It was not that too much was asked of them but too little."[5] Ms. Friedan had no understanding of the pivotal fact that the "little" asked of women was not housework but submission to sexual regulation. The male's reproductive marginality forced him to offer the female the extremely one-sided bargain upon which Ms. Friedan poured her scorn. The benefits of this bargain are being lost to men because women will not keep the marriage contract and the courts will not enforce it. They are being largely lost to women by their insistence on sexual autonomy and their consequent withdrawal of sexual loyalty from the nuclear family, which then ceases to provide what Ms. Friedan deemed a free ride for woman.. With that withdrawal they can no longer offer men what men must have if they are to participate responsibly in reproduction.

From the feminists' point of view subsidization by an ex-husband is as good as subsidization by a husband. From the man's point of view the difference is total. The husband who works to support his family works to secure his own role and to stabilize the civilization made possible by patriarchy. When he works to subsidize his ex-wife he is undermining the institution of the family and the patriarchy of which his ex- family was once a part—working (under compulsion of the legal system) to wreck civilized society rather than stabilize it. He is an unwitting and

---

5. Betty Friedan, *The Feminine Mystique* (New York: W. W. Norton, 1963), 338, 252.

unwilling (but helpless) recruit in the warfare of the ages, that between matriliny and patriliny, pressed into service to fight for the enemy, matriliny.

Betty Friedan has suggested that the feminist movement is a new biological breakthrough, "the next step in human evolution"[6]:

> Lately, I've been thinking that the ultimate implications of the women's movement are more profound than we dare realize.[7]

> I think [the family] is just evolving to new forms. Otherwise, like the dinosaur, it would become extinct.[8]

> ...these phenomena of changing sex roles of both men and women are a massive, evolutionary development....[9]

> Evolution itself...seems to be moving in what might be called a "feminine" direction.[10]

The feminist/sexual revolution is not a breakthrough but a throwback. The breakthrough was the creation of patriarchy a few thousand years ago, since when the primary business of society has been to maintain patriarchy by stabilizing the male role within the family, a role now being undermined by the enforced subsidization of ex-wives by ex-husbands—in other words the enforced subsidizing of matriliny with money formerly (and properly) used to subsidize patriarchy.

Feminists protest against the double standard required by the regulation of female sexuality. The double standard is an essential part of the patriarchal system. Male sexuality requires less regulation because it is less important. Male unchastity sets a bad example and demoralizes wives who find out about it, but otherwise damages society little. Female unchastity destroys the marriage contract, the family, the legitimacy of children,

---

6. *The Feminine Mystique* (New York: W. W. Norton, 1963), p. 378.

7. *It Changed My Life* (New York: Random House, 1976), p. 290.

8. *Ibid.*, p. 323.

9. *The Second Stage* (New York: Summit Books, 1981), p. 142.

10. *Ibid.*, p. 246.

their patriarchal socialization, the security of property and the motivation of work—destroys civilized society.

(Men accept a double *work* standard, requiring them to be more dependable, more committed to their jobs, willing to accept more arduous and dangerous labor and to exercise more self-discipline—the things which account for their earning more than women in the job market.)

A man who wants a woman to marry him would get nowhere by telling her, "If you will marry me, I will guarantee that you will be the mother of your children." He is offering her nothing, since it is impossible that she should not be the mother of her own children. A woman who wants a man to marry her would be talking sense if she said to him, "If you will marry me, I will guarantee that you will be the father of my children"—talking sense, though her personal guarantee is insufficient, because women notoriously change their minds, because the Promiscuity Principle claims for women the right to renege on their promise of sexual loyalty, and because the legal system supports this right. In the words of Mary Ann Glendon, the duty of an exiled ex-husband "to provide for the needs of [his] minor children [in Mom's custody]...is so important that it cannot be excluded by contract.[11] In other words, the woman's promise is worthless and the law will grant the man no rights under the contract of marriage. A century ago John Stuart Mill wrote "They are by law *his* children." Today they are by law *hers* and the man can do nothing about it—and nothing to protect the paycheck which he earns and she claims by a biological right which "cannot be excluded by contract." If men consent to this spoilation, the patriarchal system is doomed. The only salvation is to get the legal system to understand that it must support the man's right to have a family and deny the woman's right to wreck it at her pleasure. In other words, it must regulate female sexuality—or rather allow the father to regulate it by allowing him control over his own paycheck, a control not subject to revocation by a divorce court.

This hated double standard places a burden on women, but rewards them lavishly for accepting it. It gives them the

---

11. Mary Ann Glendon, *Abortion and Divorce in Western Law: American Failures, European Challenges* (Cambridge, MA: Harvard University Press, 1987), p. 94.

bargaining power which makes men willing to raise their standard of living by an estimated 73 percent.[12] Female sexual autonomy forfeits this bargaining power; legal regulation of women (enforced by a guarantee of father-custody in divorce) maintains it. Feminist books are written about the unwillingness of men to "make a commitment" to support women and about the unmarriageability of educated and economically independent women, those with the highest divorce rate. These women would be beneficiaries of sexual regulation, which would make them non-threatening to men and therefore marriageable. Their superior education and talents—often combined with superior personal attractiveness—would become assets to themselves, to their families and to society if there existed an assurance that these assets did not act, as they now commonly do, as incentives to divorce.[13]

Would it not be fairer to regulate both male and female sexuality with equal strictness? No; male sexuality isn't important enough. If ninety percent of male sexuality were regulated the unregulated ten percent would create as much sexual confusion and illegitimacy as the ninety percent—if females were unregulated. The regulation of ninety percent of female sexuality would, on the contrary, prevent ninety percent of sexual confusion and illegitimacy, and that is why society must insist on the double standard, which both stabilizes society and gives women greater bargaining power because it makes them more valuable to their families and to society. The woman's chastity gives the man assurance of a secure role within this family, gives the woman a higher standard of living. This is the complementariness which makes patriarchal civilization possible. The arrangement is now being destroyed by the removal of the man's assurance of a secure role within his family.

The feminist/sexual revolution and the betrayal of the family by the legal system are the two chief causes of this destruction of the family and (a generation later) the skyrocketing of crime, second-generation illegitimacy and other social pathology. Other causes are the social acceptance of non-family groupings as

---

12. See Chapter VIII.
13. See the quotation from Nickles and Ashcraft, Chaper II. Page 13.

"families"; the abandonment of the idea of marriage as a legal contract; the abolishing of the distinction between "good" and "bad" women; the consequent abolishing of the distinction between responsible and recreational sex; the acceptance of Screwtape's view that marriage is less important than a storm of emotion called "being in love";[14] the creation of reverse-rites-of-passage to prevent the transition to adulthood (e.g., trial marriage, Esalen-type group therapy in which participants break down and have a happy cry when they learn that self-discipline is not required of them); the alliance of sexual anarchists in academe and the media with feminists and other anti-patriarchal, anti-social groups; the sentimental chivalry of lawmakers; the feminist-legal attempt to make divorce into a viable alternative to marriage (for women); improved computerized techniques for extorting child support money from ex-husbands, techniques which make divorce attractive to women and marriage unattractive to men; the lowered status given to maternal functions and the higher status given to career-elitism for women; the increasing education (albeit diluted education) of women; their growing economic independence; the growth of the Backup System (welfare, day care programs, etc.); sex miseducation of children, including pre-adolescent children, who are robbed of their latency stage and pressured into premature preoccupation with sexuality; the censorship of facts and ideas unpalatable to feminists—and the placing of feminists in positions in bureaucracies and the media where they can exercise this censorship; the qualitative erosion of education since the 1960s, including the creation of Mickey Mouse programs such as Women's Studies; the abolition of shame, guilt and field direction (doing what everyone else does) as social controls (illustrated, e.g., by actresses flaunting their illegitimate children as status symbols); the inversion of "cultural flow" (in dress, hair

---

14. Demon Screwtape writes to Demon Wormwood that "humans who have not the gift of continence can be deterred from seeking marriage as a solution because they do not find themselves 'in love,' and, thanks to us [demons], the idea of marrying with any other motive seems to them low and cynical. Yes, they think that. They regard the intention of loyalty to a partnership for mutual help, for the preservation of chastity, and for the transmission of life, as something lower than a storm of emotion." (C.S. Lewis, *The Screwtape Letters* [New York: Macmillan, 1961], pp. 83f.

style, music, ideas, language), formerly from the higher ranks of society to the lower, now from the lower to the higher....And so forth.

Small wonder feminists and sexual anarchists celebrate the demise of the family and the restoration of matriliny and promiscuity.

They inform us that the word "family" refers to many different groupings, of which the nuclear, patriarchal family is merely one, not the best. Mary Jo Bane writes what is intended to be a reassuring book arguing that "American families are here to stay....Americans seem deeply committed to the notion that families are the best places to raise children." But her reassurance is based on the fact that "the proportion of children living *with at least one parent*" has not declined.[15] Ms. Bane has no comprehension of what is taking place: it is the one-parent (read: female-headed) family that is destroying the real family and reinstating matriliny.

The Hirschensohn case illustrates the manner in which the patriarchal system is being undermined. Michael Hirschensohn, a Santa Monica businessman committed adultery with one Carole D., wife of (though separated from) Gerald D., their adultery resulting in the birth of a girl named Victoria born in May, 1981. The paternity of Hirschensohn is established by blood tests said to be 98 percent reliable. Some time after the birth of Victoria, Carole D. and Gerald D. reconciled and moved from California to New York. Hirschensohn, upset over losing contact with Victoria, filed a lawsuit, which eventually reached the Supreme Court, demanding the right, which he says has been unfairly denied him, to prove his paternity in court, asserting "I think I'm entitled to see my daughter....I'm not asking to be treated other than like a divorced father."

The existing law states that the woman's husband must be presumed to be the child's father, a legal rule-of-thumb intended to strengthen families and avoid custody battles. Hirschensohn's lawyer, Joel Aaronson, says the state's rule is old fashioned and outdated and fails to take into account recent changes in the American family.[16]

---

15. Mary Jo Bane, *Here to Stay: American Families in the Twentieth Century* (New York: Basic Books, 1976), p. 70; emphasis added.

16. Details from the *Los Angeles Times*, 1 March, 1988.

What Hirschensohn is demanding is the right to proclaim his daughter a bastard, the right to confuse her concerning her social and family identity, the right to advertise to Gerald D.'s relatives and neighbors and the public that Gerald D. is a cuckold and his wife an adulteress, the right, based upon his status as an adulterer, to perpetually intrude himself into Gerald D.'s household for purposes of visitation, to embarrass and humiliate and weaken the family bonds between Gerald D. and his wife and daughter, the right to deny to Gerald D. *his* right, which would be unquestioned with respect to non-adulterers, of protecting his home and family from the intrusion of people he doesn't want to associate with.

Hirschensohn says he is only asking to be treated like a divorced father, which is to say he is only asking the courts to declare that marriage confers no rights on *husbands.* He says that the current law, holding Victoria to be legitimate, fails to take into account "recent changes in the American family." The recent changes referred to are those which replace the Legitimacy Principle by the Promiscuity Principle, and its corollary, the denial to men of any right to procreate and possess legitimate children under the contract of marriage.

That the Supreme Court would even consent to hear such a claim is a dereliction on the part of the profession whose responsibility ought to be the safeguarding of the family but which has instead become the principal agent of the family's destruction.

According to Michael L. Oddenino of the National Council for Children's Rights, Inc., who supports Hirschensohn, "modern society has essentially redefined our notion of the family unit."[17] Indeed it has, and that is why we have a Garbage Generation.

Hirschensohn and Carole D. are offenders against sexual law-and-order who have brought suffering to Gerald D. and Victoria (and of course themselves) and have worked to undermine the institution of marriage and the stability of society. But the worst villains are the practitioners of the legal system and the propagandists of the feminist/sexual revolution and its Promiscuity Principle. The Promiscuity Principle assured Carole D. that she alone was entitled to make decisions concerning her

---

17. *Los Angeles Times,* 5 March, 1987.

reproductive activity; and her believing this, combined with the Supreme Court's willingness to consider the claimed right of an adulterer to perpetually intrude himself into the privacy of another man's family, have already worked to weaken Victoria's perception of her social and familial identity—her legitimacy. The patriarchal system and the Legitimacy Principle would have given the girl reassurance concerning these things by maintaining the fatherhood of the man whom she called father, who functioned as her father, who was the husband of her mother and who provided for the family of which Victoria was a member—Gerald D.

No more. "Modern society has essentially redefined our notion of the family unit"; "A woman has a sacred right to control her own sexuality"; and "There is no such thing as an illegitimate child." If Victoria spends her life thinking otherwise, thinking that there are illegitimate children and that she is one of them, she can thank the unchastity of her mother, the chutzpah of Hirschensohn and the weakness and lack of cognitive skill of the justices of the Supreme Court in making it a matter of controversy whether the rights conferred upon Gerald D. by marriage and the Legitimacy Principle are as meaningful and socially desirable as the rights conferred upon Carole D. by the Promiscuity Principle and the rights conferred upon Hirschensohn by adultery.

"Divorce," says Bishop John Spong, "has become part of the cost that society must pay for the emancipation of women."[18] The cost would be too high even if the emancipation were a desideratum. It is the responsibility of society not to emancipate women but to regulate them (and men too, of course) in order that reproduction may take place within families, in order that children may be legitimate and may be socialized according to patriarchal principles, in order than men may be motivated to work and create the wealth and social stability which make civilization possible, in order that property may be secure and may be securely transmitted to the following generation.

---

18. John Spong. *Living In Sin? A Bishop Rethinks Human Sexuality* (San Francisco. Harper and Row, 1988). p. 64.

"In non-industrial societies," says the homosexual agitator Arthur Evans,

> prostitutes are often treated with great religious re-
> spect, and their activities are considered as religious
> activities....[T]he ritual worship of sex and nature was
> once the case throughout the world, and still is in the
> societies that industrialized academics call "primitive."[19]

That's why the societies are "primitive" and "non- industrial"; sex for these people is recreational and nothing else; they haven't figured out how to regulate it and put it to work. "In the ancient Middle East," says Evans,

> the land of Canaan, later invaded by the Israelites, was
> originally peopled by a society where Gay male prostitu-
> tion was very prominent. These prostitutes were located
> in the temples. As with medieval witches, men and
> women who impersonated sexual deities were literally
> thought to become them, and having sex with these
> people was viewed as the highest and most tangible form
> of religious communion with the deity.[20]

So they thought. That is why the Bible denounced Canaanite worship as "whoring after strange gods" and why W. Robertson Smith described it as "horrible orgies of unrestrained sensuality, of which we no longer dare to speak in unveiled words."[21] "In these societies," says Evans,

> as in the case of the witches, women and Gay men
> generally enjoyed a high status, Gay people of both sexes
> were looked upon with religious awe, and sexual acts of
> every possible kind were associated with the most holy
> forms of religious expression. Admittedly, there were
> also great diversities and variations in the beliefs and

---

19. Arthur Evans, *Witchcraft and the Gay Counterculture* (Boston: Fag Rag Books, 1978), pp. 110f.
20. P. 110.
21. W. Robertson Smith, *The Old Testament in the Jewish Church* (London: A. and C. Black, 1892), p. 350.

practices of these societies, but there was one great common feature that set them off in sharp distinction to the Christian/industrial tradition: their love of sexuality.[22]

Meaning their love of horrible orgies of unrestrained sensuality of which we no longer dare to speak in unveiled words. Evans contrasts this sexual chaos with the patriarchal system. In patriarchy, he says,

Sex itself is locked up in secrecy, privacy, darkness, embarrassment, and guilt. That's how the industrial system manages to keep it under control. Among nature peoples, as we have seen, sex is part of the public religion and education of the tribes. It becomes a collective celebration of the powers that hold the universe together. Its purpose is its own pleasure. Any group of people with such practices and values can never be dominated by industrial institutions.[23]

Right. They cannot be integrated into civilized society because they will not accept sexual law-and-order. Anyone who attends a rock concert or reads the classified ads in a homosexual publication must be confronted by the thought that our society is becoming just such a "nature people" as Evans describes, partly because it has stopped using "embarrassment and guilt" to regulate sexuality,[24] mostly because the legal system, created to maintain and stabilize families, is now busily working to destroy them and (mindlessly, to be sure) to restore matriliny.

It is judges who create most female-headed households, the breeding places of the next generation's crime, illegitimacy, demoralization, and poverty. They deprive households of their male breadwinners and then expect these displaced breadwinners to make compensation for the damage *they* have inflicted.

"The property which every man has in his own labor," says Adam Smith,

---

22. P. 111.
23. P. 130.
24. Shame and guilt are two of the most effective and humane regulators of behavior. It is a common error to suppose that because they are unpleasant emotions they are bad things.

as it is the original foundation of all other property, so it is the most sacred and inviolable. The patrimony of a poor man lies in the strength and dexterity of his hands; and to hinder him from employing this strength and dexterity in what manner he thinks proper without injury to his neighbor, is a plain violation of this most sacred property.[25]

The extortion of child support money from ex-husbands constitutes an obvious violation of this "most sacred property," and men ought to resist it.

Many wives couldn't afford to throw their breadwinners out if the displaced breadwinners didn't pay them to do so. A father who sends his ex-wife child support money is subsidizing the destruction of his own family. He is perpetuating the system of child-support-extortion which has wrecked tens of millions of other men's families. He is paying to have his children placed in a female-headed household where they are several times more likely to be impoverished and delinquent and demoralized and neurotic and underachieving and sickly and sexually confused and drug-addicted.[26]

The father's paycheck is the stabilizer of marriage. Wives, as pointed out in Chapter VIII, overwhelmingly consider a husband's primary function to be that of breadwinner.[27] The legal system has adopted the feminist view that an ex-husband should perform the same breadwinning functions, a notion which is placing the two-parent family and the entire patriarchal system at risk. Dr. Lenore Weitzman thinks the divorce court should try "to maintain the standard of living that prevailed during the marriage and, insofar as practicable, to place the parties in the financial position in which they would have been had their marriage not broken down."[28] In other words, she thinks the

---

25. Adam Smith, *An Inquiry into the Nature and Causes of the Wealth of Nations* (New York: P. F. Collier and Son, 1901; original publication, 1776), p. 197; emphasis added.

26. The evidence is given in the Annex to Chapter I.

27. See Vance Packard, *The Sexual Wilderness*, quoted in Chapter VIII, note 24.

28. Lenore Weitzman, *The Divorce Revolution* (New York: The Free Press, 1985), p. 194.

purpose of the twin institution of marriage-cum-divorce is to take everything from the man and give everything to the woman—to strap the man into a milking-machine forever.[29]

This forced labor for the benefit of another person—which differs in no essential and no particular from slavery[30]—is illegal but judges impose it anyway because they figure the American male is so docile he will submit, and because it is what he has always done in the past and what all other judges do—like mindless caterpillars following one another around the rim of a saucer, each supposing he is doing the right thing because he is doing what the others do, what he has always done in the past. They cannot see that the rise in the divorce rate from a few thousand in the mid-19th century to a mind-numbing fifty percent today has altered the nature of divorce from a tragedy affecting isolated members of society to a program for abolishing patriarchy and returning to matriliny. They cannot see that the main reason for this rise in the divorce rate is the certainty of wives that the anti-male bias of the divorce court is absolutely dependable.

The present divorce debacle is created by combining the Sanctity-of-Motherhood principle with the Mutilated Beggar principle. In the typical case Mom divorces Dad knowing that the court will assign custody on the Sanctity-of-Motherhood principle, allowing her to drag the kids into risk of poverty and delinquency and exploit their predicament to extort money from Dad. "It is already established," writes Mary Ann Glendon,

> That there is a legal duty to provide for the needs of one's minor children, that this duty must be shared fairly between both parents, and that the duty is so important that it cannot be excluded by contract. What has to be

---

29. Even the cadaver of the ex-husband must be made to pay. According to Susan Ross:

You should make special arrangements for the life insurance to insure that there will be a viable policy to cover alimony and child support if your husband [read: ex-husband] should die. (Susan Ross, *The Rights of Women: The Basic ACLU Guide to Women's Rights* (New York: Avon Books, 1973), p. 221.)

30. Correction: Slaves get something in exchange for the enforced labor exacted from them--food, clothing, shelter. Ex-husbands get nothing.

made more specific and forceful is that in divorces of couples minor children, this duty must be given the *foremost* consideration.[31]

In other words, the marriage contract confers no rights on fathers, only obligations. Mom plays the Motherhood Card and the legal system straightway becomes her willing handmaiden, transferring her children from the patriarchal system to the matriarchal system where their increased chances of poverty and delinquency make them better Mutilated Beggars.

Dr. Glendon intends that, even without the Mutilated Beggars, Mom should be rewarded by Dad "to compensate, so far as possible, for the disparity which the disruption of the marriage creates in the conditions of their respective lives."[32] The compensation, says Dr. Glendon,

depends on the establishment of the fact of a disparity between the situations of the ex-spouses, and its aim is to enable both of them to liver under approximately equivalent material conditions.[33]

Why *should* they live under approximately equivalent material conditions? Why should there *not* be a disparity in their material conditions if the man *earns* his standard of living and if the woman does *not* earn hers and if she *withdraws* the reciprocal services which during marriage justified her sharing his? Why should she be compensated for what she does not earn? The feminist movement began by Ms. Friedan heaping scorn on the parasitic wives who performed only minimal services in exchange for a virtually free ride. Why should a parasitic ex-wife receive a wholly free ride for performing no services at all? What happened to Ms. Friedan's rhetoric about women needing to gain self-respect by standing on their own feet and facing life's challenges "without sexual favor of excuse"?[34]

---

31. Mary Ann Glendon, *Abortion and Divorce in Western Law: American Failures, European Challenges* (Cambridge, MA: Harvard University Press), p. 94; emphasis in original.

32. *Ibid.*, p. 84, quoting from the French code.

33. Mary Ann Glendon, *The Transformation of Family Law: State, Law, and the Family in the United States and Western Europe* (Chicago: University of Chicago Press, 1989), p. 210.

34. *The Feminine Mystique*, p. 346.

The "disparity" between the man's and the woman's earnings is the principal reason most woman marry their husbands in the first place.[35] Dr. Glendon would make it an inducement for women to divorce them. She would make the male earnings which were once (and properly) a means of strengthening marriage into a means of weakening and destroying it. If the woman can simply take the man's money, the man cannot *offer* it to her—he has lost his bargaining power, and with it his motivation to earn the income she covets. The patriarchal system is based on putting sex and the family (not sex-deprivation and the ex-family) to work as motivators of male achievement. Dr. Glendon's "compensatory payment" for divorce wrecks the system.

It is a tiresomely reiterated demand of feminists that society should get rid of the stereotype of a woman as being dependent upon a man, on the grounds that such dependence is degrading to the woman and unjustifiably burdensome to the man. Women, they insist, must make themselves economically independent and stand on their own feet.

They don't mean it. They are liars who feel protected because men are reluctant to call women liars. The expectation that husbands shall provide economic support for wives is justified by the husband's marriage vow and by the wife's performance of reciprocal services. Ex-husbands are under no such obligation once wives revoke their marriage vows and withdraw their reciprocal services. If it is (as Betty Friedan and scores of other feminists have insisted) humiliating to wives to be supported by husbands, it is trebly humiliating to ex-wives to be supported by ex-husbands.

The willingness of ex-husbands to pay child support money to ex-wives is comparable to the willingness of blacks in the South a generation ago to sit in the back of the bus. At the time it seemed to natural because everyone did it. When Rosa Parks decided she would no longer submit to this stupid indignity and chose a seat at the front of the bus, segregated seating came to an end. When American men realize not merely the stupidity, but the social destructiveness of subsidizing matriliny, the feminist/sexual revolution will come to an end and patriarchy will be restored.

---

35. See the quotation fromVance Packard, Chapter VIII, note 24.

"Children are entitled to share the standard of living of their higher earning parent," says Dr. Weitzman.[36] Very good; except that Dr. Weitzman has no intention that the children shall share Dad's standard of living unless Mom shares too. Her sharing is presumed to be just because motherhood is sacred, partaking of the divine. "Courts know," says one judge,

> that mother love is a dominant trait in the hearts of the mother, even in the weakest of women. It is of Divine Origin, and in nearly all cases, far exceeds and surpasses the parental affection of the father. Every just man recognizes the fact that minor children need the constant bestowal of the mother's care and love.[37]

Why this divinely-originating mother-love, when left to itself by the absence of a father, inflicts upon children the conditions of the ghettos is a paradox left unaddressed. But it is this divinity-of-motherhood idea that underlies judges' anti-male bias:

> One Idaho court [says Dr. Weitzman] concluded that the preference for the mother "needs no argument to support it because it arises out of the very nature and instincts of motherhood: Nature has ordained it." Similarly, a Florida court declared: "Nature has prepared a mother to bear and rear her young and to perform many services for them and to give them many attentions for which the father is not equipped."[38]

In 1974, the Utah Supreme Court

> "brushed aside" a father's equal protection challenge to a maternal preference custody statute stating that "the contention might have some merit to it in a proper case *if the father was equally gifted in lactation as the mother.*[39]

36. *Los Angeles Times*, 13 October, 1985.
37. Bruce vs. Bruce, 14 Okla. 140, 163, 285, p. 30, 37 (1930); cited in *Father's Forum*, May, 1988.
38. Lenore Weitzman, *The Marriage Contract* (New York: The Free Press, 1981), p. 101.
39. *The Marriage Contract*, p. 103; emphasis in original.

A New Jersey judge spoke of "an inexorable natural force" dictating maternal custody awards. A Maryland judge found

> The so-called preference for the mother as the custodian particularly of younger children is simply a recognition by the law, as well as by the commonality of man, of *the universal verity that the maternal tie is so primordial that it should not lightly be severed or attenuated.*[40]

We pay these dummies fancy salaries to perform this kind of reasoning, which lumps together as "young" any offspring, from a neonate, damp from the womb and groping to suckle from its mother's teat, to a teenage boy capable of committing crimes of violence (and far more likely to commit them if he has no father) or a teenage girl capable of breeding illegitimate children (and far more likely to breed them if she has no father[41]). The judges focus attention on the neonate and overlook the fact that neonates grow into teenagers who don't need Mom's lactating but do need Dad's socializing if they are to become responsible adults.

"Where the young, after birth, are still dependent on the mother," writes feminist Charlotte Perkins Gilman,

> the functions of the one separate living body needing the service of another separate living body, we have the overlapping of personality, the mutual need, which brings with it the essential instinct that holds together these interacting personalities. That instinct we call love. The child must have the mother's breast. The mother's breast must have the child. Therefore, between mother and child was born love, long before fatherhood was anything more than a momentary incident. But the common consciousness, the mutual attraction between mother and child, stopped there absolutely. *It was limited in range to this closest relation; in duration, to the period of infancy.*[42]

---

40. *The Marriage Contract,* pp. 101f.; emphasis in original.
41. See Chapter I and Annex, pages 213ff.and 238ff.
42. Charlotte Perkins Gilman, *Women and Economics: A Study of the Economic Relations Between Men and Women as a Factor in Social Evolution* (New York: Harper and Row, 1966; original publication 1898), pp. 124f.; emphasis added.

Juvenile detention centers[43] are bursting with these "primordial" citizens, thanks to judges' incomprehension of the fact that civilized society needs patriarchal socialization as well as female biology. There is no need for judges to worry about "severing" or "attenuating" Mom's biology. Mom isn't going anywhere—not if Dad has assured custody of his children and assured possession of his paycheck. She isn't going to give up her kids, her role, her status symbols and her meal tickets. Judges suppose they must support the strongest link in the two-parent family, the mother's role, because it is the strongest. They should support the weakest link, the father's role, because it is the weakest. It is by doing this that they support the two-parent family, the patriarchal system and civilization. *It is for the purpose of stabilizing the two-parent family that patriarchal society and the legal system exist.* Mom got along without patriarchal society and the legal system for two hundred million years, but Dad has got to have them, and have them on his side or there will be no two-parent family. The two-parent family isn't "natural." It isn't "biological." It isn't "primordial." It is a cultural creation, artificial, fragile, like civilization itself, both only a few thousand years old. The female-headed family is "natural" and "biological" and "primordial," and that is why it is found in the barnyard and the rain forest and in the ghetto and on Indian reservations and in surviving Stone Age societies. The two-parent family is what makes civilization possible—and vice versa—just as the breakdown of the two-parent family is what makes the ghetto possible—and inevitable. Judges don't understand this and that is why two-parent families are falling apart and why crime and drugs and gangs and illegitimacy are out of control—why there is a Garbage Generation.

"We seem to be in the process of change back to the single-parent method," says feminist Dr. Barbara Bergmann.[44] Right. This is happening in the ghettos because the welfare system

---

43. And of course adult prisons as well. There are now some 900,000 incarcerated prisoners, with 40,000 new ones coming along each year, most of them products of female-headed families.

See Chapter VI, note 23, page 114.

44. Barbara Bergmann, *The Economic Emergence of Women* (New York: Basic Books, 1986), p. 232.

makes male providers superfluous. It is happening in the larger society because judges have no understanding of how patriarchy works—of the fact that it must have the support of the legal system which they are taking away from it. Reversion to the matriliny of the Stone Age is the real program of the feminist/sexual revolution—the abandoning of the social organization based on male kinship and the return to the tribal/matrilineal organization based on female kinship.

As feminist anthropologist Helen Fisher says, men and women are returning to the kind of roles they had on the grasslands of Africa millions of years ago.[45] This is what must be stopped, and the only way to stop it is to guarantee fathers headship of families—by guaranteeing them the custody of their children and the secure possession of their paychecks.

---

45. See Dr. Fisher's fuller remarks, Chapter 1, p. 5.

XI

The Humphrey Principle

After a half dozen years of futile war in Vietnam, with nothing to show for our expenditure of lives, money, prestige and good will, with the entire world wondering whether America had gone mad, the question was put to Vice President Hubert Humphrey, Why not just acknowledge that we made a mistake—that we should just put our soldiers on board ships and bring them home and forget the stupid war?

The Vice President's reply represents the same political wisdom which prevents the solution of the problem of the Garbage Generation:

> We must not look for easy solutions.
> —Hubert H. Humphrey

The application to the problem addressed in the present book is this: If mother-headed homes generate most of our crime, delinquency, illegitimacy, educational failure, drug addiction, infantilism, gang violence, sexual confusion and demoralization—as they demonstrably do—why should not our society adopt policies which make fathers heads of families?

Annex to Chapter 1

CRIME AND DELINQUENCY:

Ramsey Clark, *Crime in America* (New York: Pocket Books, 1970), p. 39: "In federal youth centers nearly all prisoners were convicted of crimes that occurred after the offender dropped out of high school. Three-fourths came from broken homes."

Ibid. p. 123: "Seventy-five per cent of all federal juvenile offenders come from broken homes."

Margaret Wynn, *Fatherless Families: A Study of Families Deprived of a Father by Death, Divorce, Separation or Desertion Before or After Marriage* (New York: London and Maxwell, 1964), p. 147: "The loss of a father increases the risk that a child, and particularly a boy, will become a delinquent by a factor of approximately two."

Betty Friedan, *The Feminine Mystique* (New York: W. W. Norton, 1963), p. 196: "A famous study in Chicago which had seemed to show more mothers of delinquents were working outside the home, turned out to show only that more delinquents come from broken homes."

Education Reporter, December, 1986: "A study by Stanford University's Center for the Study of Youth Development in 1985 indicated that children in single-parent families headed by a mother have higher arrest rates, more disciplinary problems in school, and a greater tendency to smoke and run away from home than do their peers who live with both natural parents—no matter what their income, race, or ethnicity."

Starke Hathaway and Elio Monachesi, *Adolescent Personality and Behavior* (Minneapolis: University of Minnesota Press, 1963), p. 81: "Broken homes do relate to the frequency of delinquency. Further, if a home is broken, a child living with the mother is more likely to be delinquent than one for whom other arrangements are made. In the case of girls, even living with neither parent is less related to higher delinquency than is living with the mother."

Henry B. Biller, *Father, Child and Sex Role* (Lexington, Massachusetts: D. C. Heath and Company, 1971), p. 49: "It is interesting to note that the Gluecks found that both father-absence and mesomorphic physiques were more frequent among delinquents than among nondelinquents [Glueck. S. and Glueck, E., *Unravelling Juvenile Delinquency*. New York: Commonwealth Fund, 1950; *Physique and Delinquency*, New York: Harper and Row, 1956].

Dewey G. Cornell, et al., "Characteristics of Adolescents Charged With Homicide: Review of 72 Cases," *Behavioral Sciences and the Law*, 5, No. 1 [1987], 11-23; epitomized in *The Family in America: New Research*, March, 1988: "In a new study of 72 adolescent murderers and 35 adolescent thieves, researchers from Michigan State University demonstrate that the overwhelming majority of teenage criminals live with only one parent. Fully 75 percent of those charged with homicide had parents who were either divorced or had never been married at all; that number rises to 82 percent of those charged with nonviolent larceny offenses."

Los Angeles Times, 19 September, 1988: "In a grim portrait of youthful offenders, a federal study released Sunday indicated that nearly 39% of the 18,226 juveniles in long-term youth correctional institutions were jailed for violent crimes, and that nearly three out of five used drugs regularly....[According to Steven R. Schlesinger, director of the Bureau of Justice Statistics] 'Almost 43% of the juveniles had been arrested more than five times.'...Researchers found that many of the young adult offenders had criminal histories that were just as extensive as those of adults in state prisons. For example, more than half of the young adults surveyed—as well as a comparable sample of state prisoners—were found to be incarcerated for violent offenses....The report also painted a picture of broken homes and poor education: Nearly 72% of the juveniles interviewed said that they had not grown up with both parents, and more than half said that one of their family members had been imprisoned at least once."

Richard M. Smith and James Walters, "Delinquent and Non- Delinquent Males' Perceptions of Their Fathers," *Adolescence*, 13, 1978, 21-28: "The factors which do distinguish between delinquents and non-delinquents indicate that delinquency is associated with: (a) lack of a warm, loving, supportive relationship with the father; (b) minimal paternal involvement with children; (c) high maternal involvement in the lives of youth; and (d) broken homes. The factors which may serve to insulate youth from delinquency are: (a) a stable, unbroken home, characterized by loving, supportive, parent-child relationships; (b) a father who has a high degree of positive involvement with his son; and (c) a father who provides a stable model for emulation by his male offspring. The evidence reported herein supports that of earlier investigations that fathers appear to be significant contributors to the development of offspring who are capable of adapting and adjusting to society, and that fathers who are involved with their offspring in a warm, friendly, cordial relationship are important in the child's life for the prevention of delinquent behavior."

Los Angeles Times, 3 November, 1985 [Ronald Ward, 15, murderer of two elderly women and a 12 year old child. According to Joseph B. Brown, Jr., Ward's attorney]: "'The hardest thing in this case was that my client's a child and really had no controlling parents. The grandmother who raised him is senile, bless her soul. People oppose abortion and sex education, make no provision to deal with the resulting parentless children, then when these children go ahead and do what can be expected, people want to kill them.'...David Burnett, the circuit judge who presided at the trial, said: 'The tragedy in the Ronald Ward story is he's a victim of a society that allowed him to live in a situation where he had no guidance or control....

"[The senile grandmother's] unmarried daughter, she said, gave her the baby in late 1969, soon after he was born. The daughter 'used to come around once every two years, but then it got to a place where it was only every four or five years.' She hasn't heard from her now in years."

Marilyn Stern, John E. Northman, and Michael R. Van Slyck, "Father Absence and Adolescent 'Problem Behaviors': Alcohol Consumption, Drug Use and Sexual Activity." *Adolescence*, 19, 1984, 301-312: "The absence of the father from the home affects significantly the behavior of adolescents, and results in greater use of alcohol and marijuana and higher rates of sexual activity. The impact of the father's absence from the home is apparently greater on males than on females. The alcohol and marijuana use and sexual activity rates for father-absent males is greater than for any other group. The data underscore the significance of the father as a key figure in the transmission of values and as a role model in the life of the adolescent. In addition, the father may have a stabilizing influence within the family structure....This suggests that the father's presence may serve as a deterrent to more liberal indulgence in alcohol and marijuana use and sexual activity....Father-absent males reported the highest levels of alcohol and marijuana use the sexual activity. This group of adolescents appears to be particularly at-risk for problems associated with the three areas of alcohol, marijuana and sexual activity."

Rachelle J. Canter, "Family Correlates of Male and Female Delinquency," *Criminology*, 20, 1982, 149-167: "Consistent with earlier research, youths from broken homes reported significantly more delinquent behavior than youths from intact homes."

Robert K. Ressler, Ann W. Burgess and John E. Douglas, *Sexual Homicide: Patterns and Motives* (Lexington, Massachusetts: D. C. Heath and Company, 1988), pp. 20f.: "[I]n seventeen cases [out of 36 sexual murders] the biological father left home before the boy reached twelve years. The absence was due to a variety of reasons, such as death or incarceration, but most often the reason was separation and divorce....Given the departure of the father from the family, it is not surprising that the dominant parent to the offender during childhood and adolescence was the mother (for twenty-one cases). Some of the offenders were able to speculate on the meaning this had in their lives, as in the following case:

> The breakup of the family started progressing into somethingI just didn't understand. I always thought families should always be together. I think that was part of the downfall...I said whether I did anything good or bad. They left that totally up to my mom. We'd go out on boats and cycle riding and stuff like that, but when it came down to the serious aspects of parent-child relationship, never anything there from the male side...My brother was eighteen and moved in with my real dad. I was ten and stayed with my mother.

"Only nine murderers said the father was the dominant parent, and two said both parents had shared the parenting role....The low level of attachment among family members is indicated by the murderers' evaluations of the emotional quality of their family relationships. Perhaps the most interesting result was that most offenders said that they did not have a satisfactory relationship with the father and that the relationship with the mother was highly ambivalent in emotional quality."

Ibid., p. 92: "In attempting to explain why Warren committed the murders, the psychiatrist pointed to his background, making the following observations:

"1. Warren grew up in a home where women were in control and men were denigrated.

"2. Warren's traumatic victimization at age twelve by two older girls served to confirm his picture of the world.

"3. Warren's marriage to a woman with four children demonstrates his tendency to empathize more with children than adults and his feelings about mother figures.

"4. The timing of the murders indicated a rekindling of Warren's own childhood fears as a result of the events of pregnancy and childbirth; thus, he perceived it necessary to destroy these women in order to prevent his own destruction.

"5. The mutilation of his victims was an attempt to remove gender identification from his victims and render them nonfemale."

Douglas A. Smith and G. Roger Jarjoura, "Social Structure and Criminal Victimization," *Journal of Research in Crime and Delinquency* 25 [Feb., 1988], 27-52; epitomized in *The Family in America: New Research,* June, 1988: "Criminologists have long used race and poverty as key variables for explaining crime rates. However, researchers at the University of Maryland find that when differences in family structure are taken into account, crime rates run much the same in rich and poor neighborhoods and among black, white, and Hispanic populations. In their study of over 11,000 urban residents of Florida, upstate New York, and Missouri, Professors Douglas A. Smith and G. Roger Jarjoura found that 'the percentage of single-parent households with children between the ages of 12 and 20 is significantly associated with rates of violent crime and burglary.' The UM team points out that 'many studies that find a significant association between racial composition and crime rates have failed to control for community family structure and may mistakenly attribute to racial composition an effect that is actually due to the association between race and family structure.' Drs. Smith and Jarjoura likewise criticize theories that attribute crime to poverty since when family structure is taken into account, 'the effect of poverty on burglary rates becomes insignificant and slightly negative.'

"This new study should dispel illusions about curing the social effects of casual divorce and rampant illegitimacy through government programs that merely alleviate poverty or reduce racial prejudice."

Dr. Lee Salk, *What Every Child Would Like His Parents To Know,* cited in Doug Spangler, "The Crucial Years for Father and Child," *American Baby,* June, 1979: "Research conducted on

children whose fathers were away in the military service revealed that...boys whose fathers were absent during the first
year of life, seemed to have had more behavior difficulties than
would normally have been expected. They seem to have had
more trouble establishing and keeping good relationships, not
only with adults but with other children. Other studies showed
a reasonably close relationship between delinquent behavior in
boys and the absence of an adequate father (male) figure during
childhood."

Henry Biller, *Father, Child and Sex Role* (Lexington, Mass.:
D. C. Heath, 1971), p. 1: "Much of the current interest in the
father's role seems to have been intensified by the growing
awareness of the prevalence of fatherless families and the social,
economic and psychological problems that such families often
encounter. The fatherless family is a source of increasing concern in many industrialized countries."

Ibid., p. 39: "Bacon, Child, and Barry [Bacon, M. K., Child,
I. L. and Barry, H. III, "A Cross-Cultural Study of Correlates of
Crime," *Journal of Abnormal and Social Psychology*, 1963, 66,
291-300] discovered that societies with relatively low father
availability have a higher rate of crime than do societies in which
the father is relatively available. Stephens' data [Stephens, W.
N. "Judgments by Social Workers on Boys and Mothers in
Fatherless Families," *Journal of Genetic Psychology*, 1961, 99, 59-
64] suggest that intense, restrictive mother-child relationships
are more likely to occur in societies in which there is relatively
low father availability in childhood. Close binding mother-child
relationships appear to be negatively related to sexual adjustment in adulthood."

Ibid., p. 66: "Juvenile delinquency can have many different
etiologies, but paternal deprivation is a frequent contributing
factor. Many researchers have noted that father-absence is
more common among delinquent boys than among nondelinquent boys. Studying adolescents, Glueck and Glueck [*Unravelling Juvenile Delinquency*, 1950] reported that more than two-
fifths of the delinquent boys were father-absent as compared

with less than one-fourth of a matched nondelinquent group. McCord, McCord, and Thurber ["Some Effects of Paternal Absence on Male Children," *Journal of Abnormal and Social Psychology,* 1962, 64, 361-369] found that the lower-class father-absent boys in their study committed more felonies than did the father-present group, although the rates of gang delinquency were not different. Gregory I. Gregory, "Anterospective Data Following Child Loss of a Parent: I. Delinquency and High School Dropout," *Archives of General Psychiatry,* 1965, 13, 99-109] referred to a large number of investigations linking father-absence with delinquent behavior and also detected a strong association between these variables in his study of high school students.

"Siegman [A. W., "Father-Absence During Childhood and Antisocial Behavior," *Journal of Abnormal Psychology,* 1966, 254, 71-74] analyzed medical students' responses to a questionnaire concerning their childhood experiences. He compared the responses of students who had been without a father for at least one year during their first four years of life, with those of students who had been continuously father-present. The father absent group admitted to a greater degree of antisocial behavior during childhood. Other researchers relying on self-report procedures have also reported that individuals from fatherless families are more likely to engage in delinquent behavior [F. I. Nye, *Family Relationships and Delinquent Behavior,* New York: Wiley, 1958; W. L. Slocum and C. L. Stone, "Family Culture Patterns and Delinquent Type Behavior," *Marriage and Family Living,* 1963, 25, 202-8]. Anderson [L. M., "Personality Characteristics of Parents of Neurotic, Aggressive, and Normal Preadolescent Boys, *Journal of Consulting and Clinical Psychology,* 1969, 33, 575-81] found that a history of paternal- absence was much more frequent among boys committed to a training school. He discovered that father-absent nondelinquents had a much higher rate of father-substitution (stepfather, father- surrogate, etc.) between the ages of four to seven than did father-absent delinquents.

"Miller [W. B., "Lower-Class Culture as a Generating Milieu of Gang Delinquency," *Journal of Social Issues,* 1958, 14, 5-19] argued that most lower-class boys suffer from paternal deprivation and that their antisocial behavior is often an attempt to prove that they are masculine. Bacon, Child and Barry [Bacon, M. K., Child, I. L. and Barry, H. III, "A Cross-Cultural Study of Correlates of Crime," *Journal of Abnormal and Social Psychology*, 1963, 66, 291-300], in a cross-cultural study, found that father availability was negatively related to the amount of theft and personal crime. Degree of father availability was defined in terms of family structure. Societies with a predominantly monogamous nuclear family structure tended to be rated low in the amount of theft and personal crime, whereas societies with a polygamous mother-child family structure tended to be rated high in both theft and personal crime. Following Miller's hypothesis, Bacon, Child and Barry suggested that such antisocial behavior was a reaction against a female-based household and an attempted assertion of masculinity. A large number of psychiatric referrals with the complaint of aggressive acting-out are made by mothers of preadolescent and adolescent father-absent boys and clinical data suggest that sex-role conflicts are frequent in such boys."

Harvey Kaye, *Male Survival* (New York: Grosset and Dunlap, 1974), p. 155: "Facing economic hardship and a much higher problem of a broken home, brittle family relationships, and an absentee father, the mere struggle for existence becomes a major preoccupation, and the niceties of psychological development may become negligible or coarsened in the process. Growing up deprived also often means growing up with little impulse control. Since the capacity to internalize one's impulses is a prerequisite for progress, handicaps mount. Fragmented families frequently germinate rage-filled children; and rage plus poor impulse control equals confrontation with the law. A sorry case, calling for any bright innovations which a boy's nimble brain can devise."

Patricia Cohen and Judith Brook, "Family Factors Related to the Persistence of Psychopathology in Childhood and Adolescence," *Psychiatry*, Vol. 50, Nov., 1987, p. 344: "One-parent families and families with multiple marital disruptions are apparently unable to mount effective means of counteracting pathological reactions that have developed in their children."

Barry Siegel, *Los Angeles Times*, 3 Nov., 1985: "Most of the young convicts' stories, full of parents who ran off and unguided lives on the streets, evoke pity. Most of their deeds, full of rapes and beatings and murders, evoke horror."

Ross L. Matsueda and Karen Heimer, "Race, Family Structure, and Delinquency: A Test of Differential Association and Social Control Theories," *American Sociological Review*, 52 [Dec., 1987], 826-40; epitomized in *The Family in America: New Research*, March, 1988: "Teenagers from broken homes are much more likely to become delinquents than are teens from intact families, particularly if they are black....Given the family roots of black delinquency, the authors of this new study find it 'not surprising that simplistic policies of rehabilitation and deterrence have failed to stem the tide of rising rates of delinquency.'"

Phyllis Chesler, Mothers on Trial: *The Battle for Children and Custody* (New York: McGraw-Hill, 1986), p. 291: "Who are the women in prison?...More than half are single mothers living on welfare."

Bill Hazlett and David Shaw, *Los Angeles Times*, 31 December, 1972, citing the views of Dr. Chaytor Mason, clinical psychologist at USC: "But many mothers just can't cope with growing boys alone—especially not with growing boys who are already frustrated by the uncertainty of their own masculinity. The boys misbehave, and the mother tells them how bad they are, and the boys, in effect, tell themselves, 'If I'm going to be bad, at least I'm going to be good at it.'"

Tamara Jones, *Los Angeles Times*, 19 December, 1988: "Favoring shaved heads and crisp, military-style clothing, skinheads are thought to have doubled their ranks over the last nine months alone to claim an estimated 2,000 to 3,500 hard core members nationwide. Some even carry business cards with their particular gang's name, post office box number and racist motto....

"'What you have here is not the last, dying remnants of an old problem' says Lenny Ziskind of the Center for Democratic Renewal. 'What we have here is just the embryo of a future problem.'...

"[Eric Anderson, a Yakima, Wash., anthropologist] described the skinheads as ranging from 14 to 27, from largely middle-class neighborhoods and broken, unstable families.

"'Most are dumber than bricks, but some are real sharp,"' Anderson said. 'They're openly trying to recruit all the time, and oftentimes it's runaway kids or punks who are looking for some family unit."

Gary Bauer, "Report to the President from the White House Working Group on the Family," quoted in *Phyllis Schlafly Report,* February, 1988: "A study by Stanford University's Center of the Study of Youth Development in 1985 indicated that children in single-parent families headed by mothers have higher arrest rates, more disciplinary problems in school, and a greater tendency to smoke and run away from home than do their peers who live with both natural parents—no matter what their income, race, or ethnicity."

Margaret Cambric, Executive Director, Jenesse Center, Los Angeles, quoted in *Los Angeles Times,* 27 February, 1988: "When you're dealing with gang activity, you're dealing with the family structure. People don't tend to see it that way....All of it is domestic violence....gang violence stems from the home."

Neal R. Peirce, citing William Haskins, National Urban League Director of Human Services, quoted in *Los Angeles Times,* 30 June, 1982: "[T]here is a strong correlation between the single-parent family and child abuse, truancy, substandard achievement in school and high unemployment and juvenile delinquency. Fatherless boys figure heavily in crimes, according to police officials....Young girls are almost ostracized if they're not ready for sex. Young men won't use [contraceptives]. They say, 'That's a reflection on my manhood.'"

Dr. Carlo Abbruzzese, M. D., FASFP Chairman, Human Rights Commission, M.E.N. International, Box 6185 Santa Ana, CA 92706, unpublished memo: "The Hon. S. L. Vavuris, Judge of the San Francisco Superior Court, stated in open Court that '90 percent of all of the children in trouble are from broken homes' (Loebenstein v. Loebenstein #648527, S. F. Superior Court, July 3, 1974. And Judge Arnason of the Contra-Costa Superior Court, speaking more recently to an 'Equal Rights for Fathers' meeting in Berkeley, CA, said '70 percent of male youth offenders committed to correctional institutions are from divorce-torn homes.'"

Anthony L. Pillay, "Psychological Disturbances in Children of Single Parents," *Psychological Reports,* 61, [October, 1987]: 803-6; excerpted in *The Family in America: New Research,* April, 1988: "Children raised in a single-parent household are much more likely to suffer psychological disturbances and break the law than children from intact families....[Of 147 children taken to a psychological clinic] 89 of them—six out of every ten—came from nonintact families....[C]hildren—both male and female—are more likely to turn to drugs when they have only one parent. But problems are most serious among fatherless boys, who 'exhibited less self-control, delay in gratification, and internalized standards of moral judgement than did boys whose families remained intact,' and were 'more antisocial, impulsive and likely to belong to delinquent groups.' Because 'boys reared without their fathers appear to be substantially disadvantaged' by the 'lack [of] a significant model for sex-appropriate behavior, the current trend in awarding custody almost automatically to mothers' should be reexamined."

Henry Biller and Dennis Meredith, *Father Power* (Garden City, New York: Anchor Books, 1975), p. 341: "People with emotional disorders manifested in criminal behavior are likely to have been inadequately fathered. A study of murderers by Boston psychiatrist Shervert H. Frazier revealed that father absence or brutalization was frequent in the killers' backgrounds. Eighteen of the thirty-one murderers he studied had either suffered father absence for significant periods or had been the subject of repeated violence from the father. Many other histories of assassins and mass murderers suggest that they suffer similar backgrounds of father absence or abuse."

Dr. Bernard Laukenmann, Newsletter of Fathers United for Equal Rights of Baltimore, Maryland, February, 1973: "A memorandum of a rehabilitation program from the Florida Ocean Sciences Institute (compiled in 1970) revealed that 75 percent of the law offenders were from broken homes. Florida's Division of Youth Services acknowledges that this situation is state wide: more than two thirds of the criminal minors that the agency has been handling are from broken homes....Recently a public statement showed that 70 percent of all crimes in the city of Baltimore, Maryland, are committed by juveniles, and of that number 60 percent come from broken homes....Of the 70 percent juvenile criminals out of broken homes [most] live with their divorced, separated or abandoned mother or other female relative. News releases have it that Oswald (J. F. Kennedy's assassin) Sirhan (R. F. Kennedy's assassin), and Bremer (attempted assassin of Gov. Wallace) came from broken homes...."

Urie Bronfenbrenner, "The Psychological Costs of Quality and Equality in Education," *Child Development*, 38 [1967], 914f.: "A growing body of research evidence points to the debilitating effect on personality development in Negro children, particularly males, resulting from the high frequency of father absence in Negro families....In seeking an explanation for this relationship, several of the major investigators have concluded that the exaggerated toughness, aggressiveness, and cruelty of delinquent gangs reflect the desperate effort of males in lower-class culture to rebel against their early overprotective, feminizing environment and to find a masculine identity. For example, Miller [W. B., "Lower Class Culture as a Generating Milieu of Gang Delinquency," *Journal of Social Issues*, 1958, 14, (3), 5-19] analyzes the dynamics of the process in the following terms:

The genesis of the intense concern over "toughness" in lower class culture is probably related to the fact that a predominantly female household, and lack a consistently present male figure with whom to identify and from whom to learn essential components of a "male" role. Since women serve as a primary object of identification during preadolescent years, the almost obsessive lower class concern with "masculinity" probably resembles a type of compulsive reaction-formation....A positive overt evaluation of behavior defined as 'effeminate' would be out of the question for a lower class male."

Ibid., p. 914, quoting T. F. Pettigrew, *A Profile of the Negro American,* 1964, p. 18: "[F]ather-deprived boys are markedly more immature, submissive, dependent, and effeminate than other boys....As they grow older, this passive behavior may continue, but more typically, it is vigorously overcompensated for by exaggerated masculinity. Juvenile gangs, white and Negro, classically act out this pseudo-masculinity with leather jackets, harsh language, and physical 'toughness.'"

William McCord, Joan McCord with Irving Zola, *Origins of Crime: A New Evaluation of the Cambridge-Sommerville Youth Study* New York: Columbia University Press, 1959), p. 169: "The father's personality had an important bearing on criminality. We established that warm fathers and passive fathers produced very few criminals. Paternal absence, cruelty, or neglect, however, tended to produce criminality in a majority of boys."

Ibid., p. 170: "Paternal absence resulted in a relatively high rate of crime, especially in drunkenness."

Robert Zagar, et al., "Developmental and Disruptive Behavior Disorders Among Delinquents," *Journal of the American Academy of Child and Adolescent Psychiatry,* 28 [1989]: 437-440, epitomized in *The Family in America: New Research,* September, 1989: "Psychotic delinquents rarely come from intact families. Officials documented a familiar pattern in a recent survey of almost 2,000 children and adolescents referred by the Circuit

Court of Cook County—Juvenile Division for psychiatric evaluation. This group of troubled children included 84 orphans (4 percent), 1,272 from single-parent homes (65 percent), 269 from stepparent families (14 percent), and just 331 from intact two-parent families (17 percent)."

Francis A. J. Ianni, *The Search for Structure: A Report on American Youth Today* (New York: The Free Press, 1989), pp. 207f.: "Yet in our observations of family life and in interviews we found that many of the members of disruptive groups and almost all of the street-gang members came from broken or severely disturbed and deprived homes....Many were from single-parent families where the mother had been unable or unwilling to establish adequate behavioral controls over her male children....They soon came to be considered rebellious, unruly, even dangerous troublemakers in the school as well as in the community. Welcome and 'understood' only among others like them, they sought out the structure and the often severe strictures of organized deviant peer groups, where fidelity is to the group or gang rather than to family or school."

Ibid., p. 76: "In Green Valley and other rural areas there were also frequent cases of missing fathers, not as much so as in the urban inner city, but with sufficient frequency among the 'old families' that 'not having a man around to straighten out the kids' was a frequent reason cited by criminal justice and social service professionals in the county seat whenever we asked about delinquency, teen pregnancy, or running away."

Robert J. Sampson and W. Byron Groves, "Community Structures and Crime: Testing Social-Disorganization Theory," *American Journal of Sociology*, 94, January, 1989, 774-802, epitomized in *The Family in America: New Research*, May, 1989: "The relationship between crime and family life recently came under the scrutiny of criminologists at the University if Illinois at Urbana—Champaign and the University of Wisconsin—Green Bay. After examining data from hundreds of communities in Great Britain, the researchers concluded that family disruption—either through divorce or illegitimacy—leads to mugging, violence against strangers, auto theft, burglary, and other crimes. The new study establishes a direct statistical link between family disruption and every kind of crime examined except vandalism. In large part, this linkage can be traced to the failure of 'informal social controls' in areas with few intact families. 'Two-parent households,' the authors of the new study explain, 'provide increased supervision and guardianship not only for their own children and household property, but also for general activities in the community. From this perspective, the supervision of peer-group and gang activity is not simply dependent on one child's family, but on a network of collective family control.' Particularly in poor communities bound together by few social ties, 'pronounced family disruption' helps to 'foster street-corner teenage groups, which, in turn, leads to increased delinquency and ultimately to a pattern of adult crime.'"

Bryce J. Christensen, "From Home Life to Prison Life: The Roots of American Crime," *The Family in America*, Vol 3, No. 4 [April, 1989], p.3: "...Professor Sampson established not only that single-parent households are likely targets for crime, but that the *neighbors* of single-parent households are more likely to be hit by crime than the neighbors of two-parent households. He concludes both that 'single-adult households suffer a victimization risk higher than two-adult households' and that 'living in areas characterized by a high proportion of [single- adult] households significantly increases burglary risk' for all types of households."

Ibid., p. 3: "In a 1987 study at the University of Toronto, sociologists noted particularly high rates of delinquency among female teens in two kinds of households: 1) single-parent households; 2) households in which the mother is employed in a career or management position. Maternal employment can affect the criminality of sons, too. 'It's tougher for mothers who are busy earning a living to control their teenage boys,' according to Professor Alfred Blumstein of Carnegie-Mellon University. Criminologist Roger Thompson believes that one of the primary reasons that young boys join gangs is that 'their parents work, and if they didn't have the gang, they'd just have an empty home.'

"But family disruption overshadows maternal employment as a cause of juvenile delinquency. In their landmark study of the problem the Gluecks found a strong correlation between delinquency and parental divorce and separation."

Ibid., p. 4: "[S]ociologists at the University of Washington and Vanderbilt University underscored the importance of the family in determining juvenile delinquency. 'That the family plays a critical role in juvenile delinquency is one of the strongest and most frequently replicated findings among studies of deviance,' write Professors Walter Gove and Robert Crutchfield. In their own examination of some 600 families in Chicago, Drs. Gove and Crutchfield again confirmed that 'boys in single-parent households are much more likely to be delinquent than boys from intact families.'...

"A young male lawbreaker will probably grow even more reckless if he fathers an illegitimate child....Since the sons of single-parent households are almost twice as likely as the sons of two-parent households to become an unwed father, this crime-producing pattern could spiral wider from generation to generation.

"Seedbed for gang activity, the broken home produces many of the nation's most violent young criminals. In a study of 72 adolescent murderers, researchers at Michigan State University found that 75 percent of them had parents who were either divorced or had never married."

Martin Kasindorf, "Keeping Manson Behind Bars," *Los Angeles Times Magazine*, 14 May, 1989: "Charles Manson, born illegitimate in Cincinnati, was placed by an uncaring mother with a series of foster parents. By 1967, he had spent 19 of his 32 years in penal institutions. On parole, Manson gravitated to San Francisco's pulsating Haight-Ashbury district. Through ready administration of LSD and a messianic message, he attracted a virtual harem of adoring women he called his 'young loves,' using offers of sex with them to draw men handy with guns and dune buggies."

Gary L. Cunningham, review of *Manson in His Own Words* by Nuel Emmons, *Los Angeles Times*, 5 July, 1987: "The man who would come to symbolize the end of the '60s and what went wrong with them was born 'no name Maddox.' Unwanted, he was reared with abuse and neglect. His unwed mother eventually gave him to the courts, not because he was unmanageable, but because he was a hindrance to her life style.

....

"It was the spring of 1967, He went to San Francisco.

"There he found a 'convict's dream,' a world of drugs and sex and no rules. In it he sought and found young women who were desperately seeking someone or something to give them acceptance, direction and permission. With the help of drugs, he easily became a kind of fantasy father figure, exchanging unconditional love and binding the women to him. For the first time in his life, Charles Manson had love, acceptance, power and control. And he had a following."

History Book Club Review, September, 1989: "Billy the Kid, age 21, has killed four men personally and he shares the blame for the deaths of five others. He will not see his 22d birthday....Billy the Kid was born Henry McCarty, the son of Catherine McCarty, in New York City in 1859....The first certain record of Billy appears in Santa Fe, New Mexico where Henry McCarty and his brother Joe stood witness at the marriage of their mother Catherine to William Henry Harrison Antrim on March 1, 1873."

Robert Graysmith, *Zodiac* (New York: Berkeley Books, 1987), p. xiii: "After Jack the Ripper and before Son of Sam there is only one name their equal in terror: the deadly, elusive, and mysterious Zodiac. Since 1968 the hooded mass murderer has terrified the city of San Francisco and the Bay Area with a string of brutal killings. Zodiac, in taunting letters sent to the newspapers, has hidden clues to his identity by using cunning ciphers that have defied the greatest codebreaking minds of the CIA, the FBI, and NSA."

....

P. 321:

"PSYCHOLOGICAL PROFILE OF ZODIAC

Paranoid delusions of grandeur.
"Psychotic.
"Sexual sadist: You will find that the Zodiac probably tortured small animals as a child, had a domineering mother, weak or absent father, strong fantasy life, confusion between violence and love, is the type of person who would be a police groupie, carry police equipment in his car, collect weapons and implements of torture."

Los Angeles Times, 8 December, 1989 [describing Marc Lepine, Canadian mass murderer who invaded a University of Montreal classroom, killed 14 women and wounded 13 others before committing suicide]: "Police say his father, whom they believe to be Algerian, left his family when son Marc was 7 years old."

Hans Sebald, *Momism: The Silent Disease of America* (Chicago: Nelson Hall, 1976), pp. 180ff. [concerning the case of Jacques Vasseur, a French collaborator with the Nazis, responsible for the deaths of 230 Frenchmen]: "Jacques's childhood was a classic example of Momistic upbringing: father-absence from the socialization process, an overindulgent mother who catered to every whim of the child, and isolation from other children, neighbors, and potential male models. His mother kept him to herself, gave toys (particularly dolls) for him to play with and provided only one companion for him—herself....After the war ended and French sovereignty was reestablished, he was a hated and hunted criminal....It was not until 1962 that he was discovered; his mother had hid him for seventeen years in a garret above her second-story apartment....Approximately 200 witnesses recited the horrors they had suffered under 'Vasseur the Terror,' recounting how he beat them, tortured them, and condemned their relatives and fiances to death. One witness said he had been bull-whipped for ten hours by Vasseur; a woman testified that he had burned her breasts with a cigarettes; and others told of the mercilessness with which he handed over to the executioners their fathers, brothers, and sisters....The attending psychiatrist...explained to the court that Jacques's subservience to the Gestapo was a transferred attachment from his mother to another powerful agent, that he embraced his grisly duties because he needed the approval of the Mom surrogate, and that his power over other humans gave him the opportunity to express his suppressed virility. The psychiatrist reminded the court that Vasseur still referred to his mother as "my Mummy" and that his greatest suffering during his imprisonment was caused by seeing 'Mummy' only once a week."

A two-hour NBC T.V. program on Jack the Ripper, October 28, 1988, featured two FBI "crime profile" experts, John Douglas and Roy Hazelwood, who profiled Jack the Ripper as a single white male, with difficulty in interacting with people, especially women, of average intelligence, from a broken home, raised by a dominant female figure.

Judge Samuel S. Leibowitz, Senior Judge of Brooklyn criminal court, with A. E. Hotchner, "Nine Words that Can Stop Juvenile Delinquency," *Reader's Digest,* March, 1962; condensed from *This Week,* 15 December, 1957: "What Western country has the lowest juvenile delinquency rate? The answer, based on official reports, is Italy, where only two percent of all sex crimes and one half of one percent of all homicides are committed by children 18 and under. (The comparable figures for the United States are 13 and 9 percent.) But *why* is Italy's delinquency rate so low? For weeks I toured Italian cities, trying to get the answers. I was given remarkable cooperation. Police commissioners, school superintendents, mayors of cities told me what I wanted to know, took me where I wanted to go.
"An important police official wanted to know if it was really true that teen-agers assaulted police in America. I had to tell him it was.
"'Ah, this is very hard for us to believe,' he said. 'No Italian youth would ever lay hands on an officer.'
"A Naples school superintendent asked me if thrill murders are figments of journalists' imaginations. 'No, I informed him, 'they are all too true.'

"'We have no such crimes,' the superintendent said. 'We have the delinquency of stealing, of misbehaving, but boys in this country commit boy wrongs, within the bounds of the boy's world.'

"'But how do you keep the boy there?' I asked. And then I found what I was seeking: a basic, vital element of living that is disappearing in our country and which, to my mind, is the only effective solution to the malady of delinquency. From all parts of Italy, from every official, I received the same answer: *Young people in Italy respect authority.*

"And here is the significant thing: that respect starts in the home—then carries over into the school, the city streets, the courts. I went into Italian homes to see for myself. I found that even in the poorest family the father is respected by the wife and children as its head. He rules with varying degrees of love and tenderness and firmness. His household has rules to live by, and the child who disobeys them is punished. Thus I found the nine-word principle that I think can do more for us than all the committees, ordinances and multimillion-dollar programs combined: *Put Father back at the head of the family.*"

ASSASSINS:

James F. Kirkham, Sheldon G. Levy and William J. Crotty, *Assassination and Political Violence: A Report to the National Commission on the Causes and Prevention of Violence* (New York: Bantam Books, 1970), pp. 65f.: "Although we cannot unravel the significance of the similarities between the assassins, we could make this statement: we could predict after President Kennedy's assassination that the next assassin would probably be short and slight of build, foreign born, and from a broken family—most probably with the father either absent or unresponsive to the child."

Patricia Cayo Sexton, *The Feminized Male* (New York: Random House, 1969), p. 4: "Sirhan and Oswald, both reared under the maternal shadow, grew to be quiet, controlled men and dutiful sons. Estranged from their fellows, fathers, and normal male associations, they joined a rapidly growing breed—the 'feminized male'—whose normal male impulses are suppressed or misshaped by overexposure to feminine norms. Such assassins often pick as their targets the most virile males, symbols of their own manly deprivation. The assassin risks no contest with this virility. His victim is caught defenseless by the sniper's bullet and is unable to strike any blows in self-defense. A cheap victory—no challenger and no risk of defeat. Their desire to get out is simply the natural male impulse to cut maternal ties and become a man. The black revolt is a quest by the black male—whose social impotence has exceeded even that of the white woman—for power, status, and manhood. He does not want to be a 'boy' any longer: *I am a man* is the slogan of his revolt. These rebellions are alarms, alerting us to the social forces that dangerously diminish manhood and spread alienation and violence."

Ibid., p. 67: "David Rothstein, for example, has analyzed twenty-seven inmates of the Medical Center for Federal Prisoners in Springfield, Mo., who had indicated an intention to attack the President. The threatmakers bore similarities to Lee Harvey Oswald. Most came from unhappy homes. They had domineering mothers and weak, ineffectual fathers. Most joined the military service at an early age, yet their experiences proved to be unhappy. Rothstein interprets their actions in threatening the President as the manifestation of a hostility towards their mother redirected against authority symbols—the government and, more specifically, the President."

Dr. Fred B. Chartan, "A Psychiatric History: What Assassins Have in Common," *The Birmingham News,* 7 July, 1968: "The [U.S. presidential] assassins were all men (there has never been a woman political assassin[1]), all loners, and all lacking fathers through death, divorce, work schedule, or at least through a very poor parental relationship. It is also significant that the assassins were either bachelors or did not get along with women."

---

1. This was written before Lynette Fromm and Sara Jane Moore had made their attempts.—D.A.

RAPISTS AND CHILD MOLESTERS:

Michael Petrovich and Donald I. Templer, "Heterosexual Molestation of Children Who Later Became Rapists," Psychological Reports, 1984, 54, 810: "Forty-nine [of 83] (59%) of the rapists had been heterosexually molested. Of these, 12 had been so molested by two or more females for a total of 73 'cases' of heterosexual molestation. In 56 (77%) of these cases, the molesting person did so on more than one occasion. The ages at the time of molestation ranged from 4 to 16 yr.; the ages of the older persons ranged from 16 to 54 yr....Note that in 15 (21%) of the cases the women who molested had a special mission to nurture, counsel or protect."

Los Angeles Times, 16 December, 1986: [According to researchers at North Florida Evaluation and Treatment Center] "The pattern of the child molester is characterized by a singular degree of closeness and attachment to the mother."

Raymond A. Knight and Robert A. Prentky, "The Developmental Antecedents and Adult Adaptations of Rapist Subtypes," *Criminal Justice and Behavior,* Vol 14 [Dec., 1987], 403-26; epitomized in *The Family in America: New Research,* April, 1988: "As families have broken down, rape has become an increasingly frequent crime. That is no coincidence, according to information in a new study. In a recent survey of 108 violent rapists—all of them repeat offenders—researchers found that a sizable majority of 60 percent came from single-parent homes. The authors state that single-parent households account for 60 percent of those rapists described as 'sadistic' and nearly 70 percent of those described as 'exploitative.' Exploitative rapists display 'the most antisocial behavior in adolescence and adulthood,' while the sadists are marked by 'both more aggressive and more deviant sexual activity.' Among rapists motivated by 'displaced anger,' fully 80 percent come from single-parent homes, and over half were foster children."

SUICIDE:

S. C. Bhatia, et al., "High Risk Suicide Factors Across Cultures," *The International Journal of Social Psychiatry*, 33, [1987], 226-236; epitomized in *The Family in America: New Research*, July, 1988: "Weaker family ties are apparently one reason that suicide occurs more frequently in the United States than in India. In a recent analysis, a team of Indian psychiatrists tried to account for the difference between a suicide rate of 12.2 suicides per 100,000 Americans and a rate of only 6.5 suicides per 100,000 per 100,000 Indians. While conceding that the official statistics were unreliable because of underreporting in both countries, the psychiatric team cited 'lack of family and social support' as a primary reason that suicide now ranks eighth among causes of death in America.

The Indian researchers found it particularly striking that while suicide rates run higher among married Indians than among the unmarried, the American pattern is very different, with suicide rates running twice as high among singles as among the married and four to five times as high among the divorced and widowed as among the married."

Evangelos Papathomopoulos *et al.*, "Suicidal Attempts by Ingestion of Various Substances in 2,050 Children and Adolescents in Greece," *Canadian Journal of Psychiatry*, 34, 1989, 205-209; epitomized in *The Family in America: New Research*, November, 1989: "The divorce of parents often pushes teenagers into suicidal despair. In a paper recently presented to the Canadian Psychiataric Association, medical authorities from Greece reported their investigation of suicidal attempts by ingestion of drugs or other chemicals among Greek children and adolescents. In an analysis of 600 such cases, the Greek researchers found that family conflict was the reason for 353 (59 percent) of the attempted suicides."

Professor Victor R. Fuchs, Stanford University, *Los Angeles Times*, 24 October, 1988: "Compared with those of the previous generation, today's children are more than twice as likely to commit suicide, perform worse at school and use much more alcohol and drugs; they are twice as likely to be obese, and show other signs of increased physical, mental and emotional distress. The poverty rate among children (under age 18) is almost double the rate for adults—a situation without precedent in American history....If Americans do not have enough children (the fertility rate has been below replacement level every year since 1973) and if children do not become healthy, well-educated adults, the country's future is bleak, regardless of progress with other issues."

Carmen Noevi Velez and Patricia Cohen, "Suicidal Behavior and Ideation in a Community Sample of Children: Maternal and Youth Reports," *Journal of the American Academy of Child and Adolescent Psychiatry* 273 [1988]: 349-356; epitomized in *The Family in America: New Research,* Sept, 1988: "The latest evidence is found in a new study by psychiatrists at the New York State Psychiatric Institute. Upon surveying 752 families at random, the researchers divided the children into those who had never attempted suicide and those who had done so at least once. The two groups, they found, differed little in age, family income, race, and religion. But those who attempted suicide were 'more likely to live in nonintact family settings than were the nonattempters. More than half of the attempters lived in households with no more than one biological parent, whereas only about a third of the nonattempters lived in such a setting.'"

John S. Wodarski and Pamela Harris, "Adolescent Suicide: A Review of Influences and the Means for Prevention," *Social Work,* 32, No. 6 [November/December, 1987] 477-84; epitomized in *The Family in America,* May, 1988: "The growing incidence of family dissolutions, and the resulting single-parent households along with the attendant life-style, makes childhood a difficult period.' Increasingly, sociological researchers 'view the phe-nomenon of adolescent suicide as a reflection of this turmoil in American families....There is a trend toward devaluation of family and children and an atmosphere that lacks intimacy and affection. Experiences in environments that are nonsupportive and overtly hostile contribute to the development of suicidal personality characteristics.' This view is borne out, [Wodarski and Harris] note, by studies comparing youths who attempt suicide with those who do not. Among those who attempted suicide, 'family disruption and disintegration played a signifi- cant role' with the suicidal often feeling that their mothers were less interested in them than did the non-suicidal."

Lynda W. Warren and C. Tomlinson-Keasey, "The Context of Suicide," *American Journal of Orthopsychiatry,* 57, No. 1 [January, 1987], p. 42; epitomized in *The Family in America: New Research,* May, 1987: "In an in-depth analysis of eight women suicides, Lynda W. Warren and C. Tomlinson-Keasey state that one of their 'most striking findings' is 'the strong influence exerted by mothers, coupled with lack of involvement of fathers in the subjects' lives. Absence of paternal involvement was characteristic of all eight cases....When a parent played a critical role in the subjects' lives, it was the mother who did so.' Drs. Warren and Tomlinson-Keasey stress that 'this finding of a high incidence of early father loss is consistent with previous reports of an association between early father loss and adult depression and suicide.'"

SEXUAL CONFUSION:

Sara S. McLanahan, "Family Structure and Dependency: Reality Transitions to Female Household Headship," *Demogra- phy* 25, Feb., 1988, 1-16: "Daughters from female-headed house- holds are much more likely than daughters from two-parent families to themselves become single parents and to rely on welfare for support as adults....[L]iving with a single mother at age 16 increases a daughter's risk of becoming a household head by 72 percent for whites and 100 percent for blacks. The contrast becomes even sharper if the comparison is between daughters continuously living in two-parent families with daughters living with an unmarried mother *at any time* between ages 12 and 16: 'Exposure to single motherhood at some point during adoles- cence increases the risk [of a daughter's later becoming a household head] by nearly 1-1/2 times for whites and...by about 100 percent for blacks.' The public costs of this differential emerge in figures showing that a daughter living in a single-parent household at any time during adolescence is far more likely (127 percent more likely among whites, 164 percent among blacks) to receive welfare benefits as an adult, compared to daughters from two-parent households."

Brent C. Miller and C. Raymond Bingham, "Family Configuration in Relation to the Sexual Behavior of Female Adolescents," *Journal of Marriage and the Family* 51, 1989, 499-506; epitomized in *The Family in America: New Research,* November, 1989: "Among young women reared in single-parent households, sexual intercourse outside marriage occurs much more often than among young women reared in intact families."

William Marsiglio, "Adolescent Fathers in the United States: Their Initial Living Arrangements, Marital Experience and Educational Outcomes," *Family Planning Perspectives,* 19, November/December, 1987, 240-51; epitomized in *The Family in America: New Research*, May, 1988: "Researchers have known for some time that girls raised in a female-headed household are much more likely to become unwed teen mothers than are girls raised in two-parent families. In a major new study, Professor William Marsiglio of Oberlin College has documented a parallel pattern for unmarried teen fathers. In a survey of more than 5,500 young American men, Dr. Marsiglio found that 'males who had not lived with two parents at age 14 were overrepresented in the subsample of teenage fathers. Only 17 percent of all young men surveyed lived in one-parent households at age 14; yet, among boys who had fathered an illegitimate child as a teenager, almost 30 percent came from single-parent households. In other words, teen boys from one-parent households are almost twice as likely to father a child out of wedlock as teen boys from two-parent families."

Suzanne Southworth and J. Conrad Schwarz, "Post-Divorce Contact, Relationship with Father, and Heterosexual Trust in Female College Students," *American Journal of Orthopsychiatry,* 57, No. 3 [July, 1987], 379-381; epitomized in *The Family in America:New Research,* October, 1987: "In surveying 104 female college students from divorced and intact families, Drs. Suzanne Southworth and J. Conrad Schwarz discover evidence that 'the experience of divorce and its aftermath have long-term effects on young college women's trust in the opposite sex and on their plans for the future.' Particularly, the [University of Connecticut, Stors] team find that 'daughters from divorced homes are more likely to anticipate cohabitation before marriage' than are daughters of intact marriages. Among daughters of intact homes it was found that 'only daughters who had a poor relationship with the father planned to cohabit,' while among daughters of divorced parents 'plans to cohabit were uniformly high and unrelated to the father's acceptance and consistency of love.'"

Single mother quoted in *SMC* (Single Mothers by Choic newsletter), January, 1987: "Most of us were raised by our mothers alone."

Allan C. Carlson, "School Clinics Don't Prevent Pregnancies," *Human Events,* 31 January, 1987: "Researchers have discovered, for instance, that black girls from father-headed families were twice as likely to be 'non-permissive' compared to those from mother-headed units."

Beverly Beyette, *Los Angeles Times,* 10 April, 1986: [Girl mothers at Los Angeles's El Nido Services, a child and youth counseling agency]: "They are rather casual about pregnancy— no, they would not choose *not* to be pregnant. And, no, they do not expect, nor do they want, to marry their babies' fathers. Camilla, a sophomore, said, 'I tell him it isn't his baby so he won't call.'...

"For most girls, counselor Mathews said, 'There's very little awareness of the responsibility—and the consequences. Their mothers become the mothers. And they keep on doing what they're doing.'...

"Almost 70% of the girls lived with their single mothers while pregnant and, both during pregnancy and after the birth of their babies, their parents, welfare and the baby's father were their primary sources of financial support, with welfare the number one source after birth of the baby....

"[Stacy] Banks [project director] said the nature of the problem is somewhat different in South Central, where 'family violence is a big issue' and where the maternal grandmother is commonly the head of household, and often a resentful one. It is not unusual, said Banks, to learn that the grandmother had herself been a teen parent, that she had hoped to go back to school but is now expected to take care of a grandchild while the mother goes to school.

"Sometimes, Davis [Fritzie Davis, project director] said, 'The grandmother is 30 years old. She's asking, 'What's in it for me?' They're angry. They still have needs but don't know how to articulate them.'

"In 1986, social stigma is not the problem. Indeed, Leibowitz [Paul Leibowitz, project director] noted, 'Over 90% have made the decision they're going to keep their babies.'"

Henry B. Biller, *Paternal Deprivation: Family, School, Sexuality, and Society* (Lexington, Mass.: D. C. Heath, 1974), p. 114: "Inappropriate and/or inadequate fathering is a major factor in the development of homosexuality in females as well as in males."

Yuko Matsuhashi et al., "Is Repeat Pregnancy in Adolescents a 'Planned Affair?'" *Journal of Adolescent Health Care,* 10 [1989], 409-412; epitomized in *The Family in America: New Research,* December, 1989: "The [University of California at San Diego] researchers discovered that most of the teen mothers in their study had neither a father nor a husband in their lives. Among the girls pregnant for the first time, only 14 percent lived with both parents; among the girls in a repeat pregnancy, only 2 percent lived with both parents."

Henry B. Biller, *Father, Child and Sex Role* (Lexington, Mass.: D. C. Heath, 1971), p. 47: "Imitation of masculine models is very important. The development of a masculine sex-role adoption, especially in the preschool years, is related to imitation of the father. A young boy's masculinity is positively related to the degree to which his father is available and behaves in a masculine manner (decision making, competence, etc.) in his interaction with his family."

Ibid., p. 58: "A later study with kindergarten boys indicated that father-absent boys had less masculine sex-role orientations and sex-role preferences than did father-present boys, even though the two groups were matched in terms of IQ [Biller, H. B., "Father-Absence, Maternal Encouragement, and Sex- Role Development in Kindergarten Age Boys," *Child Development,* 1969, 40, 539-46]. Also, matching for IQ in a study with junior high school students, we found that boys who became father-absent before the age of five had less masculine self-concepts than father-present boys [Biller, H. B. and Bahm, R. M., "Father-Absence, Perceived Maternal Behavior, and Masculinity of Self-Concept Among Junior High School Boys," *Developmental Psychology,* 1971, 4, 107].

Ibid., p. 71: "The paternally deprived boy's search for a father-figure can often be involved in the development of homosexual relationships. West [West, D. J., "Parental Relationships in Male Homosexuality," *International Journal of Social Psychiatry,* 1959, 5, 85-97] and O'Connor [O'Connor, P. J., "Aetiological Factors in Homosexuality as Seen in R. A. F. Psychiatric Practice," *British Journal of Psychiatry,* 1964, 110, 381-391] found that homosexual males, more often than neurotic males, had histories of long periods of father-absence during childhood. West [D. J., *Homosexuality,* Chicago: Aldine, 1967] reviewed much evidence which indicates that paternal deprivation is a frequent precursor in the development of homosexuality....Difficulty in forming lasting heterosexual relationships often appears to be linked to paternal deprivation."

Henry B. Biller and Richard S. Solomon, *Child Maltreatment and Paternal Deprivation: A Manifesto for Research, Prevention and Treatment* (Lexington, Mass.: D. C. Heath and Company, 1986), p. 140: "Difficulty in forming lasting heterosexual relationships often appears to be linked to father-absence during childhood. Andrews and Christensen's (1951) data suggested that college students whose parents had been divorced were likely to have frequent but unstable courtship relationships....Jacobson and Ryder (1969) did an exploratory interview study with young marrieds who suffered the death of a parent prior to marriage. Death of the husband's father before the son was twelve was associated with a high rate of marital difficulty. Husbands who had been father-absent early in life were described as immature and as lacking interpersonal competence. Participation in 'feminine' domestic endeavors and low sexual activity were commonly reported for this group. In general, their marriages were relatively devoid of closeness and intimacy....Other researchers have reported evidence that individuals who have experienced father-absence because of a broken home in childhood are more likely to have their own marriages end in divorce or separation....Research by Pettigrew (1964) with lower-class blacks is consistent with the supposition that father-absent males frequently have difficulty in their heterosexual relationships. Compared to father-present males, father-absent males were 'more likely to be single or divorced— another manifestation of their disturbed sexual identification' (p. 420)....A great deal of the heterosexual difficulty that many paternally deprived, lower-class males experience is associated with their compulsive rejection of anything they perceive as related to femininity. Proving that they are not homosexual and/ or effeminate is a major preoccupation of many lower-class males. They frequently engage in a Don Juan pattern of behavior, making one conquest after another, and may not form a stable emotional relationship with a female even during marriage. The fear of again being dominated by a female, as they were in childhood, contributes to their continual need to exhibit their masculinity by new conquests. The perception of child rearing as an exclusively feminine endeavor also interferes with their interaction with their children and helps perpetuate the depressing cycle of paternal deprivation in lower-class families....[E]arly father-absence particularly seems to interfere with the development of a secure sex-role orientation."

Ibid., p 147: "There is anthropological evidence suggesting that low father availability in early childhood is associated with later sex-role conflicts for girls as well as for boys....In Jacobson and Ryder's (1969) interview study, many women who had been father-absent as young children complained of difficulties in achieving satisfactory sexual relationships with their husbands....Case studies of father-absent girls are often filled with details of problems concerning interactions with males, particularly in sexual relationships....The father-absent girl often has difficulty in dealing with her aggressive impulses....In a clinical study, Heckel (1963) observed frequent school maladjustment, excessive sexual interest, and social acting-out behavior in five fatherless preadolescent girls. Other investigators have also found a high incidence of delinquent behavior among lower-class father-absent girls....Such acting-out behavior may be a manifestation of frustration associated with the girl's unsuccessful attempts to find a meaningful relationship with an adult male. Father-absence generally increases the probability that a girl will experience difficulties in interpersonal adjustment.

"The devaluation of maleness and masculinity so prevalent in paternally deprived, matrifocal families adversely affects many girls as well as boys."

Ibid., p. 150: "Daughters of divorcees were quite low in self-esteem, but daughters of widows did not differ significantly in their self-image from daughters from father-present homes. nevertheless, both groups of father-absent girls had less feeling of control over their lives and more anxiety than did father-present girls....The daughters of divorcees seemed to have especially troubled heterosexual relationships. They were likely to marry at an earlier age than the other groups and also to be pregnant at the time of marriage. After a brief period of time, some of these women were separated or divorced from their husbands."

Diane Trombetta and Betsy Warren Lebbos, "Co-Parenting: The Best Custody Solution," *Los Angeles Daily Journal,* June 22, 1979, p. 20: "Delinquent girls, and those pregnant out of wedlock, are also more likely to come from broken homes, in most cases meaning father-absent homes. Girls from father-absent homes have been found to engage in more and earlier sexual relationships than father-present girls.

"Insecurity in relating to males has been reported among girls who became father-absent before the age of five....

"Among males, father-absence and resulting maternal dominance has been associated with secondary impotence, homosexuality, alcoholism, and drug abuse."

Neil Kalter, "Long-Term Effects of Divorce on Children: A
Developmental Vulnerability Model," *American Journal of
Orthopsychiatry*, 57 (4), October, 1987: "The weight of evidence
suggests that boys who do not have an ongoing and close
relationship with their fathers are more vulnerable to encoun-
tering difficulties related to the development of a stable and
valued internal sense of masculinity. Problems bearing this
stamp have been associated with boys growing up in post-divorce
households. They include inhibition of assertiveness, deficient
impulse control, and lowered academic performance. Research
and clinical evidence indicate that a boy's identification with
father is the primary vehicle for the internalization of an appropriate sense of masculine identity. Further, it has been suggested that the absence of an appropriate male model for such
identification   leaves a boy open to developing pronounced
feminine identifications which, in most instances, must be
defended against vigorously in adolescence. In sum, the position
of a father in his son's development appears crucial, and disruptions in the father-son relationship have been linked to a multi-
tude of developmental interferences."

Los Angeles Times, 17 October, 1986: "Planned Parenthood
has identified teens at highest risk for becoming pregnant: those
with mothers or sisters who became pregnant while teen-agers,
those reared in single-parent homes, those who do not do well in
school and seek self-esteem elsewhere."

Eleanor J. Bader, *The Guardian*, 1 April, 1987: "'Glamor was
a great reason to have a baby. It works at first. People say "Oh,
that's great." You're famous. Then you're nine months pregnant, waddling around, and after the baby's born they put their
eyes down. You're on your own. After the baby's born the only
one who sticks around is welfare.'
"The woman speaking is 16, Black and angry. She had to
drop out of school, she says, to care for her son, and has to subsist

on less than $400 a month, a sum that is mostly gobbled up by diapers, formula, baby clothes and rent.

"But these dire conditions are not the only reasons for her anger. 'When you're a young mother people look at you like you're bad.'"

Los Angeles Times, 10 April, 1986: "Almost 70% of the girls [teen-aged mothers] lived with their single mothers...."

Susan Newcomer and J. Richard Udry, "Parental Marital Status Effects on Adolescent Sexual Behavior," *Journal of Marriage and the Family*, 49, No. 2 [May, 1987], pp. 235-40; epitomized in The *Family in America: New Research*, August, 1987: "Daughters in one-parent homes are much more likely to engage in premarital sex than are daughters in two-parent homes....Adolescent girls reared without fathers are much more likely to be sexually active than girls raised by two parents. Girls raised in single-parent homes are also much more likely to be involved in 'other age-graded delinquencies' than are girls in two-parent homes....The research team also found that the sexual activity of sons increases markedly when a two-parent home breaks up through divorce or separation."

Los Angeles Times, 16 May,, 1988: "Ed Griffin, planning officer at the [Los Angeles] Housing Authority, said that at the poorest projects, 'a young woman's idea of upward mobility is having a baby and getting her first welfare check from Aid to Families with Dependent Children. Then she leaves her mom's and gets a place of her own—in the project, of course.'"

Bettye Avery, *off our backs*, April, 1986: "Girls who refuse to have sex are accused of being virgins or dykes."

Henry Biller, *Father, Child and Sex Role* (Lexington, Mass.: D. C. Heath and Company, 1971), p. 129: "[P]aternally deprived individuals are overrepresented among individuals with psychological problems."

George A. Rekers, "Inadequate Sex Role Differentiation in Childhood: The Family and Gender Identity Disorders," *The Journal of Family and Culture,* 2, No. 3 [Autumn, 1986], 8-31; epitomized in *The Family in America: New Research,* March, 1987: "...George A. Rekers, professor of neuropsychiatry at the University of South Carolina School of Medicine, reports on the findings of the Gender Research Project he has directed for the National Institute of Mental Health. As part of his research, Dr. Rekers and his colleagues performed comprehensive psychological evaluations of 70 boys suffering from 'gender disturbance,' manifest in 'cross dressing [transvestism]' play with cosmetic articles; "feminine" appearing gestures; avoidance of masculine sex-typed activities; avoidance of male peers; predominant ratio of play with female peers...and taking predominantly female roles in play.'

"Upon examination, 'all 70 of the gender-disturbed boys were found to be normal physically...with the single exception of one boy with one undescended testicle.' However, in assessing the family backgrounds of the 70 boys, Dr. Rekers and his colleagues found 'a consistent picture' of father absence or father neglect:

> In the boys who were classified as the most profoundly disturbed, father absence was observed for all cases. In the remaining *less* disturbed cases father absence was found in 54% of the cases.

Helen Colton, *Sex After the Sexual Revolution* (New York: Association Press, 1972), p. 140: "Next to punishment and guilt, a common reason for premarital pregnancy is the need of the male to prove his masculinity. Reuben Pannor, a social worker at Vista Del Mar Child Care Center in West Los Angeles, author of notable studies on the young unwed father, has found that many of them came from homes that were female-dominated due to death or divorce or because the father had abdicated his responsibility, leaving the son with 'weak or distorted masculine identity.' Such boys often become involved in sexual relationships 'to prove their manhood.'"

Monica Sjoo and Barbara Mor, *The Great Cosmic Mother: Rediscovering the Religion of the Earth* (San Francisco: Harper and Row, 1987), p. 67: "Indeed, the further back one goes in time the more bisexual, or gyndndrous, is the Great Mother. As Charlotte Woolf says in *Love Between Women*, perhaps the present-day Lesbian woman is the closest in character to ancient women—with their fierce insistence on strength, independence, and integrity of consciousness.

"The first love-object for both women and men is the mother; but in patriarchy, the son has to reject the mother to be able to dominate the wife as 'a real man'—and the daughter must betray her for the sake of "submitting to a man." In matriarchal society this double burden of biological and spiritual betrayal does not occur. For both women and men there is a close identification with the collective group of mothers, with Mother Earth, and with the Cosmic Mother. And, as psychoanalysts keep repeating, this identification is conducive to bisexuality in both sexes. But homosexuality in tribal or pagan men was not based on rejection of the Mother, or the female, as is often true in patriarchal culture; rather, it was based on brother-love, brother-affinity, as sons of the mother. And lesbianism among women was not based on a fear and rejection of men, but on the daughter's desire to reestablish union with the Mother, and with her own femaleness."

Itabari Njeri, *Los Angeles Times*, 25 July, 1989: "Perhaps the crucial message in her book [Bebe Moore Campbell's *Sweet Summer*]—one still not fully understood by society, Campbell says—is the importance of a father or a father-figure in a young girl's life.

"'Studies show that girls without that nurturing from a father or surrogate father are likely to grow up with damaged self-esteem and are more likely to have problems with their own adult relationships with men,' Campbell says."

Peter M. Weyrich, *The Human Costs of Divorce: Who Is Paying?* (Washington, D. C.: Free Congress Foundation, 1988), pp.33f., citing George Rekers, "The Formation of a Homosexual Orientation," presented at the Free Congress Foundation "Hope and Homosexuality" Conference, 1987: "Research suggests that in order for boys to develop their masculine identity properly, they need a strong male role model, such as a father (biological or substitute) or an older brother. In 1983, Rekers, Mead, Rosen, and Brigham studied a group of gender-disturbed boys, and found a high incidence of absent fathers. The average age of the boys when they were separated from their fathers was approximately 3.5 years old. Eighty percent were 5 years old or younger when the separation took place, and the reason for the fathers' absence was separation or divorce in 82% of the cases. The male gender disturbances varied from moderate to severe in the study, but those who showed deep gender disturbances had neither a biological father nor a father substitute living at home. Of the fathers who did live at home, 60% were described as psychologically remote or apart from the other members of the family."

Kathleen Fury, "The Troubling Truth About Teen-Agers and Sex," *Reader's Digest,* June, 1980 [Condensed from *Ladies' Home Journal,* March, 1980], pp. 153f.: "Demographers at Johns Hopkins University have found that young, white, teen-age girls living in fatherless families were 60 percent more likely to have had intercourse than those living in two-parent homes."

EDUCATIONAL UNDERACHIEVEMENT

Newsweek, 13 May, 1985: "It is easy enough to spot them, the so-called children of divorce. Often, teachers say, the boys become extremely sloppy in their dress and study habits, even for boys—and former class clowns are given to spontaneous crying. Junior-high-school girls, on the other hand, sometimes begin wearing heavy makeup and jewelry, affecting a hard-bitten look, as if to advertise the current lack of parental attention. First graders suddenly forget that they're been toilet trained for years. And on any given day every single one of them, from kindergarten to high school, seems to have left home, wherever home may be at the moment, without lunch money.

"Nor is there anything mysterious about this behavior. As Chuckie Marshall, a fourth grader from Denver, recently told his divorced mother, 'I think about you and Daddy a lot at school'—and such thoughts lead inevitably to insecurity and anger, depression and, perhaps most often, guilt....[T]he Los Angeles County Board of Education now runs seminars to help teachers deal with the problems of children from 'reconstituted homes': their predictable academic declines and sudden behavior swings....[S]ome kids who appear to be coping eventually display 'time-bomb symptoms' such as drug use and precocious sexual activity years after a family has broken up and resettled."

B. Sutton-Smith, B. G. Rosenberg and Frank Landy, "Father-Absence Effects in Families of Different Sibling Compositions," *Child Development*, 39 (1968), p. 1213: "In general, father absence has a depressive effect throughout, with the greatest effects during the early and middle years; boys without brothers are more affected than those with brothers, girls with a younger brother more affected than other girls, and only girls more affected than only boys."

Rex Forehand, *et al.*, "Family Characteristics of Adolescents Who Display Overt and Covert Behavior Problems," *Journal of Behavior Therapy and Experimental Psychiatry*, 18, [December, 1987]: 325-328; epitomized in *The Family in America*, April, 1988: "The kid who causes the most trouble in school most likely comes from a divorced family. In a new study of 23 white adolescents, their mothers, and their teachers, researchers set out to examine two types of antisocial behavior in children—'overt' (fighting, temper tantrums) and 'covert' (stealing, lying, truancy, falling in with bad companions). Their findings: the worst troublemaker, the child who engaged in both kinds of behavior (both fighting and stealing, for instance) was far more likely to come from a broken home than was the child who engaged in only one type or was well-behaved. Out of seven of the worst troublemakers in this survey, six came from divorced families."

Paul G. Shane, "Changing Patterns Among Homeless and Runaway Youth," *American Journal of Orthopsychiatry*, 59,

April, 1989, 208-214: "In general, homeless youth are more likely to come from female-headed, single-parent, or reconstituted families with many children, particularly step-siblings."

R. F. Doyle, *The Rape of the Male* (St. Paul, Minn: Poor Richard's Press, 1976), p. 145, citing Starke Hathaway and Elio Monachesi, *Adolescent Personality and Behavior*, p. 81: "More than one in three children of broken families drop out of school."

Yochanan Peres and Rachel Pasternack, "The Importance of Marriage for Socialization: A Comparison of Achievements and Social Adjustment Between Offspring of One- and Two-Parent Families in Israel," in *Contemporary Marriage: Comparative Perspectus of a Changing Institution,* ed. Kingsley Davis in association with Amyra Grossbard-Schechtman (New York: Russell Sage Foundation, 1985), pp. 162ff.: "Table 6.2 shows that in all three subject matters [Arithmetic, English, Hebrew] children of matrifocal families have significantly lower scholastic achievement than children raised in two-parent families....

"To make sure that these differences in achievement are not due to background factors, we applied a multivariate regression analysis to the data. Table 6.3 indicates that when many relevant background factors are controlled, children of intact families performed significantly better in arithmetic than children from matrifocal families....Similar regressions run on English and Hebrew scores also showed a highly significant new effect of parental marital status on achievement. In addition, regressions run on a sample from which children of hostile families and their controls were excluded (thus allowing us to assess the effect of 'pure' matrifocality) demonstrate that matrifocality has highly significant (negative) influence on all three measures of children's scholastic achievements. A similar overall detriment from father absence has been reported by several investigators over the last two decades."

Dale J. Hu *et al.,* "Healthcare Needs for Children of the Recently Homeless," *Journal of Community Health,* 14, 1989, 1-7; epitomized in *The Family in America: New Research,* November, 1989: "Homeless children are usually fatherless children as well. In a recent survey of thirty parents with children in a homeless shelter in San Diego, researchers talked with only two fathers and with relatively few married mothers. Nine of the homeless parents interviewed had never married, while ten were separated, divorced or widowed, making a total of 63 percent of the homeless parents interviewed who were living without a spouse."

James Coleman, "Educational Achievement: What We Can Learn from the Catholic Schools," Associates Memo, *Manhattan Institute for Policy Research*, No. 15, November 4, 1988: "It is important to remember that schools as we know them have never been very successful with weak families. These days many more families have become weak, either because they are single-parent families or because both parents are working and the family cannot devote sufficient time and attention to children."

Henry B. Biller and Richard S. Solomon, *Child Maltreatment and Paternal Deprivation: A Manifesto for Research, Prevention and Treatment* (Lexington, Mass.: D. C. Heath and Company, 1986), p. 136: "[C]omparison of children who have from an early age been consistently deprived of paternal influence with those who have had actively and positively involved fathers clearly reveals that the former are generally less adequate in their functioning and development."

Ibid., p 151: "The first investigator to present data suggesting an intellectual disadvantage among father-absent children was Sutherland (1930). In an ambitious study involving Scottish children, he discovered that those who were father- absent scored significantly lower than did those who were father-present....A number of more recent and better controlled studies are also generally consistent with the supposition that father-absent children, at least from lower-class backgrounds, are less likely to function well on intelligence and aptitude tests than are father-present children....

"Maxwell (1961) reported some evidence indicating that father-absence after the age of five negatively influences children's functioning on certain cognitive tasks. He analyzed the Wechsler

Intelligence Test scores of a large group of eight- to-thirteen-year-old children who had been referred to a British psychiatric clinic. He found that children whose fathers had been absent since the children were five performed below the norms for their age on a number of subtests. Children who had become father-absent after the age of five had lower scores on tasks tapping social knowledge, perception of details, and verbal skills. Father-absence since the age of five was the only family background variable which was consistently related to subtest scores....Compared to father-present students, those who were father-absent performed at a lower level in terms of verbal, language, and total aptitude test scores.

"In a related investigation, Landy, Rosenberg, and Sutton-Smith (1969) found that father-absence had a particularly disruptive effect on the quantitative aptitudes of college females. Total father-absence before the age of ten was highly associated with a deficit in quantitative aptitude. Their findings also suggested that father-absence during the age period from three to seven may have an especially negative effect on academic aptitude....

"For both boys and girls, father-absence was associated with relatively low ability in perceptual-motor and manipulative-spatial tasks (block design and object assembly). Father-absent boys also scored lower than did father-present boys on the arithmetic subtest....In a study with black elementary-school boys, Cortes and Fleming (1968) also reported an association between father-absence and poor mathematical functioning."

Ibid., p 154: "The high father-present group was very superior to the other three groups. With respect to both grades and achievement test scores, the early father-absent boys were generally underachievers, the late father-absent boys and low father-present boys usually functioned somewhat below grade level, and the high father-present group performed above grade level.

"The early father-absent boys were consistently handicapped in their academic performance. They scored significantly lower on every achievement test index as well as in their grades....

"Santrock (1972) presented additional evidence indicating that early father-absence can have a significant debilitating effect on cognitive functioning. Among lower-class junior high and high school children, those who became father-absent before the age of five, and particularly before the age of two, generally scored significantly lower on measures of IQ (Otis Quick Test) and achievement (Stanford Achievement Test) that had been administered when they were in the third and sixth grades than did those from intact homes. The most detrimental effects occurred when father-absence was due to divorce, desertion, or separation, rather than to death....

"Hetherington, Cox and Cox...also reported data indicating that early father-absence can impede cognitive development. They found differences between the cognitive functioning of young boys (five- and six-year-olds) who had been father-absent for two years because of divorce and that of boys from intact families Boys from intact families scored significantly higher on the block design, mazes, and arithmetic subtests of the WIPSI as well as achieving higher Performance Scale Intelligence scores and marginally higher Full-Scale Intelligence scores. Other data from this study clearly suggest that the decreasing availability of the divorced fathers for their sons during the two years following the divorce was a major factor in these boys' lower level of performance compared with boys from intact families."

Ibid., p. 155: "There is evidence that early paternal deprivation has a cumulative impact as the child grows older. In her excellent review, Radin (1981) noted several studies that indicated few if any cognitive differences associated with father-absence for black children entering first grade, but evidence of clear-cut superiority of father-present children by the later elementary-school years. Differences in academic performance as a function of variations in the quality of early father involvement seem to become more apparent as children grow older...."

Henry B. Biller, *Father, Child and Sex Role* (Lexington, Mass.: D. C. Heath and Company, 1971), p. 57: "Investigators have found that among lower-class black children, those who are father-absent score lower on intelligence and achievement tests than do those who are father-present."

Ibid., p. 59: "Boys from high father-present families are more likely to actualize their intellectual potential than are boys from families in which the father is absent or relatively unavailable."

Ibid., p. 60: "Barclay and Cusumano's data [Barclay, A. G. and Cusumano, D., "Father-Absence, Cross-Sex Identity, and Field- Dependent Behavior in Male Adolescents." *Child Development*, 1967, 38, 243-50] point to difficulties in analytical functioning being associated with father-absence. Using Witkin's rod and frame procedure, these investigators found that, among adolescent males, those who were father-absent were more field-dependent than those who were father-present. Field dependence relates to an inability to ignore irrelevant environmental cues in the analysis of certain types of problems."

Ibid., p. 63: "For example, among children in the lower class, father-absence usually intensifies lack of exposure to experiences linking intellectual activities with masculine interests. Many boys, in their intense efforts to view themselves as totally masculine, perceive intellectual tasks and school in general as feminine. When the school presents women as authority figures and makes strong demands for obedience and conformity, it is particularly antithetical to such boys' desperate attempts to feel masculine."

John Guidubaldi and Joseph D. Perry, "Divorce, Socioeconomic Status, and Children's Cognitive-Social Competence at School Entry," *American Journal of Orthopsychiatry* 54 (3). July, 1984, 459-68: "The direction of the relationships indicates that children from single-parent homes tended to have significantly lower academic and personal-social competencies than did children from two-parent families....This study provides evidence that children from divorced family homes enter school with significantly less social and academic competence than those from intact families....[S]ingle-parent status resulting from divorce predicts poor academic and social school entry competence in addition to and independent of SES [socio-economic status]."

Rex Forehand, *et al.*, "Adolescent Functioning as a Consequence of Recent Parental Divorce and the Parent-Adolescent Relationship," *Journal of Applied Developmental Psychology*, 8, [1987], 305-15; epitomized in *The Family in America: New Research*, June, 1988: "University of Georgia researchers found that those from broken homes had greater difficulties both with their classes and with their relations with their peers. 'Adolescents from intact homes had higher grades and were perceived as more socially competent by teachers,' the authors report. Their explanation: 'When parents divorce, their use of effective monitoring and disciplinary procedures, as well as their positive relationship with their children, may diminish. As a consequence, the social competence and cognitive performance of the child...may deteriorate.'"

Patricia Moran and Allan Barclay, "Effects of Fathers' Absence on Delinquent Boys: Dependency and Hyper-masculinity," *Psychological Reports* 62 [1988], 115-121; epitomized in *The Family in America: New Research*, June, 1988: "[W]hen the father is absent from the home, young black males experience 'less internalization of society's norms.' Drs. Moran and Barclay suggest that it is precisely this 'lack of internalized norms' which may be responsible for 'behavior of an antisocial and delinquent nature.'
"Intriguingly, the new study found that black delinquents whose fathers were absent were 'more overtly masculine in their expressed interests and behavior' than were black adolescents whose fathers were present.' The authors speculate that 'delinquency represents defensive coping' among black youth who develop attitudes of 'hypermasculinity' to compensate for the absence of their fathers."

David H. Demo and Alan C. Acock, "The Impact of Divorce on Children," *Journal of Marriage and the Family*, 50 [August, 1988], 619-48; epitomized in *The Family in America: New Re-*

search, November, 1988: "Young children, particularly boys, are hard hit by divorce. Children of various ages are disadvantaged in school performance. Children 'in disrupted families experience problems in peer relations, while adolescents in such families tend to be more active in dating and sexual relations.' And 'research on antisocial behavior consistently illustrates that adolescents in mother-only households and in conflict-ridden families are more prone to commit delinquent acts.'"

Gary Bauer, "Report to the President from the White House Working Group on the Family," quoted in *Phyllis Schlafly Report,* February, 1988: "A two-year study funded by Kent State, the William T. Grant Foundation and the National Association of School Psychologists, found that there were substantial differences between children of intact families and those of divorced families. "Children of divorce also are absent from school more frequently and are more likely to repeat a grade, to be placed in remedial reading classes and to be referred to a school psychologist,' says the study of 699 randomly chosen first, third and fifth graders in 38 states. In addition, John Guidubaldi, Professor of Early Childhood Education and director of the study, noted 'far more detrimental effects of divorce on boys than on girls. Disruptions in boys' classroom behavior and academic performance increased 'noticeably' throughout elementary school. Boys, he speculated, are much more affected by their parents' divorce because children fare better with single parents of the same sex, and 90 percent of all custody rights go to mothers."

Gilbert C. Hentschke [dean of the school of education, USC] and Lydia Lopez, co-chairpersons of the Education Working Group of the 2000 Partnership, *Los Angeles Times,* 30 August, 1989: "After several years of education reforms, it is more evident than ever that our Los Angeles public schools are failing....About 60% of the district's children come from impoverished families. While some poor children do succeed, poverty is closely correlated with failure, especially for children from single-parent families, according to a recent national study. The study also notes that poor students are three times more likely than others to become dropouts.

"These children who are failing swell the ranks of functionally illiterate adults (now estimated to be 20% of the population in Los Angeles County). They enter the economy at the bottom where they are likely to stay."

Henry Biller and Dennis Meredith, *Father Power* (Garden City, N. Y.: Anchor Books, 1975), p. 236: "The high father-present boys consistently received superior grades and performed above grade level on achievement tests. The late father-absent and low father-present boys scored a little below grade level on achievement tests. The lowest scores were achieved by the early father-absent group."

Maxine Thompson, Karl L. Alexander, and Doris R. Entwisle, "Household Composition, Parental Expectations, and School Achievement," *Social Forces,* 67, Dec., 1988, 424-451; epitomized in *The Family in America: New Research,* April, 1989: "Married black couples expect better school performance from their children than do single black parents—and their children respond accordingly. In a recent study conducted at the Johns Hopkins University and North Carolina State University, researchers found that black first-grade students from married-couple households outperform their peers from single-parent households....The researchers stress that these gaps cannot be explained by economic differences nor by any discernible differences in initial ability levels."

Frank J. Sciara, "Effects of Father Absence on the Educational Achievement of Urban Black Children," *Child Study Journal,* 5, No. 1, 1975, p. 45: "The analysis of variance revealed significant differences favoring the academic achievement of both boys and girls from father present homes in the two test areas. Father absence had a much greater effect on the achievement scores of boys and girls in this study whose IQ was above 100."

Ibid., p. 52: "From the analysis of the results, it would appear that for the 1,073 fourth grade Black children represented in this study, those from father present homes attained a significantly higher educational achievement level than those children from the same group coming from father absent homes. This finding was consistent in both the reading and the arithmetic tests, affecting both boys and girls. When the group was analyzed by the three levels of IQ, the father absent children achieved lower reading and arithmetic scores than those from father present homes."

Betty Arras, *California Monitor of Education* [now *National Monitor of Education*], February, 1985: "As a kindergarten teacher in the late fifties in a ghetto school in Oakland, California, I can personally testify to the negative impact of the broken home upon school achievement and emotional stability. My observation shared by virtually all my colleagues in that school was that broken homes hurt children in every way—emotionally, academically, and socially. Obviously, there are children from single parent homes who grow up with few emotional scars but generally speaking, the elements for personality disintegration are more common in the broken home. Because of increasing numbers of families in which both parents work spending less time at home, children in both these and single-parent homes tend to experience a lack of nurturing. All children need psychological nourishment whether it be in the form of supporting them in their feelings, soothing their anxieties, helping them with homework, or just sharing conversation. What is frequently missing in the broken home is a lack of parental supervision which can result in feelings of isolation, excessive freedom or responsibility which the child cannot handle, and/or lack of attention and affection. In broken homes of the welfare variety there is the problem of no father figure with whom the sons can identity.

"On February 5, ABC-TV national news aired the first in a series about violent crime in the cities. A New York City policeman who was interviewed pointed out that nearly all juveniles who commit violent crimes come from broken homes."

PSYCHOLOGICAL PROBLEMS

Neil Kalter, "Long-term Effects of Divorce on Children: A Developmental Vulnerability Model," *American Journal of Orthopsychiatry,* 57 (4), October, 1987: "A large national survey revealed that more than twice as many children of divorce, compared to youngsters from intact families, had seen a mental health professional. In a representative national sample, men and women who were 16 years of age or younger when their parents divorced reported significantly higher divorce rates, more work-related problems, and higher levels of emotional distress than did their counterparts who grew up in intact families. In addition to these rigorous cross-sectional studies, recent findings from two conceptually and methodologically diverse longitudinal research projects also indicate that divorce-related difficulties persist over time for many children....Clinical and research investigations have indicated that children of divorce constitute a population at risk for developing particular emotional, social, and behavioral problems that either persist or first appear years after the marital rupture. Prominent among these are aggressive and antisocial (externalizing) problems, sadness, depression, and self-esteem (internalizing) problems; and difficulty establishing and maintaining mutually enhancing heterosexual relationships."

Adelaide M. Johnson and S. A. Szurels, "The Genesis of Antisocial Acting Out in Children and Adults," *Psychoanalytic Quarterly,* 1952, 21: 323-343; quoted in Betty Friedan, *The Feminine Mystique* (New York: W. W. Norton, 1963), p. 297: "Regularly the more important parent—usually the mother, although the father is always in some way involved—has been seen unconsciously to encourage the amoral or antisocial behavior of the child. The neurotic needs of the parent...are vicariously gratified by the behavior of the child. Such neurotic needs of the parent exist either because of some current inability to satisfy them in the world of adults, or because of the stunting experiences in the parent's own childhood—or more commonly, because of a combination of both of these factors."

Carol Z. Garrison, "Epidemiology of Depressive Symptoms in Young Adolescents," *Journal of the American Academy of Child and Adolescent Psychiatry*, 28, 1989, 343-351; epitomized in *The Family in America: New Research*, November, 1989: "Teens living in single-parent or step-family households are more likely to suffer from depression than teens living in intact families.... Persistent symptoms of depression showed up significantly less often among young teens living with both natural parents than among peers living with only one parent or with one parent and a stepparent."

John Beer, "Relation of Divorce to Self-Concepts and Grade Point Averages of Fifth Grade School Children," *Psychological Reports*, 65 [1989], 104-106; quoted in *The Family in America: New Research*, December, 1989: "Children from divorced homes score lower on self-concept than do children from nondivorced homes."

Berthold Berg and Lawrence A.. Kurdek, "Children's Beliefs About Parental Divorce Scale: Psychometric Characteristics and Concurrent Validity," *Journal of Consulting and Clinical Psychology*, 55, [October, 1987], 712-18; epitomized in *The Family in America: New Research*, January, 1988: "In a recent study of 170 children (ranging in age from six to 17) with divorced parents, psychologists at the University of Dayton and Wright State University uncovered a disturbing pattern. The research team found that many of the children surveyed expressed one or more 'problematic beliefs' about their parents' divorce. Over one-fourth of the children blamed themselves for their parents' divorce and suffered 'low self-concepts.' Over one-fourth of children also harbored illusory hopes that 'once my parents realize how much I want them to, they'll live together again.' Approximately one-third express 'fear of abandonment' by their parents, a fear which actually appears higher among children whose divorced mothers have remarried than among children whose divorced mothers have not remarried."

Tony Campolo, "Too Old, Too Soon: The New Junior Higher," Youthworker, 4, [Spring, 1987], 20-25; epitomized in *The Family in America: New Research,* August, 1987: "...Dr. Compolo observes that young Americans now 'do things in their early teens that a generation ago were reserved for older high schoolers.' The primary reason for this 'transformation of junior highers,' he believes, is the 'diminishing presence of parents' in the lives of young adolescents. Because many of them live in single-parent homes or in two-income homes where both parents are 'out of their homes much of the time,' young teenagers are 'left with the freedom to do what they want to do.'...Dr. Campolo reports that many young teenagers become 'emotionally disturbed and psychologically disoriented' when given personal autonomy prematurely."

Carolyn Webster-Stratton, "The Relationship of Marital Support, Conflict and Divorce to Parent Perceptions, Behaviors, and Childhood Conduct Problems," *Journal of Marriage and the Family,* 51 [1989], 417-30, quoted in *The Family in America: New Research,* October, 1989: "Compared with the maritally distressed [households in which couples reported relatively unsatisfactory marriages] and supported [households in which mothers reported satisfactory marriages] mother groups, single mothers reported more parenting stress and perceived their children as having significantly more behavior problems."

Robert Zagar, et. al., "Developmental and Disruptive Behavior Disorders among Delinquents," *Journal of the American Academy of Child and Adolescent Psychiatry,* 28 (1989), 437-440; epitomized in *The Family in America: New Research,* September, 1989: "Psychotic delinquents rarely come from intact families. Officials documented a familiar pattern in a recent survey of almost 2,000 children and adolescents referred by the Circuit Court of Cook County—Juvenile Division for psychiatric evaluation. This group of troubled children included 84 orphans (4 percent), 1,272 from single-parent homes (65 percent), 269 from stepparent families (14 percent) and just 331 from two- parent families (17 percent).

"As the court officials noted in reporting their findings, there was nothing new about the linkage between delinquency and broken homes."

Statement of William P. Wilson, M. D., Professor of Psychiatry, Duke University Medical Center, Durham, N. C. to the House Select Committee on Children, Youth, and Families, 10 November, 1983; printed in *Paternal Absence and Fathers' Roles*, U. S. Government Printing Office, 1984, pp. 12ff.: "As you know, it is estimated that 40 percent of children born in America today will grow up in a broken home. In 1974 only 14 percent of children could anticipate this fate. At that time 18 million children experienced a disruption of parental relationship. Since 85 percent of the parents remarried, and of these 40 percent divorced a second time, a huge percentage of children could expect to experience the trauma of a broken home more than twice.

"These children are at risk psychiatrically. The risks are as follows: First, the child may become psychiatrically disturbed; second, that they may turn away from marriage as a satisfactory mode of human relationships; and third, the children of divorce can develop psychiatric disorders in later adult life that have as their origin the broken home which is at the least a contributing factor.

....

"Now, after children of divorce marry many problems arise in role modeling. Young men often have problems because the mother projects a variety of role models. Sometimes she has turned her son into a substitute husband. Other times she takes out all of her hostility and anger on him and attributes to him the same problems that his father had, the same personality patterns. If he tries to live up to her expectations he finds that it is beyond his capacity. Children of divorce also have poor impulse control.

"Many mothers feel incapable of administering firm discipline. If you have a 6 foot 2 son and the mother is 5 foot 4, it is difficult for her to discipline that child and deal with him in a way that is effective.

"Since the behavior of parents before, during, and after divorce most often reflects a disparate value system, the child also grows up with poorly defined values.

"In the past our interest has been in comparing the homelife of normal people with people with mental problems. We came to the conclusion that normal people come from homes where there is a stable, harmonious marriage of the parents, where there is love and order in the home, where there is administration of consistent and just discipline, where roles are well defined, and where the presentation of a traditional value system is presented, and where there is a philosophy to live by, this gives some structure to their thinking and to their lives.   "The studies of people like Grinker, Valliant and ourselves have clearly demonstrated the influence of these particular basic principles of home life.

"In contrast, the observations of Sheldon and Eleanor Glueck of people who have been delinquent—have clearly demonstrated that you can grow up in the ghetto, and if you have a well-structured home life, your chances of being a normal person and being out of that ghetto in a few years—is extremely high. Whereas if you grow up in a broken home with an harassed mother where value systems are poorly presented and where discipline is often harsh and unjust and inconsistent, you will grow up to be delinquent. At the end of 20 years' followup, you will still be delinquent and still living in the ghetto.

"The same thing can be said to be true about heroin addicts and alcoholics. In our study of over 450 alcoholics and 80 heroin addicts—we found that the absent father is a very common phenomenon. As a matter of fact, it is the rule rather than the exception.

....

"We find also that there is enormous distortion in the structure of the homes of manic depressive patients and schizophrenic patients. There father operates in roles which are grossly distorted. Many times they are emotionally absent.

"In a different version, Frances Welsing had emphasized that the biggest problem facing blacks in America today is the absence of the father from the home and the role reversals found in the black family. Her observations now are beginning to apply equally to all families, whether they are black or white or other racial origins.

....

"Finally I would add that we also have looked at the family structure of abused children who have grown up. Most of these children are now what we call borderline personality disorders. They too often have a father who is in and out of the home or is not available on a consistent basis.

"Now, just to summarize what I had to say, and I did not prepare any long statements because I think the data and the literature speaks for itself. The absence of the father from the home has the following effects on a growing child:

"After the second year of life it profoundly distorts the development of normal role assumption. A person really does not come to know who he is within his own sex. Second, it is a primary cause of low self-esteem....[Coopersmith's] work and the work of Rosenberg has shown that the father's presence in the home is an absolute necessity for the development of good self-esteem in males. Our own studies have demonstrated quite clearly that it is also necessary for the mother to be in the home for a female to develop good self-esteem.

"Third, it created a model of separation and/or divorce for the management of marital conflict in their own lives as they become adults.

"Fourth, it also distorts values development so that the child has a tendency to adopt peer values rather than the conventional values of the parent with whom they continue to live. We find this very frequently among heroin addicts and alcoholics."

Ibid., p. 97: "[A]bout half of the kids who come from broken homes end up with a broken home fairly promptly after they contract their first marriage."

Ibid., pp. 79ff.: Statement of Henry B. Biller, Ph.D, Professor of Psychology, University of Rhode Island to House Committee on Children, Youth, and Families, 10 November, 1984: "There is much evidence that paternally deprived children are more at risk for cognitive and behavioral adjustment difficulties and are more vulnerable to negative developmental influences than are adequately fathered children.

....

"Father-absent males seem particularly likely to develop insecurity in their self-concept and sexuality. There is some evidence that males are more affected by father absence than are females, but there is a growing body of research which supports the conclusion that by adolescence, females are at least as much influenced in their interpersonal and heterosexual development by father absence as are males.

"Research points to a particularly high frequency of early and continuing father absence among emotionally disturbed children and adults. Of course, in some cases constitutionally atypical children contribute to the development of marital stress, conflict and parental separation.

"Some data indicate that individuals who suffered early father loss because of their father's death are more likely to show symptoms of inhibition, lack of assertiveness, anxiety and depression, but are less likely to have the cognitive, academic and impulse control problems often found in children of divorced parents.

....

"Much of the interest in paternal deprivation has been an outcome of growing concern with the psychological, social and economic disadvantages often suffered by fatherless children. There is much evidence that paternally-deprived children are more at-risk for cognitive and behavioral adjustment difficulties, and are more vulnerable to negative developmental influences than are adequately fathered children.

....

"Father absence before the age of four or five appears to have a more disruptive effect on the individual's personality development than does father absence beginning at a later period. For example, children who become father absent before the age of four or five are likely to have more difficulties in their sex role and sexual adjustment than either father-present children or children who become father-absent at a later time. Father-absent males seem particularly likely to develop insecurity in

268

their self-concept and sexuality even though they may strive to be highly masculine in more manifest aspects of their behavior.

"Other data have indicated that early father absence is often associated with difficulties in intellectual and academic functioning (particularly analytical and quantitative abilities), a low level of independence and assertiveness in peer relations, feelings of inferiority and mistrust of others, antisocial and delinquent behavior, and difficulties in later occupational performance.

....

"Both boys and girls need to learn how to relate with adult males. Many children who are paternally deprived become enmeshed in a cycle of difficulty in establishing intimate relationships that continues into adulthood and interferes with the development of a stable family life. The experience of divorce is likely to be a family heirloom that extends into the next generation. Growing up with divorced parents does relate to increased risks in development, although certainly some children who have been subjected to divorce, and broken homes, strive and succeed as adults to have very stable, positive marital and family relationships.

"But in a general way there may be a kind of generation-to-generation effect relating to the divorce experience not only in disadvantaged families, but also among the affluent."

Ibid., pp. 86ff., Statement of Michael E. Lamb, Professor, Department of Psychology, Psychiatry and Pediatrics, University of Utah to House Select Committee on Children, Youth, and Families, 10 November, 1984: "As Dr. Biller reported, it appears in general that boys whose fathers are absent, usually due to divorce, tend to manifest problems in the areas of achievement, motivation, school performance, psychological adjustment, and heterosexual relationships. They also tend to manifest less stereotypically masculine sex roles and may have difficulties in the areas of self-control and aggression.

"The effects seem to be most marked when the father's absence begins early, and at least some effects can be ameliorated by having substitute relationships with males such as stepfathers, grandfathers, and so on. At least in the areas of sex role and achievement, the effects of psychological father absence appear qualitatively similar to, although quantitatively less than, the effects of physical father absence.

"The effects of father absence on girls have been less thoroughly studied and appear to be less severe than the effects on boys. Problems in heterosexual relationships may emerge in adolescence even though, as in boys, the effects again are more severe when father absence began earlier.

Ibid., p. 111. Statement of David W. Bahlmann, Executive Vice President of Big Brothers/Big Sisters of America, and Chair of the National Collaboration for Youth: "Present research indicates that children from one-parent homes show lower achievement and present more discipline problems than do their peers. It also shows that they tend to be absent from school more often, late to school more often, and may show more health problems than do their peers."

Ibid., p. 128. Statement of Rev. Herman Heade, Jr., National Director of Urban Affairs and Church Relations, Prison Fellowship, Washington,D.C.: "[P]aternally deprived individuals are overrepresented among individuals with psychological problems."

Heather Munroe Blum, et al., "Single Parent Families: Academic and Psychiatric Risk," *Journal of the American Academy of Child and Adolescent Psychiatry,* 27 [1988], 214-219; epitomized in *The Family in America:New Research,* July, 1988: "The children of broken homes are frequently emotionally disturbed and academically incompetent. In a new study of nearly 3,000 Canadian children (ages 4-16), researchers found that 'children with psychiatric disorder are 1.7 times more likely to be from a single-parent family than a two-parent family.' One major disturbance—'conduct disorder'—was found to be well over twice as common in children of single parents. The same children who are suffering emotionally are also suffering educationally: 'single-parent children are 1.7 times as likely to demonstrate poor school performance as are two-parent children.'

"Perhaps fearful of antagonizing some feminists, the authors suggest that it is poverty, not divorce and illegitimacy, that is the cause of the children's problems. They state that, when household income is allowed for, single-parent family status 'does not have a significant independent relationship with either child psychiatric disorder or poor school performance, *except in particular subgroups*'(emphasis added). But the list of 'particular subgroups' who suffer in one-parent homes regardless of income turns out to be surprisingly inclusive: "rural children, girls, and older boys.' Since when were *girls* merely a 'particular subgroup' of the young population? Furthermore, the authors concede, 'the younger boys might also develop problems' in later years."

Richard Polanco, *Los Angeles Times,* 7 May, 1989: "As of 1988, more than 35,000 adolescents nationwide were in psychiatric treatment in the private sector. This figure has doubled since 1980, and the numbers are growing....The absence of involvement of the father in so many post-divorce families, coupled with the overburdened state of many single mothers, seems at least partly responsible for the prevalence of externalizing, aggressive behavior problems among children of divorce."

Elyce Wakerman, *Father Loss: Daughters Discuss the Man that Got Away* (Garden City, N. Y: Doubleday, 1984), p. 109: "A study of teenage girls by Dr. E. Mavis Hetherington revealed that daughters of divorced parents had lower self-esteem than those of intact or widowed families. By aligning with mother's anger, they may have blunted the reconciliation wish, but it was at the cost of their own self-image. Describing the self-defeating pattern, Deidre Laiken writes, 'Being one with Mother means relinquishing our natural and necessary longings for Father...[But] low self-esteem is a natural and very evident result of a merger with the...parent who was left...' Identifying with the rejected female, as most daughters of divorce do, has two other, far-reaching influences on the young girl's developing attitudes. First, she may incorporate her mother's bitterness and distrust of men. And she is reluctant to succeed where her mother has failed. Having lost her father, she is acutely dependent on her mother's continued affection, and to surpass her in the romantic arena would be to risk separation from her one remaining parent."

Ibid., p. 169: "It is little wonder that fatherless girls are visibly anxious around men. In fact, both fatherless groups in the Hetherington study scored a higher overall anxiety level on the Manifest Anxiety Scale than did girls with fathers at home. Craving male attention, they are equally resolved to remain invulnerable. They would like to be loved, without the threat posed by loving. That way, the need for approval may be safely gratified and the attachment to father unrelinquished."

Sara McLanahan and Larry Bumpass, "Intergenerational Consequences of Family Disruption," *American Journal of Sociology*, 4 [July, 1988], 130-52; epitomized in *The Family in America: New Research*, October, 1988: "In a new study at the University of Wisconsin, sociologists found that daughters raised in single-parent households do not do well in building successful family life as adults. A particularly striking pattern emerged among white women who had lived in a single-parent family created through divorce or illegitimacy. Compared to white women raised in intact families, these women were '53 percent more likely to have teenage marriages, 111 percent more likely to have teenage births, 164 percent more likely to have premarital births, and 92 percent more likely to experience marital disruptions.' Overall, 'there appears to be some lower family orientation associated with one-parent childhood experience.'...The study concludes that the present upheaval in the American family is liable to have aftershocks which will be felt for generations to come: 'More than half of today's children will have had family experiences that are likely to have negative consequences for their subsequent marital and fertility life courses.'"

Alfred A. Messer, "Boys' Father Hunger: The Missing Father Syndrome," *Medical Aspects of Human Sexuality*, 23, January, 1989, 44-47, epitomized in *The Family in America: New Research*,

July, 1989: "Nightmares often trouble the sleep of young boys who have lost their fathers. A psychiatrist at Northside Hospital in Atlanta, Georgia, Alfred A. Messer describes 'father hunger' as 'the newest syndrome described by child psychiatrists.' Dr. Messer reports that this syndrome, which occurs in boys ages 18 to 36 months, 'consists primarily of sleep disturbances, such as trouble falling asleep, nightmares, and night terrors, and coincides with the recent loss of the father due to divorce or separation....In boys who exhibit the father-hunger syndrome, these sleep disturbances usually begin within one to three months after the father leaves home.'

"Young boys suffer from troubled sleep because of 'the abrupt loss of a father' during a 'critical period of gender development.' Dr. Messer explains that 'children recognize the difference between maleness and femaleness as early as 14 months of age' and that between the ages of 18 to 36 months, a young boy 'learns to establish his physical and gender role identity.' 'If the young boy is deprived of the father's presence, the result can be deeply traumatic,' Messer emphasizes. When the father is absent, the young boy may 'remain in a prolonged state of dependence on the mother, with "sissy" behavior often a concomitant.'"

Henry Biller, *Father, Child and Sex Role* (Lexington, Mass: D. C. Heath and Company, 1971), p. 3: "In a very thorough investigation, Stolz et al. [Stolz, L. M., et al. *Father Relations of War-Born Children*. Stanford: Stanford University Press, 1954] gathered data concerning four- to eight-year-old children who from approximately the first two years of their lives had been separated from their fathers. Interview results revealed that the previously father-separated boys were generally perceived by their fathers as being 'sissies.' Careful observation of these boys supported this view. They were less assertively aggressive and independent in their peer relations than boys who had not been separated from their fathers; they were more often observed to be very submissive or to react with immature hostility."

Ibid., pp. 6f.: "A study of lower-class fifth grade boys by Santrock [Santrock, J. W., "Influence of Onset and Type of Paternal Absence on the First Four Eriksonian Developmental Crises," *Developmental Psychology,* 1970, 3, 273-4.] revealed that boys who became father-absent before the age of two were more handicapped in terms of several dimensions of personality development than were boys who became father-absent at a later age. For example, boys who became father-absent before age two were found to be less trusting, less industrious, and to have more feelings of inferiority than boys who became father-absent between the ages of three to five. The impact of early paternal deprivation is also supported by Carlsmith's findings [Carlsmith, L., "Effect of Early Father-Absence on Scholastic Aptitude," *Harvard Educational Review,* 1964, 34, 3-21] concerning cognitive functioning. Additional evidence is consistent with the supposition that early father-absence is associated with a heightened susceptibility to a variety of psychological problems."

Ibid., p. 14: "However, many boys separated from their fathers between the ages of 6 and 12 exhibited a feminine-aggressive pattern of behavior. A feminine-aggressive pattern of behavior can be a consequence of sex-role conflict and insecurity. It is interesting that Tiller [Tiller, P. O., "Father-Absence and Personality Development of Children in Sailor Families," *Nordisk Psyckologi's Monograph Series,* 1958, 9, 1-48] described a somewhat similar pattern of behavior for Norwegian father-separated boys."

Ibid., p. 18: "Comparisons of father-absent and father- present boys suggested that availability of the father is an important factor in the masculine development of young boys. There is evidence that the young father-absent boy is more dependent, less aggressive, and less competent in peer relationships than his father-present counterpart. He seems likely to have an unmasculine self-concept."

Ibid., p. 65: "In societies in which fathers have little contact with their young children, there is more of a tendency to blame others and/or supernatural beings for one's illness. Blaming one's self for illness was strongest in nuclear households and least in polygamous mother-child households. Such evidence is also consistent with the view that paternal deprivation can inhibit the development of trust in others."

Ibid., p. 65: "Father-absent boys consistently scored lower than father-present boys on a variety of moral indexes. They scored lower on measures of internal moral judgement, guilt following transgressions, acceptance of blame, moral values, and rule-conformity."

Ibid., p. 65: "A number of clinicians including Aichorn [Aichorn, A., *Wayward Youth*, New York: Viking Press, 1935] and Lederer [Lederer, W. "Dragons, Delinquents, and Destiny," *Psychological Issues*, 1964, 4, (Whole No. 3)] have speculated about inadequacies in the conscience development of the father-absent boy. In his experience as a psychotherapist, Meerloo [Meerloo, J. A. M., "The Father Cuts the Cord: The Role of the Father as Initial Transference Figure," *American Journal of Psychotherapy*, 1956, 10, 471-80] found that a lack of accurate time perception is also common among father-absent children. Meerloo assumed that the father represents social order and that his adherence to time schedules gives the child an important lesson in social functioning. The paternally deprived boy may find it very difficult to follow the rules of society. Antisocial acts are often impulsive as well as aggressive, and there is evidence that inability to delay gratification is associated with inaccurate time perception, lack of social responsibility, low achievement motivation, and juvenile delinquency....the father-absent boy may lack a model from whom to learn to delay gratification and to control his aggressive and destructive impulses. A boy who has experienced paternal deprivation may have particular difficulty in respecting and communicating with adult males in positions of authority. There is some evidence that perceived similarity to father is related to positive relationships with authority figures....The boy whose father has set limits for him—in a nurturant and realistic manner—is better able to set limits for himself. Investigators have found that boys who receive appropriate and consistent discipline from their fathers are less likely to commit delinquent acts even if they are gang members."

Irma Moilanen and Paula Rantakallio, "The Single Parent Family and the Child's Mental Health," *Social Science and Medicine,* 27 [1988], 181-6; epitomized in *The Family in America: New Research,* October, 1988: "The evidence mounts that children without two parents are much more likely to develop psychiatric problems....Finnish researchers found that children from single-parent homes were at significantly greater risk from most psychiatric disorders than children from intact homes. Those who had only one parent through the child's life were at greatest risk: boys were three times as likely to be disturbed as their counterparts from intact families, and girls were four times as likely to be disturbed. Nor was the harm strictly mental."

Patricia Cohen and Judith Brook, "Family Factors Related to the Persistence of Pshchopathology in Childhood and Adolescence," *Psychiatry* 50 [November, 1987]: 332-345; quoted in *The Family in America,* April, 1988: "One-parent families and families with multiple marital disruptions are apparently unable to mount effective means of counteracting pathological reactions that have developed in their children."

R. G. Robertson, et al., "The Female Offender: A Canadian Study," *Canadian Journal of Psychiatry,* 32 [December, 1987], 749-755; epitomized in *The Family in America,* April, 1988: "Two thirds had children, but almost as many had never been married, and less than one in 10 was married at the time of her arrest. The majority...were single or divorced mothers. Most came from broken homes...."

Viktor Gecas, "Born in the USA in the 1980's: Growing Up in Difficult Times," *Journal of Family Issues* 8 [December, 1987], 434-436; epitomized in *The Family in America: New Research,* July, 1988: "What are the consequences of these family trends [rising levels of divorce, illegitimacy and maternal employment] for child rearing? Not good. At the very least, these trends suggest decreasing contact between parents and children, and decreasing parental involvement in child rearing....Poor cognitive and emotional development, low self-esteem, low self-efficiency, antisocial behavior, and pathologies of various kinds are some of the consequences.'

"Professor Gecas blames family breakdown for the disturbing levels of drug use, teen pregnancy, teen suicide, delinquency, and academic failure now found in America. Nothing, he urges, could be more important than to strengthen the family 'if the next generation is to have much of a chance.'"

Richard Dalton, et al., "Psychiatric Hospitalization of Preschool Children: Admission Factors and Discharge Implications," *Journal of the American Academy of Child and Adolescent Psychiatry*, 26, No. 3 [May, 1987], 308-12; epitomized in *The Family in America: New Research*, August, 1987: "When preschoolers end up in psychiatric wards, they typically come from homes where there is no father and where the mother is herself mentally disturbed....In assessing the 'family situation' of all of the preschool children admitted to the psychiatric units of two New Orleans hospitals over a 34-month period, [Dalton's] study found a depressingly uniform pattern. When preschool autistic patients were excluded from the sample, it was found that the fathers were not living in the homes of almost 80 percent of the preschool patients and that the mothers suffered with 'major psychiatric disorders' in over 90 percent of the homes. The authors of the study observe that 'the data reflect the fact that most of the preschoolers were hospitalized because their severe symptoms could be neither contained nor successfully treated within their disturbed and unsupported family settings.'"

Boris M. Segal, "A Borderline Style of Functioning—the Role of Family, Society and Heredity: An Overview," *Child Psychiatry and Human Development*, 18 [Summer, 1988], 219-238; epitomized in *The Family in America: New Research*, November, 1988: "According to psychiatrist Boris M. Segal, the 'borderline style of functioning' (a diagnosis used 'to describe conditions which lie between psychosis and neurosis') should be understood as a symptom of a broader social malaise. Dr. Segal concludes that 'borderline organization' is increasing among Americans in part because of the 'decline of paternal authority.' 'The decline of the father-centered family...has left children to develop their own standards of behavior. This new freedom has been conducive...to such modern phenomena as lack of discipline and lack of a feeling of duty, overindulgence, narcissism, hedonism, sexual permissiveness, intolerance to frustration, [and] sex role confusion....All these behavioral patterns meet certain criteria of borderline organization.' Dr. Segal observes that 'disorganization of the family lead[s] to the loss of its protective functions....Children who have been brought up in "broken homes"...tend to develop a high rate of borderline pathology.'"

Irwin Garfinkel and Sara S. McLanahan, *Single Mothers and Their Children: A New American Dilemma* (Washington, D. C.: The Urban Institute Press, 1986), pp. 1f.: "Half of all American children born today will spend part of their childhood in a family headed by a mother who is divorced, unwed, or widowed....About half of them are poor and dependent on welfare. The mothers and children in such families also have poorer than average mental health and use a disproportionate share of community mental health services. Most important, perhaps, compared with children who grow up in two-parent (husband-wife) families, the children from mother-only families are less successful on average when they become adults. They are more likely to drop out of school, to give birth out of wedlock, to divorce or separate, and to become dependent on welfare."

Paul G. Shane, "Changing Patterns Among Homeless and Runaway Youth," *American Journal of Orthopsychiatry,* 59, 1989, 208-214; epitomized in *The Family in America: New Research,* July, 1989: "Teenagers who turn to state officials for shelter typically come from broken families. In a recent study of over 500 homeless and runaway youth in New Jersey, Paul Shane of Rutgers University discovered a clear pattern implicating 'family breakdown as a major cause of homelessness among youth.' Professor Shane found that a remarkably low 14 percent of the youth in his study come from 'a family with both biological parents.'"

Betty Friedan, *The Feminine Mystique* (New York: W. W. Norton, 1963), p. 288: "[I]n recent years the 'symbiosis' concept has crept with increasing frequency into the case histories of disturbed children. More and more of the new child pathologies seem to stem from that very symbiotic relationship with the mother, which has somehow kept children from becoming separate selves. These disturbed children seem to be 'acting out' the mother's unconscious wishes or conflicts—infantile dreams she had not outgrown or given up, but was still trying to gratify for herself in the person of her child....Thus, it would seem, it is the child who supports life in the mother in that 'symbiotic' relationship, and the child is virtually destroyed in the process."

HEALTH PROBLEMS

Ronald Angel and Jacqueline Lowe Worebey, "Single Motherhood and Children's Health," *Journal of Health and Social Behavior*, 29 [March, 1988], 38-52; epitomized in *The Family in America: New Research,* July, 1988: "[S]ingle mothers report poorer health in their children than do mothers in intact marriages. The authors cite a number of factors to account for this disparity. Living in poverty, many children of single mothers decline in health because of simple deprivation. Because many were low-birth-weight babies, they suffer from chronic illnesses. And some may be developing psychosomatic illnesses owing to the general misery of their lives."

Nicholas Eberstadt, researcher at Harvard's University's Center for Population Studies and the American Enterprise Institute, *Los Angeles Times,* 3 November, 1989: "An enormous—and growing—number of American children suffer from a serious health threat inflicted on them by their parents. Bluntly put, their health is at risk because they have been born out of wedlock.

"In some circles, it is fashionable to see illegitimacy merely as an 'alternataive life style,' as good as any other. From the standpoint of the children in question, this view is tragically wrongheaded. Illegitimacy, and the parental behavior that accompanies it, directly endangers the newborn and may even cost a baby its life....

"Indeed, if it were a medical condition rather than a social disorder, illegitimacy would be seen as one of the leading killers of children in America today."

Sara A. Mullett, et al., "A Comparison of Birth Outcomes by Payment Source," *Minnesota Medicine,* 72, [June, 1988], 365-69; Wilma Bailey, "Child Morbidity in the Kingston Metropolitan Area, Jamaica 1983," *Social Science and Medicine,* 26 [1988], 1117-1124; both articles epitomized in *The Family in America: New Research,* October, 1988: "In a new study at the University of Minnesota, researchers found that an infant's birth weight depends heavily on the mother's marital status. 'Single women,' they reported, 'had smaller infants, with a mean birth weight of 3,192 grams as compared with 3,534 grams for infants of married women.'

....

"Mothers in Jamaica confront much harsher economic challenges than those in Minnesota. Yet in a recent study in Kingston, Jamaica, geographer Wilma Bailey at the University of the West Indies found a parallel pattern of impaired health among children in female-headed households compared to children in two- parent households. Dr. Bailey found a statistical correlation between the percentage of female-headed households in any given area and the hospital admissions of children in that same area. Her findings suggest 'that the children of young, unemployed and single women may be particularly vulnerable' to ill health and malnutrition. Dr. Bailey interprets her work in light of American studies which have 'documented the vulnerability of families of female-headed households in the U.S.A.'"

Lorian Baker and Dennis P. Cantwell, "Factors Associated with the Development of Psychiatric Illness in Children with

Early Speech/Language Problems," *Journal of Autism and Developmental Disorders,* 17 [1987], 499-507; epitomized in *The Family in America: New Research,* July, 1988: "Children with speech problems, according to a growing body of evidence, are at risk of developing psychiatric problems. Now a new study suggests that broken homes are causing or aggravating speech-related problems. Researchers from the University of California at Los Angeles studied 600 children who were patients at a Los Angeles speech clinic, finding half of them to be psychiatrically ill. While the background of the ill children differed little from the mentally healthy in most respects—gender, parental education and occupation, birth order, language background, etc.— one distinction stood out: the 'ill' children were nearly twice as likely to have unmarried parents."

DRUGS

Judith A. Stein, et al., "An 8-Year Study of Multiple Influences on Drug Use and Drug Use Consequences," *Journal of Personality and Social Psychology,* 53, No. 6 [December, 1987], 1094-1105; epitomized in *The Family in America,* March, 1988: "[N]ewer research...suggests that the family is often the most important factor in whether or not a teenager abuses drugs. In an eight-year study of 654 young people, psychologists at the University of California at Los Angeles found that early parental influence—especially parental drug use—'exerted a potent and pervasive influence on a teenager that apparently continues for many years into adulthood.' The authors also suggest that 'inadequate family structure and a lack of positive familial relationships' often lead to 'substance use...as a coping mechanism to relieve depression and anxiety.' The study stresses that parental divorce can often foster teen rebelliousness, which leads to poor selection of friends and to social perceptionsconducive to drug use."

Bryce Christensen, "From Home Life to Prison Life: The Roots of American Crime," *The Family in America,* April, 1989, pp. 5f.: "In two new studies on drug use conducted at the

University of California at Los Angeles, researchers have provided new evidence of the importance of the family. In 1987, UCLA psychologists published an eight-year study of 654 young people. Their findings demonstrate that 'inadequate family structure and a lack of positive familial relationships' often caused young people to use drugs as 'a coping mechanism to relieve depression and anxiety.' The authors also stressed that parental divorce can foster teen rebelliousness, leading to poor selection of friends and self-destructive attitudes. In a different study published just last year, UCLA psychiatrists examined drug use among 443 young people, concluding that paternal authority was decisive. In families with strict fathers, only 18 percent of the youth studied used drugs and alcohol, compared to 27 percent where fathers were less strict and 40 percent in homes with permissive fathers. Frequent drug use occurred in 35 percent of mother-dominant homes. Overall, the UCLA researchers concluded that 'with regard to youthful drug use, fathers' involvement is more important' than mothers'."

Clarence Lusane, staff aide to Rep. Walter Fauntroy, and Dennis Desmond, staff aide to D. C. Counmcilmember Hilda Mason, *The Guardian,* 25 October, 1989: "Women, particularly women of color, are disproportionately victimized by the drug epidemic. For the first time, health officials see more women drug users than men. In New York, Washington, D.C., Kansas City and Portland, women outnumber men in drug abuse. Girls as young as 12 trade sex for crack as prostitutes in crack houses.

"This has led directly to the rise in boarder babies— abandoned babies born of drug-addicted parents. According to the Wall Street Journal, about 375,000 babies a year are born exposed to drugs. D.C. General, Harlem Hospital and other hospitals nationally have opened prenatal clinics for women addicts. At some Washington, D.C. hospitals, 40% of women having babies are drug addicts. This has resulted in the highest infant mortality rate in the nation at 32 per 1000 live births. In central Harlem, 21% of all pregnant crack users receive no prenatal care. Howard University hospital had no boarder babies until May, 1988; this year it had 21 in one week, five with AIDS.

"These infants' care costs $100,000 each per year. More than half of these babies develop smaller heads and smaller abdomens. They sometimes suffer strokes in the womb. Boarder babies stay in the hospital an average of 42 days while the normal stay is three days. At the human level, these children will probably grow up without love or closeness."

Carmen N. Velez and Jane A. Ungemack, "Drug Use Among Puerto Rican Youth: An Exploration of Generational Status Differences," *Social Science and Medicine* 29, 1989, 779-89; epitomized in *The Family in America:New Research,* November, 1989: "Researchers from Columbia University and the University of Puerto Rico recently took a hard look at the drug problem among Puerto Rican youth in Puerto Rico and in New York City. They discovered more drug use among Puerto Rican students living in non-intact households than among students living in intact homes. Among students living in a nonintact household, three quarters live in female-headed households, suggesting to the researchers that greater vulnerability to drug use may be one 'effect of living in a female-headed family.'"

CHILD ABUSE

Los Angeles Times, 16 December, 1986: "Child molesters have a stronger relationship to their mothers during childhood than rapists do, a study of sex offenders suggests.

"Researchers at the North Florida Evaluation and Treatment Center interviewed 64 convicted sex offenders—21 rapists and 43 child molesters, Psychiatric News has reported.

"'Whereas the general pattern with both groups is characterized by a lack of fathering,' the study said, 'the pattern of the child molester is characterized by a singular degree of closeness and attachment to the mother.

"'Almost 83% of this group claimed to have had a close or very close relationship with their mothers.'"

L. Mitchel, "Child Abuse and Neglect Fatalities: A Review of the Problem and Strategies for Reform," Working Paper 838.

Monograph of the National Center on Child Abuse Prevention Research, National Committee for the Prevention of Child Abuse, Chicago, Illinois, 1987, p. 6; quoted in R. L. McNeely and Gloria Robinson-Simpson, "The Truth About Domestic Violence Revisited: A Reply to Saunders," Social Work, March/April, 1988, p. 186: "Active victims are typically males, under two years of age, living in low socioeconomic status families with multiple young siblings, and who die at the hands of a single mother."

Terrence Cooley, Inter-Office Communication, County of Milwaukee, "AFDC/Child Abuse Information," [11 September, 1989]; epitomized in *The Family in America: New Research,* December, 1989: "Child abuse typically occurs in impoverished single-parent households. In a recent survey, social-service officials established that of all 1,050 ongoing substantiated child abuse and neglect cases in Milwaukee County in May 1989, 83 percent involved households receiving Aid to Families with Dependent Children (AFDC). Since AFDC goes predominantly to single-parent households (generally the households of unmarried mothers), this survey reveals a remarkably high risk of child abuse in such homes. This new survey also clarifies the great difficulty of curtailing child abuse without reducing illegitimacy and divorce."

Richard J. Gelles and Murray Straus, *Intimate Violence: The Causes and Consequences of Abuse in the American Family* (New York: Simon and Schuster, 1988), p. 112: "One skeptical reader of our study, Frederick Green, noted that he was seeing more child abuse now than ten years ago. Since he also reported that he sees a largely minority, single-parent, and poor population, this is not surprising."

Henry B. Biller and Richard S. Solomon, *Child Maltreatment and Paternal Deprivation: A Manifesto for Research, Prevention and Treatment* (Lexington, Mass.: D. C. Heath, 1986), pp. 21f.: "Upwards of 25 percent of children in our society do not have a father living at home. Children in such families are overrepresented in terms of reported cases of physical abuse and other forms of child maltreatment."

Persuasion at Work, August, 1985: "The constant media focus on abusive parents from intact, suburban families belies the fact that a greatly disproportionate number of the serious physical abuse cases are found in the otherwise celebrated 'female-headed families,' commonly involving the illegitimate father or mother's current boy friend."

Los Angeles Times, 16 September, 1985: "Most [victims of child molestation] were from single parent families or were the children of [pedophile] ring members."

Additional Note

There has arisen a murmuring and a discontent among academic feminists who sense a threat to the feminist/sexual revolution in the public's awareness of the social pathology of female-headed families, a pathology whose existence they would like to deny. According to Terry Arendell,

> The long-held view that the absence of a father adversely affects children has increasingly been challenged. For example, a study of nearly nine hundred school-aged children found that single-parent families were just as effective in rearing children as traditional two-parent families. *After controlling for socioeconomic variables and matching groups of children in father-present and father-absent families,* they found no significant differences between the two groups [Feldman, H. 1979. "Why We Need a Family Policy." *Journal of Marriage and the Family* 41 (3): 453-455]. Another scholar argues: "*Studies that adequately control for economic status* challenge the popular homily that divorce is disastrous for children. Differences between children from one- and two-parent homes of *comparable status* on school achievement, social adjustment, and delinquent behavior are small or even nonexistent" [Bane, M. 1976. *Here to Stay: American Families in the Twentieth Century,* p. 111].[1]

This is like saying that pygmies are no shorter than other people *with whom they have been matched for height.* "After controlling for socioeconomic variables" means after leaving out

---

1. Terry Arendell, *Mothers and Divorce: Legal, Economic, and Social Dilemmas* (Berkeley: University of California Press, 1986), pp. 4f.; emphasis added. The quotation ascribed to Bane does not occur on page 111 of her book.

most of the evidence. Arendell wants to limit her comparison to female-headed homes where divorce or illegitimacy does not produce economic deterioration and lowered standards of living. But the whole thrust of her book and of Lenore Weitzman's *Divorce Revolution* and of half a library of other feminist literature is that divorce, father-absence and illegitimacy do lower the standard of living of ex-wives and "their" children; so Arendell is saying that there is no deterioration in school achievement, social adjustment, etc.—*except in almost every case.*

Arendell's framing of her assertion contains the *suggestio falsi* that the problem of single women is wholly economic and that therefore it can be solved by further amercing the ex-husband or ex-boyfriend who, for the purpose of making him justifiably amerceable, must be misrepresented (by the gerrymandering of evidence discussed in Chapter VIII) as enriched by divorce or non-marriage.

What she is here acknowledging is that money, a good thing, commonly keeps company with other good things—high status, high educational achievement, social stability and so forth. She explains what happens when these good things are expelled along with Dad:

> The children could not help being adversely affected by the reduced standard of living and new economic stresses that confronted their mothers. They were affected most directly by the conflict between their own needs and the demands of their mothers' new jobs. Being put into child care, being without supervision before and after school, having to remain home alone when ill, or having to deal with mothers who felt chronically fatigued and overburdened were all major adjustments for many of them.[2]

The children suffer both paternal and maternal deprivation—paternal deprivation inflicted by Mom's throwing Dad out of the house, maternal deprivation by Mom's absenting herself as a wage earner because she no longer has Dad as a provider.

"There is," say Henry B. Biller and Richard S. Solomon,

---

2. Arendell, p. 152.

ample documentation of the association between socioeconomic status and various aspects of children's cognitive and social functioning. Many researchers have
argued that the impact of father-absence and divorce on
children's development is, for the most part, an artifact
of lowered socioeconomic status. Some research, however, suggests that, in fact, single-parent status may
actually be a more powerful predictor of the academic
and social functioning of young children at school entry
than is socioeconomic status or any other family background, developmental history, or health variable.
Guidubaldi and Perry [Guidubaldi, J., and Perry, J. D.
1984. "Divorce, Socioeconomic Status, and Children's
Cognitive-Social Competence at School Entry," *American Journal of Orthopsychiatry,* 54, 459-468] reported
striking evidence that single-parent status accounts for
much statistically independent variance, and is highly
predictive of performance on various indexes of academic and social competence, even when socioeconomic
status is controlled through regression analyses. Although family structure in itself was not associated with
intellectual ability measures, children from single-parent homes were found to be much more at risk for poor
academic performance and sociobehavioral difficulties
upon entering school than were children from two-
parent families [Guidubaldi, J.. 1983. "The Impact of
Divorce on Children: Report of the Nationwide NASP
Study," *School Psychology Review,* 12, 300-323; Guidubaldi and Perry, 1984].

According to Elizabeth Herzog and Cecilia Sudia,

It is often implied or stated that the causal element in
the reported association of father's absence and juvenile
delinquency is lack of paternal supervision and control.
Studies that inquire into family factors confirm the

importance of supervision, but not the *indispensability*
of the father to that element of child-rearing.[3]

No one would assert the father's presence is indispensable to
the proper socializing of children. Many single mothers do an
excellent job of child-rearing on their own or with the assistance
of a father-surrogate. So do many orphan asylums. What the
evidence cited in the Annex shows is that there exists an
ominous correlation between father-absence and delinquency.
Herzog and Sudia maintain merely that the correlation is less
than one hundred percent—which is unquestionable, but irrelevant.

The same faulty logic occurs in the following:

The questions here are merely whether the father is
the *only* available source of masculine identity and
whether absence of a father from the home *necessarily*
impairs a boy's masculine identity. The studies reviewed do not, in our view, provide solid support for such
a thesis.[4]

No one would suppose the father was the "only" source or
that his absence "necessarily" impaired the boy's masculine
identity. No one would suppose, in other words, that there
existed a hundred percent correlation between father-absence
and impaired masculinity in sons. But having thus trium-
phantly disproved what was never asserted, Herzog and Sudia
affect to believe that they have disproved what is asserted, that
there exists a significant correlation between father absence and
impaired masculinity in sons.

They continue:

Family-oriented studies usually include father's absence as part of the family configuration rather than as
a sole and separate factor. Some of them find father's

---

3. Elizabeth Herzog and Cedilia E. Sudia, "Children in Fatherless Families," in
Review of Child Development Research, Vol. 3: Child Development and Social Policy, ed.
Bettye M. Caldwell and Henry N. Ricciuti. (Chicago: University of Chicago Press, 1973),
p. 148; emphasis added.
4. *Ibid.*, p. 184; emphasis added.

absence significantly related to juvenile delinquency and some donot. A recurrent finding, however, is that other factors are more important, especially competent supervision of the child and general family climate or harmony.

The correlations established in the Annex show that the father's presence is often not merely "another factor," but the most relevant factor, that the absence of the father often means the absence of more competent supervision and its replacement by less competent supervision. Herzog and Sudia's argument is comparable to saying that the absence of the father's paycheck is not as important as "other factors" such as adequate income. It is the father's paycheck which commonly provides the adequate income children need; and it is the father' socialization which commonly provides the competent supervision children need.

It is often, say Herzog and Sudia,

difficult to know whether reported differences related more strongly to family factors (including fatherlessness) or to SES [socioeconomic status]—the more so since family factors and SES are intricately intertwined.[6]

They had better be. The intertwining of family factors and SES is an essential part of the patriarchal system, which motivates males to create wealth, in exchange for which it guarantees them a secure family role. It is for this reason that families must be headed by fathers and why fathers must not permit their paychecks to be taken from them for the purpose of subsidizing ex-wives and fatherless families.

According to the feminist sociologists Patricia Van Voorhis, Francis T. Cullen, Richard A. Mathers and Connie Chenoweth Garner, "Marital status (single versus two-parent home) and marital conflict were weak predictors of delinquency."[7] No one

---

5. *Ibid.*, p. 148.
6. P. 159.
7. "The Impact of Family Structure andQuality onDelinquency: A Comparative Assessment of Structural and Functional Factors." *Criminology*, Vol. 26, No. 2, May, 1986, p. 241.

would suppose otherwise. The correlation between broken home and delinquency is nowhere near high enough to *predict* that a particular child from such a home will become delinquent—any more than the Highway Patrol can predict which drunk will have an accident. What can be predicted is that children from broken homes will be overrepresented in the class of delinquents and that people who drink will be overrepresented among those who .have accidents. Assertions that evidence concerning the problems of fatherlessness "are a dubious predictor...most of these studies...typically show overprediction of problems"[8] are irrelevant.

Herzog and Sudia's insistence that father-absence is not of primary importance because "other factors are more important, especially competent supervision of the child and general family climate or harmony" is inconsistent with another point they make when they are grinding a different axe and wish their readers to believe in the *in*ability of single mothers to provide what they previously insisted they *could* provide. The mothers cannot provide the "competent supervision...and general family climate or harmony" because of their "sense of incompleteness and frustration, of failure and guilt, feelings of ambivalence between them and their children, loneliness, loss of self-esteem, hostility toward men, problems with ex-husbands, problems of income and how to find the right job, anxiety about children and their problems, and a tendency to overcompensate for the loss to their children....This anxious picture seems related to the findings of M. Rosenberg...and J. Landis...that children of divorce show less self esteem....Among low-income mothers, Rainwater...found a majority of female respondents saying that a separated woman will miss most companionship or love or sex, or simply that she will be lonesome. Descriptions of AFDC mothers repeatedly stress their loneliness and anxiety, which breed and are bred by apathy, depression, and lethargy."[9]

Is it any wonder that women family heads such as these generate a disproportionate amount of social pathology?

---

8. Van Voorhis et al., p. 184.
9. P. 204.

When the single mothers do properly socialize children along patriarchal lines, they fall foul of other feminists like Phyllis Chesler, who rails at them for perpetuating patriarchy and "sexism":

Aren't patriarchal mothers still complicity [*sic*] in the reproduction of sexism? Don't they, in Sarah Ruddick's words, carry out "The Father's Will"—even or especially in His absence? Aren't patriarchal mothers, in Mary Daly's words, their own daughters' "token-torturers?"[10]

It is acknowledged that there is an "officially recognized" correlation between delinquency and father-absence but this is said to be the result of prejudice: police and social workers and teachers *expect* fatherless children to be more delinquent and they stereotype them and discriminate against them on the basis of their stereotype. "Teachers and other social agents," say Van Voorhis, Cullen, Mathers and Garner,

are more likely to expect and ultimately perceive poor behavior from the children of divorced parents.[11]

"Since agencies of juvenile justice routinely include the stability of the home as a criterion for legal intervention," says feminist Margaret Farnsworth,

such evidence may reflect a self-fulfilling prophecy.....That is, decision-making policy based on the assumption that broken homes lead to delinquency could, in itself, account for the higher official rate of delinquency observed among juveniles from broken homes.[12]

---

10. *off our backs*, January, 1989.
11. Van Voorhis et al., p. 239.
12. Margaret Farnsworth, "Family Structure, Family Attributes, and Delinquency in a Sample of Low-Income, Minority Males and Females." *Journal of Youth and Adolescence*, 13 No. 4, 1984, p. 350.

Why *do* social workers, teachers and juvenile authorities—
the people who interact day in and day out with disturbed kids—
why *do* they expect those without fathers to be more frequently
messed-up? These people are far more qualified as experts than
academic feminists sitting in offices and writing tendentious
articles enveloped in impenetrable jargon[13] and statistical mys-
tifications. "My observation," writes Mrs. Betty Arras (quoted in
the Annex above), *"shared by virtually all my colleagues in that
school* [in the Oakland ghetto] was that broken homes hurt
children in every way—emotionally, academically, and socially."

---

13. Sample: "In this context, this study endeavors to contribute to the criminological
family literature by conducting a multivariate analysis of the comparative effects on self-
report delinquency of family structure and theoretically relevant measures of family
quality (including supervision, affection, conflict, child maltreatment, and overall home
quality)." (Van Voorhis et al., p. 238)

14. *California Monitor of Education* [now *National Monitor of Education*], February,
1985. See the fuller quotation in Annex to Chapter I, p. 000 above.

Index

295